FERN GROWERS MANUAL

FERN GROWERS MANUAL

Barbara Joe Hoshizaki

Alfred A. Knopf | New York | 1975

THIS IS A BORZOI BOOK
PUBLISHED BY ALFRED A. KNOPF, INC.

Library of Congress Cataloging in Publication Data

Hoshizaki, Barbara Joe.
Fern growers manual.

Bibliography: p.
Includes index.
1. Ferns.   I. Title.
SB429. H64   635.9'37'31   75-8220
ISBN 0-394-49687-6

Manufactured in the United States of America

First Edition

CONTENTS

PREFACE

In recent years, ferns have found new popularity not only with hobbyists but with a broad spectrum of the general public. Commercial growers have responded to this interest by seeking out and offering a new and wider variety of ferns. Even more active, however, have been amateur growers, introducing new species into greenhouses and gardens even faster than they can be identified by botanists. All this attention to ferns has in turn generated a need for fresh and accurate information on fern culture. It is this need that *Fern Growers Manual* aims to satisfy, by bringing together in one easily accessible reference book material hitherto available only in widely scattered technical papers, and providing the sort of basic fern knowledge beginners and experts alike require.

In the past it has been difficult, for example, to locate the name of a fern or the ingredients of a nutrient solution unless one had access to technical literature and the proper background to interpret it. Since ferns are considered—quite wrongly in my opinion—to be an especially difficult and arcane branch of horticulture, most conventional gardening books ignore them. But although the lack of a book like this one has been obvious for some time, I, like most professional plant people, have been reluctant to write it. For one thing, the subject of fern taxonomy appears to be in a constant state of flux. But in the end there seemed to be no alternative, if only because of the amount of time I was already spending answering plaintive inquiries from growers.

Thus this book includes discussion of such topics as soil mixes, fertilizers, propagation, insecticides, and fungicides, how to grow particular fern groups, and importing ferns, along with the necessary background information. I have also assembled descriptions and photographs of the fern genera cultivated in the United States. There has been no attempt made to describe and illustrate *every* species known in cultivation—such an attempt would be far beyond the scope of this book. However, most of the cultivated species and representative cultivars will be found here. My organization of genera follows that of accepted modern authorities, except for such genera as are still in an unsettled state; those cases are treated conservatively.

Fern Growers Manual is intended to be a handbook or reference book, written in such a way as to be most useful to anyone cultivating these fascinating plants. It should be noted that although I have for convenience' sake used trade names from various products mentioned in the text, I am not endorsing the particular brands. And though the advice contained here has been brought together with care, I cannot guarantee results. The reader acts on his own responsibility.

The contents of this book represents suggestions and help from many people through many years. These kind people include hobbyists, commercial growers, and professionals. It would be very difficult for me to list all the hobbyists who have contributed to this work through the past twenty-five years. But I do wish to express my deep appreciation to all of them. Their enthusiasm, their generosity with specimens, and their many personal kindnesses to me have made this work most enjoyable. For helping me check the temperature tolerances of ferns in different parts of the country I wish to thank Mrs. Virginia Ault, Mr. Neill Hall, Mrs. Margedant Hayakawa, and Mrs. Gerda Isenberg. I wish to thank Mr. Dean Gardner of the U.S. Department of Agriculture, Plant Protection and Quarantine, for reading and adding valuable information to the section dealing with plant imports. Commercial growers with their direct experiences and their willingness to share their knowledge with others have added immeasurably to this work. Among some of the professional growers who have assisted in one way or another I wish to thank Mrs. Virginia Ault and Mrs. Yolanda Orta, who read and checked parts of the manuscript, Mr. Albert Angeli, Mr. Bob Cole, Mr. Bill Cook, Mr. Art Dias, Mr. John Ekstrand, Mrs. Gerda Isenberg, Mrs. Sylvia Leatherman, Mr. Charles Luger, Mr. Tom Mentelos, Mr. J. L. Merkel, Mr. R. Plath, Mr. and Mrs. Leo Porter, Mr. Tom Porter, Mr. Sam Potter, Mr. Alfred Roberts, Miss Hildegard Sanders, Mr. Con Slack, Mr. Rolfe Smith, the late Mr. George Spaulding, Mr. and Mrs. Steve Talnadge, Mr. and Mrs. H. F. Woodley, Mr. John Wright, and Mr. Rudy Ziesenhenne.

I owe special thanks to the many botanists I have called on through the years to assist in the identification of problem ferns. I am deeply appreciative of the time they took away from their own duties to perform this time-consuming and difficult task of identifying cultivated plants. I wish to acknowledge in particular the help I received from the late C. V. Morton of the U.S. National Museum in Washington, D.C., who from the time I first knew him in 1950 until his death in 1972 was one of the main sources of help with cultivated species. Others who have generously assisted in identification or provided material for study are Dr. Rolla Tryon, Gray Herbarium, Cambridge, Massachusetts; Dr. David Lellinger, U.S. National Museum, Washington, D.C., Dr. Alan R. Smith, University of California, Berkeley, California; Dr. David Bierhorst, University of Massachusetts, Amherst, Massachusetts; Dr. G. Brownlie, University of Canterbury, Christchurch, New Zealand; Dr. Donovan Correll, Fairchild Tropical Garden, Coral Gables, Florida; Dr. Elias De la Sota, Museo de La Plata, La Plata, Argentina; Dr. Gene Delchamps, Homestead, Florida; Dr.

Charles E. Devol, National Taiwan University, Taipei, Taiwan; Dr. Murray Evans, University of Tennessee, Knoxville, Tennessee; Dr. R. E. Holttum, Royal Botanic Garden, Kew, Richmond, Surrey, England; Dr. Donald G. Huttleston, Longwood Garden, Kennett Square, Pennsylvania; Dr. F. M. Jarrett, Royal Botanic Garden, Kew, Richmond, Surrey, England; Dr. Anne Johnson, Nanyang University, Singapore; Dr. Frank Lang, Southern Oregon College, Ashland, Oregon; Dr. Robert Lloyd, University of Ohio, Athens, Ohio; Dr. Bruce McAlpin, Las Cruces Botanical Garden, San Vito de Java, Costa Rica; Dr. John Mickel, New York Botanical Garden, Bronx, New York; Dr. R. E. G. Pichi Sermolli, Universita Delgi Studi, Genova, Italy; Dr. E. A. Schelpe, University of Capetown, Capetown, South Africa; Dr. M. G. Shivas, The University, Newcastle upon Tyne, England; Dr. Mary D. Tindale, Royal Botanic Garden and National Herbarium of New South Wales, Sydney, Australia; Dr. Warren H. Wagner, Jr., University of Michigan, Ann Arbor, Michigan; and Dr. Ira L. Wiggins, Stanford University, Palo Alto, California.

Dr. John Mickel has also helped in reading the manuscript and giving many valuable and helpful suggestions, particularly on the section dealing with the fern genera. My husband, Dr. Takashi Hoshizaki, of California State University, Fullerton, California, assisted in many aspects of this book, particularly the parts dealing with plant physiology. Mr. Arthur Takayama of Los Angeles, California, has combined his artistic and technical skills in producing many of the fine photographs. His contributions are particularly important, for ferns are known to be difficult photographic subjects. I also wish to thank Misses Marilyn Bundick and Carol Hoshizaki and Mrs. Bee Olson for their editing and typing help and Mr. Jon Hoshizaki for many of the line drawings. Dr. Mildred Mathias of the University of California, Los Angeles, California, has made the facilities of her institution available to me through the years, and this has been very important in bringing the work to completion.

BARBARA JOE HOSHIZAKI

Los Angeles, California

FERN GROWERS MANUAL

1. ABOUT FERNS

Ferns bring to mind pleasant, cool glens and shaded forests. We recall such things when we use ferns in our gardens and homes. The ferny look is well known and beloved. Some of us are content to sit back and relax as we enjoy the soft green array of patterns and textures in ferns. But there is more to appreciate about ferns than their mere appearance.

Ferns are plants which are usually recognized by their finely divided leaves, a type of leaf so readily associated with ferns that it is called a ferny leaf. However, there are many plants with ferny leaves that aren't ferns and many ferns that don't have ferny leaves. What, then, makes a fern a fern? Ferns never have flowers or seeds; they bear only spores. The so-called asparagus fern, for example, despite its finely divided appearance, is not a fern—it bears flowers and seeds. Seeds and spores are very different. Spores are simple one-celled microscopic structures, whereas seeds are complex, many-celled structures usually seen easily by the unaided eye. And though such plants as algae, fungi, and mosses may also produce spores, they are distinguished from ferns by the fact that they do not have the relatively large, thin, true leaves of ferns. Ferns are further separated from these plants by their development of tissue to conduct food and water and to provide support. Such tissues enable ferns to grow far taller than other spore bearers.

Unlike seed plants, ferns are dependent upon water to complete their typical life cycle. They grow only in places where, when the time comes to reproduce, there will be enough water to permit the sperms to swim to the egg. Seed plants such as pines and flowering plants produce cones or flowers which are able to utilize the wind or insects to complete their life cycle; they therefore can grow under a variety of conditions, dominating the landscape.

Nevertheless ferns, though fewer in number and less adaptable than plants with seeds, do surprise us with their ability to get along in climatic extremes. Though few desert ferns exist, a few may be found growing in the shade of rocks and boulders, utilizing every bit of water available. Their roots grow deep into the soil between the cool rocks, and their fronds are often covered with woolly hairs or scales to protect them from water loss. When water is not sufficient for new growth, these desert ferns may curl up or shed their leaflets and suspend growth until the next rain. Alpine ferns are also adapted to climatic extremes. Like desert ferns, they are small and tend to have hard-textured fronds which can endure the cold dry winds. They grow during the short period in the year when the weather permits.

Moist temperate forests favor ferns. Most of the ferns found in temperate regions grow in the ground or on rocks, and only a few species grow on trees. In temperate areas of the United States there are approximately 200 species of ferns. Temperate to subtropical areas noted for their abundance of ferns include parts of the Himalayas, Australia, New Zealand, and Japan. Of all areas, the tropical areas of the world have the largest number of ferns, particularly on the cooler mountain slopes. Here the mountain fog encourages an abundance of ferns. Ferns grow on the ground, on rocks, in trees, or on other ferns. Tree fern trunks are often covered with smaller ferns and other plants. There are upright ferns, creeping ferns, scrambling ferns, climbing ferns, tree ferns, coarse ferns, fine ferns—a staggering variety of sizes, shades, and shapes. Tropical areas noted for their richness in ferns include Central America (particularly Costa Rica), the West Indies (particularly Jamaica), the northern part of South America, tropical Africa, and the Indo-Malayan area.

New ferns are still being discovered even in the better-known parts of the world, so in the more remote parts much remains to be discovered. There are about 10,000 identified species, and many of them are yet to be introduced into horticulture. Places which may have still-to-be-discovered ferns suitable for temperate gardens in the United States include Japan and the cooler slopes of the subtropical and tropical parts of the world.

Compared to some other groups of plants, ferns have few economic uses. Though they have been credited with forming much of the coal, evidence seems to indicate that seed ferns, an extinct group of plants midway between ferns and seed plants in development, were the more important contributors to this fossil fuel. Few species of ferns are edible. Fiddleheads of ferns are eaten, the ostrich fern in the United States and the bracken fern in the Orient. The foliage of the water fern and *Diplazium esculentum* are eaten in the tropics. (An early Oregon agricultural bulletin told how to make "creamed bracken"; however, recent research indicates that bracken may contain cancer-producing agents.) *Osmunda* and tree ferns have been shredded to make a planting media for orchids and other epiphytic plants. More recently, tree fern trunks have been used to make planter containers for hanging basket ferns. Tree ferns have also been used to line roads and to build small buildings. Some fern rhizomes and rachises are flexible and tough enough to be used in basketry. Other uses of ferns include thatching roofs and making tea. Folklore ascribes many uses to ferns, such as restoring hair, making oneself invisible, and providing lucky amulets. The use of the male fern to treat worm infections is an example of one such tale being true. Some ferns—the bracken fern, gleichenias, and the hay-scented ferns—are considered weeds. In science, ferns have been used as subjects or tools to investigate organ development, plant hormones, genetics, evolution, plant responses to light, and in many other ways. But of all their uses, ferns are by far most important for their ornamental value.

2. THE STRUCTURE OF FERNS

Like sunflowers, oaks, or pines, ferns have true stems, roots, and leaves. These parts form the familiar fern plant. Yet their character and function may take unfamiliar forms. Much of this chapter may seem complicated, but you will find a basic understanding of fern structure extremely useful preparation for the rest of this book.

STEMS

The stems of ferns may grow erect and be quite conspicuous, or they may go unnoticed. Inconspicuous stems may be short, partly buried in the soil, or densely covered with leaf bases, hairs, or scales. If the stem is erect and stout it may be called a rootstock (*Fig. 2.1a*). If it lies horizontally on the ground and is anchored to the soil by roots it may be called a rhizome (*Fig. 2.1b, c, d, e,*). Some rhizomes are long, branch freely, and may climb or scramble over soil, rocks, or trees. Fronds may be close together or far apart on rhizomes. Some rhizomes may grow into the soil and send out new fronds in unexpected places. Some rhizomes branch frequently and may form very dense clumps. These dense clumps usually produce fronds in whorls, in irregular clusters, or arranged in a two-rank fashion. Erect stems generally produce fronds in a whorl or a vaselike cluster. The very slender long stems seen on Boston ferns are called stolons (*Fig. 2.1f*). Stolons spring from the main stem or rootstock and are capable of producing new plantlets at their tips or from side buds. Tree fern stems are so large that they may be called trunks (*Fig. 2.1g*). Some may grow to 60 feet. Where tree ferns are abundant they have been used to build small buildings, and the starch in their stems has been used for food. Some ferns have thick hollow stems which house ants. The ants presumably protect the fern and provide some nutrients to the fern in exchange for shelter.

Whether the stems of ferns are erect or horizontal, long or short, thick or thin, branched or unbranched, they serve the plant in basic ways. First, the stem tip produces the new growth by forming new stems, leaves, and roots. Damage to this tip may result in the death of the entire fern,

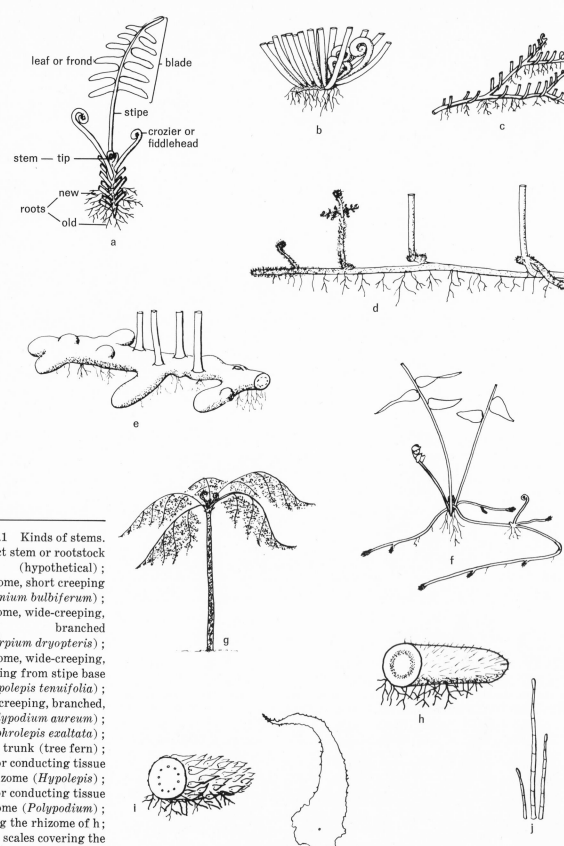

Fig. 2.1   Kinds of stems.
a. erect stem or rootstock
(hypothetical) ;
b. rhizome, short creeping
(*Asplenium bulbiferum*) ;
c. rhizome, wide-creeping,
branched
(*Gymnocarpium dryopteris*) ;
d. rhizome, wide-creeping,
branching from stipe base
(*Hypolepis tenuifolia*) ;
e. rhizome, creeping, branched,
fleshy (*Polypodium aureum*) ;
f. stolons (*Nephrolepis exaltata*) ;
g. trunk (tree fern) ;
h. vascular or conducting tissue
within rhizome (*Hypolepis*) ;
i. vascular or conducting tissue
within rhizome (*Polypodium*) ;
j. hairs covering the rhizome of h ;
k. scales covering the
rhizome of i

particularly if the stem does not form branches. Second, the stem supports the leaves. Leaves may be supported in large clusters at great heights as with the stems of tree ferns. However, most leaves are supported on short or long creeping stems. Whatever the pattern of support, the leaves are always held up to the light and air. Third, stems conduct water and food between the roots and leaves. For this purpose they are equipped with strands or bundles of special tissue known as vascular or conducting tissue. The vascular tissue may be arranged in many different patterns within the stem (*Fig. 2.1h, i*). Fourth, stems which are thick and fleshy serve the plant by storing food and water (*Fig. 2.1e*). Stems such as stolons and branching rhizomes also function to reproduce plants or increase the colony.

ROOTS

The roots of adult ferns grow from the stem. Fern roots are mostly fine, fibrous, densely branched, thick masses. They grow close to the surface of the soil and therefore are easily injured when the soil is tilled or disturbed. Young, actively growing roots have yellowish-colored tips. Older roots are dark brown or black. Many young roots are a good sign of active growth. Creeping or reclining rhizomes produce new roots as they grow forward. These roots are located on the underside of the rhizome just behind the tip. Ferns with erect stems produce new roots from the stem base. Erect stemmed ferns may have their bases covered with old leaf bases, making it hard for the emerging roots to establish themselves into the soil. If, however, the old leaves should decay away and a fine layer of forest litter accumulates around the stem, emerging roots will find a rooting medium. In cultivation it may be necessary to remove the old leaf bases of erect stems and replant the fern deeper into the soil to give the emerging roots a better chance to establish themselves and prolong the life of the fern.

Older tree ferns often have masses of roots on their stems. These roots are called aerial roots and form a fibrous outer core around the stem. They absorb rain water, but also aid in giving strength and rigidity to the stem

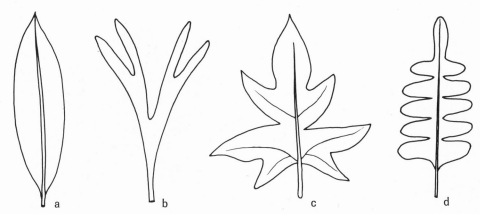

Fig. 2.2   Simple fronds.
a. simple and entire;
b. bifurcate;
c. tripartite;
d. pinnatifid

Fig. 2.3   Compound fronds. a. pinnate, the pinnae broadly attached;
b. pinnate; c. pinnate-pinnatifid; d. bipinnate; e. tripinnate;
f. palmate; g. pedate; h. pedate, the pinnae pinnate;
r = rachis; p = pinna; sp = secondary pinna or pinnule; tp = tertiary pinna

which must support the huge crown of fronds. Several trunks of some tree ferns—for example, the Hawaiian tree fern (*Cibotium glaucum*)—readily send out new roots when planted. The function of roots in all plants is to absorb moisture and minerals as well as secure the plant in place. A few fern species have thick, fleshy roots which benefit the plant by storing food and water. Some fern roots produce new plants and thereby function as a method of reproduction.

LEAVES

The leaves of ferns are called fronds and are produced from the tip of the stem. Most fronds uncoil in such a way that the young fronds are called fiddleheads or monkey tails. Technically, they are called croziers, from the term for a shepherd's crook. Croziers are very tender and vulnerable to drying and damage. They are often protected by a covering of hairs or scales.

When a crozier has uncoiled, it produces a frond which typically has two parts—the stipe (petiole) and blade (*Fig. 2.1a*). The stipe is the stalk; the thin leafy part it supports, the blade. The stipe commonly bears hairs or scales which are sometimes very important in identification of the fern, particularly tree ferns. In some ferns the stipes may be dark and highly polished, as in the maidenhair ferns. The stipes may also be long, short, or entirely absent (sessile). If the stipe naturally breaks or separates from the stem along a predetermined line or joint, it is said to be jointed or articulate. If you cut across the stipe with a razor blade the vascular or conducting tissue (stipe bundles) may be seen. Many fern genera may be identified by the patterns made by this tissue.

The blade may come in many shapes and may be undivided, little divided, or much divided into smaller parts. Names have been given to all these shapes, states of division, and their parts. The undivided state is called simple (*Fig. 2.2*). If the blade is divided to the central vein or midrib, the frond is said to be compound (*Fig. 2.3*). If each resulting leaflet is again divided to its midrib, the frond is twice compound. Tree ferns are

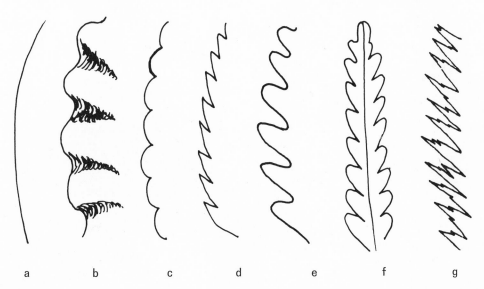

Fig. 2.4 Leaf margins.
a. entire;
b. undulate; c. crenate;
d. serrate; e. lobed;
f. pinnatifid; g. incised

a   b   c   d   e   f   g

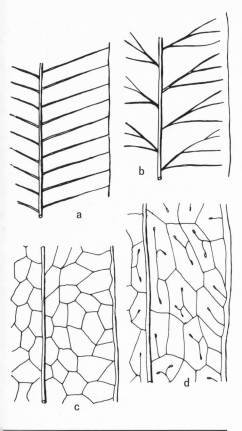

Fig. 2.5   Veins.
a. simple;
b. forked with free vein endings;
c. netted;
d. netted with enclosed veinlets

often four times compound. If the blade is cut so that the leaflets form along the midrib, the frond is said to be pinnately compound or pinnate. If the blade is cut so the leaflets join at the same point on the stipe, the frond is said to be palmately compound or palmate. If the lateral leaflets on a palmate frond are cleft into two or more segments the frond is called pedate. Most ferns are pinnately compound.

Whether the blade is pinnate, palmate, or pedately compound, the leaflet of the first division is called a pinna (pinnae is the plural). If the pinna is divided, its divisions are called pinnules or secondary pinnae and the frond is twice pinnate. If the secondary pinnae are divided, their divisions are called tertiary pinnae and the frond is thrice pinnate. A general name for these parts, whether primary, secondary, or tertiary in rank, is leaflet. If a frond is pinnately compound, its midrib appears like a continuation of the stipe and is then called a rachis. (Refer to Fig. 2.3 for more details on the names of the blade types, parts, etc.) The margins of the blade or its leaflets may be smooth, variously toothed, lobed, or wavy (*Fig. 2.4*).

The midrib of an undivided frond branches into side veins. These veins in turn branch into smaller veins or veinlets. Veinlets may be unforked (simple) or forked. Forked veins may be variously branched. Their ends may be free or joined with others to form meshes, in which case they are said to be netted. Sometimes free veins are enclosed in a mesh and the ferns are said to have enclosed veinlets. (Refer to Fig. 2.5 for details on vein patterns.) Some ferns have inconspicuous veins which are deeply immersed in the blade and are not clearly visible.

The great variety in frond shape, size, and veining does not affect the ability of the frond to fulfill its main function—to make food for the plant with the help of sunlight.

FRUITING BODIES

The underside of the frond may bear rusty patches known as sori. These are clusters of spore cases or sporangia. The sori may be round, oblong, linear, or of some other shape (*Fig. 2.6*). Some ferns do not have

Fig. 2.6   Sori.
a. along the veins
(*Coniogramme*);
b. in round clusters
(*Thelypteris torresiana*);
c. linear and marginal
(*Pteridium*);
d. linear and medial
(*Athyrium*)

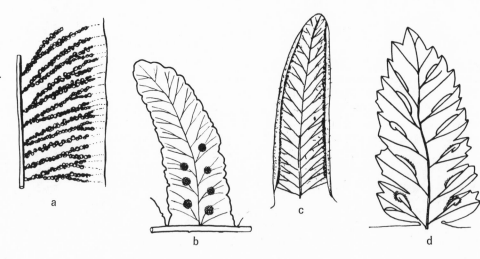

Fig. 2.7   Indusia.
a. peltate or umbrella-shaped
(*Polystichum*) ;
b. scalelike (*Humata*) ;
c. false indusium formed from
a reflexed leaf margin (*Adiantum*) ;
d. cup-shaped (*Dennstaedtia*)

the sori in definite clusters. The sporangia may be scattered along the main veins or completely cover the undersurface of the frond. The sori may be covered by a special bit of tissue called an indusium, or the covering may be the margin of the leaf rolled over the sori (*Fig. 2.7*). Such a reflexed leaf margin is called a false indusium. The shape of the sori, the kind of indusium, and the location of both are important in identifying ferns.

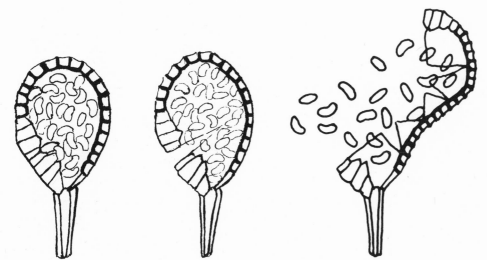

Fig. 2.8 Sporangium
shedding spores

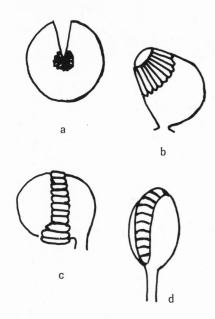

Spore cases or sporangia are easily seen with a 10X magnifying glass, but to see their finer structures requires higher magnification. They will be seen as stalked capsules or cases containing spores. If the sporangia have already shed their spores, they will appear frayed or cracked (*Fig. 2.8*). If the sporangia still contain spores the round case will be intact. In this condition you may be able to see a slightly raised dark ring of cells around the case. This ring is called the annulus and acts like a spring to open the case and release the spores. In some genera, the annulus is a cluster of cells rather than a ring (*Fig. 2.9*). All of the sporangia of a given sorus may open at about the same time in some species, while in other species the sporangia open over a period of time.

One frond may produce hundreds of thousands of spores. To the unaided eye, spores appear as a fine dust. Under the microscope, fern spores appear in two shapes. Some species have bean-shaped spores, and others have more or less pyramid-shaped spores (*Fig. 2.10*). Both shapes usually have patterns or embellishments on their outer layer. Green-colored spores are found in some species. These spores are short-lived, usually lasting a few days. Other colored spores (mostly yellow, brown or black) may live for years. But the older they become, the slower and less dependable is their germination.

The life cycle of ferns, including means of reproduction, is a matter of some complexity and considerable interest. It is discussed in Chapter 8, in connection with techniques of propagating the plants.

Fig. 2.9   Kinds of sporangia.
a. *Osmunda*; b. *Lygodium*;
c. *Gleichenia*; d. *Polypodium*

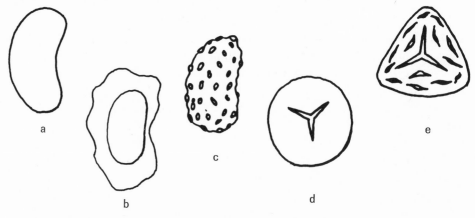

Fig. 2.10   Kinds of spores.
a–c. monolete; d–e. trilete.
a. smooth surface;
b. winged; c. tuberculate;
d. smooth surface; e. wrinkled

3. OBTAINING FERNS

FERN NURSERIES AND FERN ORGANIZATIONS

The general plant nurseries in your area usually carry a few ferns. They should also be able to direct you to specialty nurseries or mail order businesses which carry a larger variety of ferns. Local newspapers announce garden club meetings and flower shows. These will introduce you to the local plant people who may help you locate sources of ferns. Botanical gardens usually know what plant societies exist in your area and whom to contact for information. They may also have a file of more distant and foreign nurseries who may ship ferns. Fern groups have been organized in various parts of the world. These organizations send out newsletters, print journals, sponsor fern spore exchanges, conduct field trips, provide programs, and maintain a fern library for their members. Most of these fern groups are listed in Appendix II.

PURCHASING FERNS

Before you decide upon the fern you want to buy first check its climatic needs and determine whether you can provide it with the proper temperature, shade, and humidity. Second, check to see if the fern will produce the desired landscape effect, considering in particular its size at maturity. When fully grown, some ferns take up more space than you intended.

Once at the nursery, purchase the fern in a four-inch to one-gallon size container, unless you are in a hurry to have a larger plant. Leave the smaller sizes for a time when you have gained more experience in growing them. Plants larger than the one-gallon size are more expensive, and some may have passed the stage of rapid growth.

Examine the growing tip. Select a fern that has a firm, large growing tip. Avoid any that seem off-color, shriveled, or undersized for that species. If the fern is actively growing, see that the tip is forming healthy new fronds. Avoid ferns with shriveled or deformed growth. If you don't want to repot the fern in the near future, pick one that has not already overgrown its pot. The growing tip should not be pushing against the edge of the pot. If the fern is one that forms clumps of rhizomes, select the one that has the largest number of healthy rhizome tips.

Nurseries use different soil mixes. Be aware that some mixes will require more watering than others. Also, the smaller the pot and the larger the fern, the more water it will require. If the fern has been accustomed to high humidity at the nursery, it may wilt when you get it home. If you give it just enough humidity to keep it from wilting, new fronds which will develop should adapt to your less humid conditions without difficulty. If not, see Chapter 4, "Air Circulation and Humidity."

COLLECTING FERNS

If you live in areas where many native ferns grow, you will have access to species suited for your climate, but not necessarily for garden culture. Care must be taken not to collect rare or infrequently found species or to damage the natural environment in any way. Remember that growing ferns from spores often produces more adaptable plants, and this means of obtaining ferns is to be favored over collecting established plants. If you collect ferns, be certain that you observe local laws on collecting plants. Collecting native plant material is forbidden in all national parks and monuments, state parks, and most county and city parks. Permission to collect plants in national forests and on private lands must be obtained. Ask at the nearest Forestry Service Office (listed under the United States Government, Department of Agriculture) for permission to collect in a national forest. A good time to collect temperate, deciduous ferns is in the late fall to early spring. Collect other ferns just before the growing season, usually in early or midspring. Though ferns may be collected at any time, their chances of survival are best when they are moved near the end of their inactive period, or just before their active growing period, so they may have a full season to grow and establish themselves. Young mature ferns are the best to collect. If the fern branches or clumps, one piece is enough to start a plant. When collecting the rhizome, take as much of the active roots and undisturbed soil as possible. Plants with thick rhizomes have a better chance to survive. Keep the soil and foliage cool and moist in transit. Replant as soon as possible.

INTERSTATE TRANSPORT OF FERNS

Regulations about the interstate movement of plants vary between states and between counties within a state. Check with your local state and county agricultural offices before attempting shipment of plants.

IMPORTING FERNS FROM ABROAD

People who travel may find many interesting ferns. Certain parts of the world are particularly rich in them. Resist the temptation to collect indiscriminately, wastefully, and without a thought for the environment. Keep in mind that spores are easier to collect, pack, and import. If live plants must be collected, take only the number you can realistically import and grow. Remember that some countries require collecting permits, so check with the consulate of that country before you leave home, if possible. Also before leaving your home, check with the Plant Import Permit Station of the U.S. Department of Agriculture (see Appendix II for address) concerning the importing of foreign plants. They will inform you of the procedures to take regarding imports and may request that you obtain a permit before departure. This permit is issued without charge. Fern plants may be imported into the United States, but must be free of soil, insects, and disease pests and packed in approved packing materials. The size-age regulations also cite that plants be the youngest, smallest, normal, clean, healthy plants which can be successfully freed of soil, transported to the United States, and established. If the Agricultural Inspector finds insects or disease pests the shipment may require dipping or fumigation. Keep records of where you collected the ferns. This information may be helpful at the Agricultural Inspector's station and is certainly needed in fern identification. There are no regulations concerning the importing of fern spores into the United States. Spores may be scraped into envelopes, preferably glassine, and sent by ordinary mail (see Chapter 8, "Collecting Spores"). Send any green spores by air and have them planted immediately. Though growing ferns from spores is a lengthy process, spore-grown plants are generally more adaptable to cultivation than imported plants.

It is generally safer and quicker to hand-carry plants into the United States, particularly if your point of entry has an Agricultural Inspector on duty and the value of your plants is less than $250. Avoid stopovers on your return trip where local Customs may bar entry to your plants. Plants sent by air mail or by air freight may be lost in the country of origin. When they arrive by air in the United States, even those plants with a permit will have to be sent first to Customs, then to an Agricultural Inspector, and finally back by mail to you. Air freight arrivals valued at $250 or more require the services and the fee of a Custom Broker. His function is to meet the shipment, complete the formalities at Customs (pay the custom fee on your behalf), and convey the shipment to the Agricultural Inspector. If the shipment is less than $250 you may process the shipment yourself. Inquire at your local Bureau of Customs for further information on procedures.

HOLDING FERNS UNTIL DEPARTURE TIME

If you have collected ferns on the earlier part of your trip and will not be returning for a week or so, be sure to remove the plant with as little disturbance to the roots as possible, put it into a plastic bag, and keep the bag open for ventilation. Water it sparingly, and provide drainage in the bag if needed. Find a cool shady place to store plants as you travel. Just prior to departure, prepare and package the plants as discussed below.

PACKING FERNS

Water the ferns the day before packing so the excess water has time to drain away before packing. Ferns which may be imported with soil on their roots need only be wrapped in newspaper. If ferns are in pots, they may be tapped out of their pots to reduce the weight. Entry into the United States demands that all soil be removed from the plant. Dip the roots into a bucket of water so the soil will fall away with a minimum of disturbance to the roots. To protect the rhizome and roots from being crushed, pack some finely shredded newspaper loosely around the roots. Moisten lightly before wrapping. Several plants placed together in a plastic bag need no other packing material unless they are especially fragile. (But see caution about plastic bags below.) If packing other than newspaper is used and ferns are to be sent into the United States, be certain the packing material is on the approved list issued by the Plant Import Permit Station. Bring your own packaging and wrapping supplies if you are going to remote areas.

Remove all dead and broken fronds. Double-check to see that any stray insects are removed. The tip of the stem or rhizome is the most important part of the fern. If fronds have to be removed for packing, do so, but keep the roots and particularly the rhizome or crown intact.

Small plants may also be wrapped in moistened newspaper to form a cylinder or a cone with the root end folded over. If the wrapped ferns are very damp, they can be wrapped again in the wax paper used by butchers or in several layers of ordinary wax paper. Be very cautious about using plastic bags, especially in hot climates where plants rot readily or where plants will be long in transit. Put some holes in the bags or leave them open at the top. Wetness encourages rot.

Cardboard cartons lined with wax paper may be used to pack the wrapped ferns and as many as possible may be stuffed into the box. In some areas, woven baskets are easier to obtain and may be used—unless they are made of willow withes or wood which may carry boring insects; they are barred from entry into the United States. Secure the individually wrapped ferns so they will not slip or slide in the box.

4. CULTURAL NEEDS

UNDERSTANDING FERN NEEDS

Ferns have the same basic growing needs as other plants, and they grow because those needs are supplied. There is nothing about this process that is particularly mysterious, known only to people with "green thumbs"; but it is true that the best gardeners are those who *understand* plant requirements and are careful about satisfying them. Now, what are these needs?

WATER AND HUMIDITY

All plants need water. Water in the soil keeps roots from drying and is used within the plant. Besides water in the soil, most plants need water in the air. Adequate humidity keeps the plant from drying out.

LIGHT

All green plants need light. Light is the energy plants use to make their own food. Some plants need more energy than others; some can operate in both sun or shade. Most ferns prefer shade.

AIR

A raw material plants need to make their food is "stale air" containing carbon dioxide, a gas which animals exhale from their lungs as waste. Plants take this waste gas into their leaves through tiny pores. In the leaf the carbon dioxide and water are then fused by light to form the plant's food, sugar. This fusion takes place in the green parts of plants and is called photosynthesis.

Plants need some fresh (oxygen-rich) air too. The green parts of a plant don't need much oxygen from the air, because while the sun is shining they make much more oxygen than they can use (and incidentally provide humans and all animal life with enough oxygen to breathe). What do plants do with their oxygen? They use the oxygen just as we do, to release the energy stored in their food. We use it to move about, to talk, to grow, and to carry on all our life processes. Though plants don't talk or move very much, they do grow and must carry on all their life processes using oxygen to release the energy from the food.

Roots need air all the time. They get it from the air spaces between the soil particles.

MINERALS

A lot of machinery is needed by plants to make and use food. Minerals or certain chemicals supplied by soil nutrients or fertilizers form the plant's machinery. If a part of the machinery is missing the whole system may fail to work. If a mineral is missing, the plant will not grow properly.

TEMPERATURE

Some plants operate in a wide range of temperatures, while others are fussy. If the proper temperatures are not present, the machinery of the plant will not operate satisfactorily or will cease entirely.

The basic needs of plants are not hard to supply, but growing success depends on supplying these needs with care and exactitude. The remainder of this chapter is devoted to a discussion of the needs of ferns, except for mineral needs, which are discussed in Chapter 5 under "Fertilizers."

TEMPERATURE

Ferns vary greatly in their temperature requirements. Most will grow best at day temperatures of 65–80°F. Very tropical ferns will prefer ranges from 70° to 80°F during the day, and some may even tolerate similar night temperatures. However, most ferns grow best when the night temperature is about 10°F cooler than the day temperature. Some ferns need seasonal periods of cooler temperatures to grow well. There is no way to predict temperature tolerances by the looks of a fern. A knowledge of its native habitat and the temperature tolerances of its relatives will help greatly, but there always are surprising exceptions. It is helpful for gardeners to test temperature tolerances of newly introduced species, reporting their findings to specialist journals.

Ferns may be classified as hardy, semihardy, semitender, and tender. This classification refers to the coolest temperature range they can tolerate. It is arbitrary, since there are borderline cases, and many ferns can endure short periods of lower temperatures. However, the classification method ensures that the temperature preferences of a large number of ferns can easily be known. See Chapter 13 for the temperature requirements of particular species.

HARDY FERNS

Hardy ferns can be grown outdoors in temperate or colder areas of the United States. These ferns are capable of withstanding winter temperature below 32°F. The alpine species of this group can endure very cold temperatures. Hardy garden species are mostly native to North and Central Europe, North America, and North Asia. There is much literature on hardy fern cultivation, both in the United States and in Europe, which will be of interest to fern growers in temperate areas (see Bibliography). Many native eastern United States ferns are suitable for gardens. However, most hardy ferns do not do well in subtropical and tropical climates, presumably because they need cold temperatures to break dormancy.

SEMIHARDY FERNS

Semihardy ferns usually grow well when night temperatures are mostly above 40°F during the cool seasons. They can survive a freezing temperature if it is of short duration and not too severe. These ferns come from many parts of the world. Many are native to parts of Japan, Korea, and China where warm temperate climates prevail. They will grow outdoors in the southeastern parts of the United States and the warmer northern areas. They are good choices for inland valleys of southern California.

SEMITENDER FERNS

Semitender ferns grow well where night temperatures are mostly above 50°F during the cool seasons and freezing temperatures are rare. Frost may burn the foliage or kill the plant. These plants are native to subtropical and warmer areas with day temperatures of 65°F. Many come from Latin America, Australia, and New Zealand. Coastal southern California is particularly suited for these semitender species, while those that can tolerate cooler temperatures may grow inland or as far north as San Francisco.

TENDER FERNS

Tender ferns (warm or "stove species") usually display poor growth when temperatures drop to 60°F or below for successive nights. These ferns are mostly native to the lowland tropical parts of the world where year-round warmth and humidity prevail. South Florida and the Hawaiian Islands are particularly favorable places to grow such ferns outdoors. In southern California most of these species must be grown under glass with day temperatures kept near 75°F.

Some of the semitender and tender ferns prefer cooler temperatures at night and do not do well in places where it does not become cool at night. These ferns are usually native to the cooler upland areas of the tropics and include many of the tree ferns. Conversely, some lowland tropical ferns may not grow in places where the night temperatures are consistently much lower than the day temperatures.

LOCAL TEMPERATURE VARIANCE

In areas where there is a diversity of land elevation and the moderating influence of coastal temperatures, there will be a diversity of climates within a few miles. In such areas it is important to know the precise local temperature conditions. In southern California, for example, climates ranging from subalpine to subtropical may exist within a distance of forty miles. The local U.S. Department of Commerce, National Weather Service Forecast Office, will give you information on climatic conditions.

LOW-TEMPERATURE DAMAGE

If temperatures are too low for the plant, but not low enough to freeze it or cause frost damage, the plant usually turns yellow, produces little growth, and may waste away. But before you dig up a fern to move it to a warmer place, be sure it is not merely taking its normal rest period. Many ferns take a rest period, especially during the cooler winter months, when they normally turn yellow and produce little growth. However, these ferns come back vigorously in spring, while those which have suffered from low temperatures will be slow to recover and often have very undersized rootstocks or rhizomes.

Semitender and tender ferns growing in marginally favorable temperatures need to be watered very carefully during the cooler months when the growth is slow. Overwatering may bring about root rot.

Ferns damaged from freezing or frost appear wilted and then turn black. Less severely damaged fronds have a scorched or burned appearance. If injury is only to the fronds and not to the rhizomes, new growth may eventually appear. As with all other types of damage, weak plants, very young plants, recently transplanted plants, and newly emerged fronds are most vulnerable to low-temperature damage. To prepare plants for low winter temperatures, avoid heavy pruning or fertilizing in fall, as this may encourage tender growth vulnerable to cold damage. Withered fronds left on the plant will protect the fern through the winter. Transplant ferns early in the growing season so they will be well established by fall. Protect weak, young, or susceptible plants by moving them to warmer places or by building temporary shelters around them. Temporary coverings of burlap, straw, leaves, or newspaper will afford some protection to the fern during cold spells. If artificial heat must be used, be on guard for dry air injury. Electric heaters are far more drying than gas heaters.

HIGH-TEMPERATURE DAMAGE

Fern damage due to high temperatures in arid areas is difficult to separate from damage due to low humidity. However, even with high humidity, high temperatures may cause all or parts of the frond to wilt or be scorched. If the wilted parts do not recover, they will turn brown and brittle. On thicker fronds the scorched areas are usually near the margin or in places where they were most exposed. During heat waves, shade the ferns and keep the air humid and the soil moist. In greenhouses, open the vents and keep the mist nozzle operating. Water sprayed on the roof of the greenhouse will reduce the temperature appreciably.

Alpine ferns or those liking cold or cool temperatures often do not grow well in climates that are warm the year around. They do not establish themselves in warm gardens and eventually waste away. Few gardeners are prepared to raise these ferns in greenhouses equipped to produce low temperatures, so it is better to forgo attempting to grow them in warm climates.

LIGHT

HOW MUCH LIGHT?

The majority of ferns grow best in shade or filtered light. The optimal amount of light is that from the sun on a dim overcast day. This intensity measures between 200 and 600 foot-candles. Foot-candles are units of measuring light intensity. One foot-candle is equal to the amount of light cast on a surface by a standard candle one foot away from the flame. Adult ferns prefer more light than younger ones; most spores germinate and grow best in the lower light ranges. Very dense shade is not suitable for most ferns. Under these conditions fronds grow very spindly, are few in number, and are apt to yellow and die early.

Ferns growing in the lower but adequate end of the light intensity range are larger and more luxuriant. In the upper end of the intensity range, the fronds become firmer, thicker, produce more spores, and withstand environmental changes better. Ferns suffering from too much light are smaller, less luxuriant, yellowish green, and may have brown margins.

Along overcast coastal areas ferns may be planted in full sun. Inland areas may have brighter days, and the ferns will require more shade. In planting ferns, do not overlook the added intensity from light which may reflect off walks and buildings or which may result from the seasonal changes in the sun's angle. Appendix I contains the description of a method for measuring light intensity using an ordinary photographic light meter.

SHADING FERNS

Trees, laths, painted glass, fiberglass, plastic cloth, and discarded detoxified fluorescent tubes have been used to shade ferns. The plastic cloth polypropylene (or Prop-a-Lite, which superseded Saran or Lumite) is much used by the nursery trade. Different grades give 30 to 90 percent shade. In sunny southern California 73 percent shade cloth (giving 73 percent shade) has been used with good results. If ferns must be grown in an area receiving direct sun, shield them from the sun between noon and 3 p.m., these are the brightest and hottest hours.

ARTIFICIAL LIGHT

Ferns grown indoors, especially in more northern areas, often suffer from inadequate light. Supplemental or full artificial light must be given. Fluorescent lamps (cool white) are the usual choice, though Gro-lux lamps give a better light range. Ordinary electric lights may be used, but their heat output is high and may injure the plant. They are best used along with fluorescent lights to give the proper kind of light. To obtain the proper light intensities using two fluorescent tubes of 40 watts (4-foot tubes), consult Fig. 4.1. Light intensity in foot-candles is given at 6, 12, 18, and 24 inches below the light source. The light intensities are highest directly under the tubes. Also, as the tubes get older their intensities diminish. The light intensity may be increased by using reflectors and/or having two fixtures mounted side by side so the light intensities of the two are then combined. Lining the benches and sides with aluminum foil or reflecting surfaces may increase the intensity by 20 to 50 percent. Most ferns grow best at between 200 and 600 foot-candles. Light intensity is generally measured at the top of the plant.

Little is known about the photoperiodic response of ferns—how they respond to day length. Changes in day length may affect their growth or ability to form spores (Patterson and Freeman, 1963).

WATERING

HOW MUCH?

The majority of cultivated ferns prefer consistently moist soil. Moist soil feels moist, not soggy wet. Continuously wet soil is to be avoided as much as dry soil. A few cultivated ferns may prefer soil either drier or moister than the average, but these are exceptions. Water less during cool

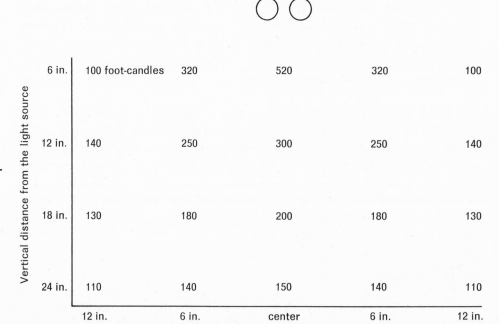

Fig. 4.1 Light intensity.

Intensity of light (foot-candles) below two 4-foot, 40-watt cool white fluorescent tubes. Use of a reflector will increase the intensity of light. The light intensity was measured on a horizontal surface with a light meter (Western illumination meter model 756)

Vertical distance from the light source	12 in.	6 in.	center	6 in.	12 in.
6 in.	100 foot-candles	320	520	320	100
12 in.	140	250	300	250	140
18 in.	130	180	200	180	130
24 in.	110	140	150	140	110

Horizontal distance from the center of the lighted area

weather, especially when ferns are not actively growing. See Chapter 13 for the requirements of specific ferns.

HOW OFTEN?

There is no precise answer to this question. Average conditions will require watering every two or three days, less during cool weather and more during warm. Plants in small pots will dry quickly and will need to be watered more frequently than those in larger pots. Plants in clay pots will need to be watered more frequently than those in plastic or glazed pots. Plants in sandy or coarse soil mixes will need to be watered more frequently than those in silty or clay soil mixes. It is wiser to learn to water a plant when it needs it than to do so on a time schedule.

TELLING WHEN WATER IS NEEDED

Don't wait for the plant to wilt. Feel the soil surface. If it is dry or starting to dry it is time to water. A second indication that the plant needs water is to lift the pot to feel if it is lighter than usual. A third test is to tap clay pots. If they are very dry they will have a ringing sound. If you still can't decide, probe the soil where you won't injure the plant and see if it is dry ½ to 1 inch below the surface.

HOW TO WATER

Once you have determined that the plant needs water, water it thoroughly with a gentle sprinkle or flow of water. Avoid forceful streams of water. Apply water until it comes through the pot's drain hole. If the plant is in the ground, be sure that the water has reached the soil around the roots. Overhead watering which wets the foliage is not recommended for some ferns, particularly those which are very finely divided or are xerophytic species. Water these ferns at the soil level. In areas with much humidity and poor air circulation, water in the early part of the day so the foliage will not remain wet for long. Prolonged wet foliage encourages certain diseases. Scant sprinklings of water will increase the humidity, but are seldom sufficient for the water needs of medium or larger ferns and may cause an accumulation of salts which are injurious to plants.

TREATING A WILTED PLANT

A plant which has wilted from drying needs water immediately. Be certain that the water has reached the roots and is not merely running between the dry ball of soil and wall of the pot. If this appears to be happening, submerge the pot in water until it is thoroughly wet. Then remove it from the water and permit it to drain. Thereafter water only to keep the soil moist. Do not be tempted to overwater. Wilted fronds which do not recover will turn brown in a few days. Remove them. Keep as many green fronds on the plant as possible. Recovery of a wilted plant at this stage will depend upon the extent of root damage and the plant's innate vigor. Generally, the thicker the rhizome the greater the chances of recovery because there is a store of food and water in the rhizome. These reserves help produce new growth to replace the damaged tissue.

TREATING AN OVERWATERED PLANT

A plant may wilt even though you have been watering it. The most common cause is overwatering which results in root injury. Soil which feels wet even two or three days after watering may be too wet for the plant; in serious overwatering, soil will feel soggy wet and may smell bad. The pot is heavy for its size when lifted due to the waterlogged soil. When it is tapped there is only a dull thud. Damage to the plant may be gradual or sudden. If gradual, the fronds first yellow and may show poor growth. The fronds may then wilt, and examination of the roots will show that they have rotted away.

If the plant hasn't wilted yet, reduce the watering. If it has wilted, determine how badly the roots and rhizomes are damaged. If most of the roots are rotted and the rhizome is soft and discolored, the plant probably will not survive and should be discarded. Otherwise trim off the rotted parts and replant the healthy part in fresh, well-aerated soil. Keep the soil moist and hope for the best. Be careful not to overwater again. The cut ends of rhizome and roots may be dusted with Captan to discourage further rotting.

HOW OVERWATERING CAUSES DAMAGE

Roots need air. The oxygen of the air is used by the roots to release their stored food energy. This energy brings minerals into the plant, moves substances within the roots, and helps the plant's life processes. Overwatering and filling the soil spaces with water doesn't allow enough air for the roots to function. Also, the lack of air in the soil favors the growth of certain bacteria and fungi which may injure the plant.

WATER QUALITY AND SALT INJURY

Water varies in quality in different areas and at different times. The amount of chlorine present in drinking water has not been reported to be detrimental to most ferns. However, do not use water discarded from swimming pools—its chlorine content and other additives are probably higher than in drinking water.

The temperature of water may be very high in garden hoses or pipes that have been exposed to sun or heat. Let the water run before using it. Very cold water should be avoided, since it slows down the nutrient intake rate. Water feeling comfortable to the hands, generally between 65° and 80°F, is suitable for use.

Do not use water containing softeners. The sodium in the water is not beneficial to the soil structure and replaces desirable nutrients. Water containing excess salt may cause salt injury to plants. This occurs when salt accumulates in the soil from the water supply, overfertilization, or soil additives such as manures containing too much salt. A crust of salt, usually whitish gray, may be seen on the soil surface or on the flower pot. The plant may have slow growth or scorched foliage, or may wilt owing to the death of the roots. Salt damage is more common in arid areas where the water supply has passed through soil high in natural salts. The salt content remains high in these soils because there is insufficient rain to wash the salts away.

To avoid salt injury, water ferns thoroughly. Light sprinklings will simply add salt to the soil, not leach it out. Provide good drainage for adequate leaching. Avoid adding manures, leaf molds, compost, or especially sedge peats, which may have a high salt content. Clean salt-encrusted pots or discard them (see Chapter 7, "Planting in Pots").

TIPS ON WATERING

Sometimes the watering of basket ferns results in damage to the ferns planted below. Damage may be caused by the physical force of water cascading on the plants below or by overwatering. To avoid this, the basket may be lifted down and watered or the plants underneath removed while the baskets are being watered. Other alternatives are to provide catch basins in the basket by building a substantial rim of moss around the top edges of the baskets. This will hold more of the water and reduce the spillover of water. Also, you may place a saucer at the bottom of the basket on top of the moss lining before planting, to act as a hidden catch basin. (See Chapter 7, "Planting in Baskets" and "Special Care.") Watering with a fine gentle spray takes longer but will result in a better soaking of the basket and less water runoff.

To keep potted ferns from drying too quickly, plant pot and all in a bigger pot. Fill the spaces between the pots with sand, planting mix, or coarse sphagnum moss. This method is known as double potting (*Fig. 4.2*). Slipping watered plants into a plastic bag will keep them sufficiently moist for a week or more depending on how wide the bag is left open. Some ventilation holes should be put in the bag if it is closed unless ample air space surrounds the fern. This is a handy way to care for ferns when you are away for a week or so.

AIR CIRCULATION AND HUMIDITY

AIR MOVEMENT

Ferns will need to be protected from hot, dry, battering winds and drafts. Though some ferns can tolerate wind, their fronds usually look ragged. A small amount of air circulation and ventilation is desirable in greenhouses or similar enclosures. Circulation of the air discourages fungi and helps to distribute humidity and temperature evenly. Small fans, partially open windows, or vents serve to circulate air adequately in the average home greenhouse.

Some outside air flowing into the greenhouse is beneficial. The outside air will replenish the supply of carbon dioxide in the air for plant growth. Incoming air is detrimental when it is very dry, very hot, very cold, or smoggy. Such air creates a stress on the plants.

HOW MUCH HUMIDITY?

Most ferns prefer 60 to 80 percent relative humidity during the day and a lower humidity at night. The more robust or older ferns can do with less humidity. More delicate or younger ferns prefer the higher ranges of humidity. Most epiphytes and of course all xerophytes can tolerate less humidity than other ferns.

LOW-HUMIDITY DAMAGE

Low humidity prevents luxuriant growth and is one of the commonest causes of poor growth indoors. If the humidity is too low (i.e., the air has very little moisture in it), older fronds yellow more quickly and emerging fronds shrivel. If the air is very dry, the fronds wilt or the margins become scorched. Also, low humidity encourages red spider infestations. Barely adequate humidity may result in thicker, smaller, harder-textured fronds which may be heavier spore bearers. Increasing the air temperature lowers the relative humidity.

Fig. 4.2   Increasing the humidity.
a. mister or humidifier;
b. grouping plants;
c. setting plants just above
the water level on
pebbles in a tray or pot;
d. planting in terrariums;
e. enclosing plants
on top and 2 or 3 sides with
plastic sheets or glass frames;
f. double potting

INCREASING THE HUMIDITY

Various ways to increase the humidity are shown in Figure 4.2. There are different mechanical devices on the market to increase both indoor and greenhouse humidity. Indoor units are controlled by electricity. Greenhouse and outdoor units are generally attached to the water line. All units produce a very fine mist. The very fine opening in the valve frequently

a

b

becomes plugged and must be routinely cleared to operate efficiently. Intermittent spraying of the air, the foliage, and the walks with a fine mist of water from a garden hose is very effective in increasing the humidity. A single misting is not adequate during a hot, dry day, as the moisture evaporates quickly. Depending on the lack of humidity, misting may need to be done several times during the drier part of the day. Venting the household clothes drier into an adjacent greenhouse makes good use of the warm humid air on days when it is needed. Grouping potted plants together or planting them in the ground will keep them more humid. But in increasing the humidity, avoid overwatering.

A simple procedure to increase the humidity indoors is to place potted plants on top of pebbles which are spread out in a shallow tray containing water. The bottom of the pot should not touch the water level. Planting smaller plants in glass or plastic containers or enclosing larger plants on the sides with plastic sheets or glass frames will also help retain the moisture and humidity. A fine mist of water may be sprayed around the foliage during the hotter, drier part of the day. Kitchens and bathrooms are the most humid places in the home, and if light is sufficient there, they are good places to grow plants. Double-potting plants (see "Tips on Watering" earlier in this chapter) will also keep more humidity around plants than single potting.

HIGH-HUMIDITY DAMAGE

Excessive humidity is not desirable for the majority of ferns and should be controlled, especially during the night when the temperature may lower

quickly. Water or mist in the earlier part of the day or increase the air circulation by opening the vents to decrease humidity. Fungus diseases and algae are encouraged by excessive humidity, and the plants grow soft, weak, and succulent. They are also vulnerable to sudden climatic changes. Under high humidity and warm temperatures some ferns with firm smooth fronds (as polypodiums) may develop brownish-purplish areas on the frond, particularly where they arch or bend. Finely divided fronds, as in some types of Boston ferns, may yellow and shed their leaflets if the humidity is too high.

SMOG AND OTHER GAS INJURY

Smog is known to be detrimental to young plants of *Blechnum gibbum* and *Microlepia platyphylla*. Damage appears about 24 hours after a heavy concentration of smog. First signs of damage are tan or purple spots near the smaller veins. These spots then turn dry and brown in about 48 hours. Parts of the frond or the whole frond may die. Since home growers will find it impractical to install desmogging devices, the only corrective measure is to close outside air vents during heavy smog attacks or to avoid planting smog-sensitive plants.

Natural and manufactured gas leaking into greenhouses has been reported to cause injury to various types of plants, presumably including ferns. Typical injuries to flowering plants would be curling of plant parts, growth of dormant buds, and early petal drop or closure. A sensitive test for the presence of gas is the early folding of carnation flower petals.

5. SOILS AND FERTILIZERS

SOILS

There are probably as many soil mixes as growers. It is the grower who determines what mix is best for him. If he waters frequently, he will use a coarser mix. If he waters less frequently, he will use a finer mix. If he fertilizes frequently, he will not add fertilizers to his mix. If he does not fertilize regularly, he will add fertilizers to his mix or use one that has rich garden soil. In every case, however, all ferns need a growing medium that will hold moisture, provide aeration, support the roots, and either provide nutrients or be receptive to their addition.

SOIL FOR POTTING

Beginners and even commercial growers may find it easier to purchase commercially prepared planter mixes (see Appendix II for sources). Most of these mixes contain one-half to three-fourths organic matter (peat moss, leaf mold, wood shavings, or bark chips) and the balance of inorganic matter (sand, perlite, vermiculite, soil, or various combinations of these). Some may also have nutrients and wetting agents added. Soilless mixes are much favored by some commercial growers, as mixes containing soil are heavy and tend to vary with the quality of the soil. Some of the standard fern mixes with or without soil are given in Table 5.1. Also see "Soil Additives," below. A very simple mix consists of 1 part peat moss and 1 part fine sand to which one tablespoon of hoof and horn is added to each gallon of the mix. After adding hoof and horn use within a week. This mix will need to be followed with regular fertilization shortly after planting. The mix may need to be screened to a finer texture for very young or small ferns. For basket ferns and terrestrial ferns requiring very good drainage, add another part or two of coarse material, such as ground bark, coarse leaf mold, or perlite. Also see the Cornell epiphytic mix, Table 5.1.

SOIL FOR OUTDOOR PLANTING BEDS

If the soil in the planting bed is loam and at least half organic matter you are fortunate. From time to time the organic matter may need to be replaced, but such a soil is ideal and easy to work for outdoor plantings.

If the soil is on the sandy side it can be improved by adding water-holding materials such as peat moss. Sandy soils will require more watering and fertilizing than other soils, but they are easy to work, provide excellent aeration, and do not accumulate excess salts. Plants grown in sandy soils respond quickly to fertilization.

Silty soils hold more water and nutrients than sandy soils but may need to have their aeration improved for good fern growth. Add organic matter, sand, or perlite to improve the aeration.

Partial or light clay soils need coarse and resilient additions to improve aeration and to keep the clay from packing and becoming hard. Add coarse-textured grades of organic matter until it makes up about half or more of the soil. Sand, perlite, or gypsum (calcium sulfate) will also be helpful additives to reduce packing of the clay.

TABLE 5.1   COMMONLY USED PLANTING MIXES

PLANTING MIXES WITH SOIL

Garden Soil Mix

Leaf mold	4 parts
Garden loam	1 part
Sand	1 part

Garden Soil Mix for Lime-loving Ferns

Leaf mold	3 parts
Garden loam	1½ parts
Sand	1½ parts
Calcium carbonate (ground limestone)	1 ounce per cubic foot of soil mix or more to bring pH to 7–8.

SOILLESS PLANTING MIXES

UC Soil Mix C (Matkin and Chandler 1957)

Peat moss, Canadian or German sphagnum, or California hypnum	5 cubic feet
Sand, fine (0.5 to 0.05 mm in diameter)	5 cubic feet
Potassium nitrate	1½ ounces
Pctassium sulfate	1½ ounces
20% superphosphate	14 ounces
Dolomite lime	2¾ ounces
Calcium carbonate (ground limestone)	14 ounces

If a moderate amount of reserve nitrogen is desired add 14 ounces of hoof and horn or blood meal to the above, but use the mixture within a week of preparation. For limestone-loving plants, add more ground limestone, up to 14 additional ounces may be needed.

It is best to remove all or most of the soil if it consists of very dense clay. Replace it with a good potting mix. Replacement need only be in pockets where the ferns are to be planted. Clay soils are difficult to dilute. Even if an equal amount of organic matter is added to heavy clay soil, the soil will be suitable for ferns for only about three years. The organic material gradually decays, and the soil becomes more and more dominated by clay, resulting in poor aeration and drainage. The growth slows, and the plant may rot, particularly during cool weather. Top applications of mulch are usually too thin to improve the clay, and thicker mulch layers may bury the ferns. In either case, little organic matter will reach the established roots.

If such a soil has reverted to heavy clay, dig out the ferns in spring, correct the soil, and replant the fern. Tree ferns and large ferns are difficult to replant, so before planting in the first place, be certain the soil is suitable.

Clay soils generally have more nutrients than sandy soils. They also hold more water. The main problems with clay soils are their harsh texture, tendency to expand when wet, and shrink when dry, and their lack

Cornell Foliage Plant Mix (Boodley 1972)

Peat moss, Canadian or German sphagnum	5 cubic feet
Vermiculite, #2 grade	2½ cubic feet
Perlite, medium-fine grade	2½ cubic feet
Dolomite lime	3 pounds
20% superphosphate	12 ounces
10-10-10 fertilizer, inorganic	1 pound
Iron sulfate	4 ounces
Potassium nitrate	6 ounces
Peter's Soluble Trace Element Mix (see Appendix II for source)	1 teaspoon

For limestone-loving plants add 3 more pounds of dolomite lime.

Cornell Epiphytic Mix (Boodley 1972)

Peat moss, Canadian or German sphagnum, shredded or screened through ¼-inch mesh	5 cubic feet
Douglas fir bark, screened through ⅛- to ¼-inch mesh	5 cubic feet
Perlite, medium-fine grade	5 cubic feet
Dolomite lime	3 pounds
20% superphosphate	2⅔ pounds
10-10-10 fertilizer, inorganic	1⅓ pounds
Iron sulfate	6 ounces
Potassium nitrate	8 ounces
Peter's Soluble Trace Element Mix (see Appendix II for source)	1 tablespoon

Commercially Prepared Mixes
A number are on the market. See Appendix II for sources.

of aeration. Though tropical ferns may grow in clay, they are usually on slopes with very good drainage where the clay seldom dries and shrinks during periods of active growth.

RAISED PLANTING BEDS

Where it is suitable, raised planting beds may be another solution to poor soil or a lack of topsoil. Raised beds may be erected over poor soil and filled with a good planter mix. If commercial planter boxes aren't used, redwood planks or rocks are suitable as retaining walls for the raised beds. Be certain that the soil is well drained. If not, provide drain holes to the sides and add a layer of broken flower pots, gravel, or coarse sand at the bottom of the planting bed.

MULCHES

Mulches are any loose material placed over the soil. For ferns this includes peat moss, leaf mold, and wood and bark products. Mulches reduce the evaporation from the soil, prevent mud from splattering on the foliage, replace soil which may have washed away from the roots, and give a neater look to the garden. Ferns benefit from the application of periodic mulches. A good time to mulch is in the spring. The major precaution is to avoid burying the crown of the fern when applying the mulch.

SOIL ADDITIVES

Soil additives are substances which may be added to soil to suit the individual needs of the fern and grower. Some of the more common additives used in soil mixes for ferns are as follows:

Bark products. Bark may be shredded, ground, or in chips. Bark products decay more slowly than wood or peat additives and are used when a well-drained, long-lasting organic mix is needed.

Charcoal. Charcoal is added to mixes which might become waterlogged. It absorbs toxic materials produced under poor aeration. However, there are limits to its capabilities, and it is better to avoid waterlogged conditions in the beginning.

Fertilizers. Fertilizers contain mineral substances needed by the plant. Fish emulsion, blood meal, and hoof and horn are examples of organic fertilizers often used in planting mixes for ferns. Planting mixes with organic fertilizers added to them should be used within a week of mixing. Inorganic fertilizers which may be added to planting mixes include potassium nitrate, potassium sulfate, superphosphate, dolomite lime, calcium carbonate, and so forth. Mixes containing inorganic fertilizers may usually be stored indefinitely.

Humus. Humus is the dark, resilient, water-holding material resulting from the partial decay of plant material. A "humusy" soil is one containing much partially decayed plant material. Any partially decayed plant material may be used as a source of humus.

Inorganic matter. Inorganic matter lacks substances derived directly from plants or animals. Inorganic matter often used in planting mixes for ferns includes perlite, vermiculite, and soils such as sand, silt, or loams.

Leaf mold. Next to peat moss, leaf mold—partly decayed leaves—is the most popular substance used in planting mixes for ferns. Quality oak leaf mold is increasingly difficult to obtain. In California it is illegal to remove leaf mold from many areas, and if taken from lowland areas it may be infected with *Armillaria* or oak root rot fungus.

Lime. See discussion in "Acid and Base Soils," below.

Loam. Loam is a soil having a mixture of sand, silt, and clay in such proportions that the characteristics of no one predominates. It is an ideal garden soil.

Organic matter. Organic matter refers to any materials derived from plants or animals or their remains. Minerals and humus may be added to the soil from organic material. Organic matter commonly used in planting mixes for ferns includes peat moss, leaf mold, sawdust, wood shavings, ground or shredded bark, compost, and manures. Manures and compost are not favored for commercial planting mixes because of their variable quality and possible contamination with plant diseases.

Oyster shell. See discussion in "Acid and Base Soils," below.

Peat moss. Peat moss is partly or wholly decomposed moss. It may be composed of a mixture of moss species or of certain species such as sphagnum moss or hypnum moss. German sphagnum is of good quality. Canadian sphagnum tends to be coarser than American sphagnum. Sedge or black peat does not contain moss and it is not recommended for fern use because it may contain salts. Peat moss provides resilience and aeration to the soil as well as water-holding capability. Moisten peat moss a day or two before use. Warm water penetrates faster than cold water. Also, the use of a wetting agent will facilitate water penetration. The peat moss may need to be worked by mixing and squeezing to ensure even distribution of the moisture. The moss used to line hanging baskets is uncut and coarse. It may be composed of sphagnum or a mixture of species often sold as green moss.

Perlite. Perlite is also known by the brand name, Sponge Rok. It is a sterile inorganic material derived by expanding siliceous rock. Perlite is light, porous, loose, and resistant to collapse. Drainage and aeration of soil is improved by additions of perlite.

Sand. Sand is a type of soil having a particular particle size range. The fine grade is recommended for potting mixes. Coarser grades of sand may be added to soils to increase the aeration and drainage. Fine sand is commercially designated as "minus 30 and plus 270," meaning that the sand has passed through a 30-mesh screen but does not pass a 270-mesh screen. Quartz sand and washed builder's sand are suitable sands. Do not use sand from oceans, beaches, or other saline areas.

Sawdust and other wood waste. Applications of sawdust and other wood waste such as wood shavings or chips increase the humus of the soil and therefore improve the soil structure. However, they contain very few mineral nutrients. Fresh or partly decayed sawdust (or other wood waste) may be used. Most fresh sawdust and wood waste contain no appreciable amount of toxic substances, and what might be present disappears by decomposition in a few weeks after application. Reports of toxicity are probably due to the failure to provide sufficient nitrogen and phosphorous to the soil after the addition of wood waste. The microorganisms which convert the sawdust to humus need mineral nutrients to grow and therefore deplete the soil of these minerals. Provide additional mineral elements for the microorganisms so the plants will not suffer. Add 12 pounds of 10-6-4 fertilizer to every 100 pounds of sawdust. Other fertilizers rich in nitrogen and phosphorous may be used. Nitrogen is the most important, and calculations are based on supplying 1.2 pounds of nitrogen per 100 pounds of sawdust. Apply the minerals at intervals through the growing season. Nitrified sawdust has nitrogen added.

Soil. Soil in the strict sense refers to sand, silt, or clay. (Also see "Loam" and "Sand," above.) For consistency in quality of a potting mix, sand is used. Silty sands and loams vary in quality but do retain more moisture and contain more nutrients than sand. Clay soils are not recommended for ferns, though they can be improved somewhat by additives (see above).

Vermiculite. Vermiculite is a sterile inorganic substance produced by expanding bits of mica. It contains some potassium and calcium. Its surfaces provide sites for favorable movement of minerals. It also retains water but tends to collapse in a relatively short time.

ACID AND BASE SOILS

Much emphasis has been placed on whether a soil is acidic or basic. The importance is not in the acidity itself, but in its effect on the availability of chemicals needed by the plants. If your plants are growing well, do not be concerned about the soil acidity. If they are not growing well and do not respond to balanced fertilizers, consider checking the acidity, but first check for other unfavorable conditions.

Determining an acidic or basic soil. Arid climatic regions tend to have basic soils; rainy regions tend to have acidic soils. The range from an acid to base condition is known as the pH range and is measured on a logarithmic scale from 1 to 14. A pH of 7 is neutral, and such a soil is neither acidic or basic. Acid soils measure less than 7 and basic soils more than 7. The greatest amount and variety of nutrients used by plants are available to them at a pH between 5.5 and 7. Therefore, most plants grow best somewhere in this range. Most ferns grow best at a pH between 6 and 7. The most inexpensive way to measure the pH of soils is to use pH paper, which turns a particular color at a particular pH. See Appendix II for source.

Limestone-loving ferns or ferns of basic soil (pH 7–8). Ferns native to basic soils, limestone bluffs, or boulders need more calcium than the average fern. To grow these ferns it may be necessary to add calcium carbonate in the form of dolomite, agricultural lime, ground limestone, or oyster shells to the soil. Hydrated forms of lime ($Ca(OH)_2$) should be used with caution, as the pH may be changed too much and be injurious to the plants. Where limestone rocks are available, ferns may be grown in soil pockets between these rocks or crushed limestone may be added to the soil. Some people have claimed success by using pieces of concrete instead of limestone rock.

It is very simple to test for calcium in the soil. Obtain a teaspoon of some strong acid, such as sulfuric acid or muriatic acid (hydrochloric acid or hydrogen chloride). Sulfuric acid may be obtained from the car battery. Muriatic acid may be obtained by using the toilet bowl cleaner Vanish. Place a teaspoon of one of these acids on a cup or less of soil and watch for bubbling. Bubbling indicates the presence of enough calcium in the form of lime (calcium carbonate). If there is no bubbling you may not have enough calcium or may have one of the few soils that has calcium but does not respond to this test, in which case you may have to have the soil tested commercially.

Acid-loving ferns (pH 4–7). Some acid-loving ferns grow in wet, marshy areas where large amounts of decaying organic material produce carbonic acid. Other acid-loving ferns may grow in well-drained soil which has been leached of its calcium or basic salts. A peaty or highly organic soil mix will provide an acid condition for growing these ferns. Also the additions of aluminum sulfate, ammonium sulfate, ammonium nitrate, or finely ground sulfur will make the soil more acid. Sulfur is the most economical and efficient additive.

STERILIZING SOILS

In the strict usage, sterilization means the complete killing of all organisms, a condition required for research but not general horticulture. The term "soil sterilization" as usually used in horticulture refers to the destruction of only the important disease organisms, insects, and weeds. It will be referred to here as soil "treatment" to distinguish it from true sterilization. Except for commercial growers, planting mixes for ferns are usually not given soil treatment unless diseases are present or the mix is used for growing fern spores or young ferns. Use of compost, manure, soils, or leaf mold in planting mixes increases the need for soil treatment. It may

be accomplished by the use of chemicals or heat whereas true soil sterilization is usually done by heat in an autoclave or oven. The commercial
grower will find the U.C. System for Producing Healthy Container-Grown
Plants, Manual 23 published by the University of California, Division of
Agricultural Sciences, 1957, a very helpful source of information regarding
soil treatments.

Chemical treatments. Chemicals such as methyl bromide, formaldehyde, or other such commercial preparations may be used to treat soil but
not around live plants. Home growers may find it easier, though not as
effective, to use fungicide drenches such as Terraclor (PCNB), Arasan
(Thiram), Captan, or Physan (Consan) (see Chapter 11, "Fungi and
Bacteria"). These products may be used around live plants.

Steam treatment. Most commercial growers use steam to treat the soil.
Steam is applied through various types of equipment until all parts of the
soil have been heated to 160°F for 30 minutes. For a better margin of
safety, heat at 180°F for 30 minutes. High heat does affect the soil and
may produce toxic conditions. If this should become a problem, let the soil
stand for a few weeks or leach it thoroughly with water.

For small amounts of soil, a home-made steam sterilizer can be devised
for steam treatment. A large cooking pot or roasting pan containing a rack
to raise the soil or pots containing the soil above the water may be covered
and heated over the stove or in the oven to produce steam. Very moist soil
wrapped in aluminum foil may also be so heated. Set the oven temperature
at 250°F or high enough to produce active steam. Be sure that the steam has
penetrated all parts of the soil for at least 30 minutes. This may require
placing the oven controls at 300°F for half an hour if there is much mass
to be penetrated. Since most plastic pots or boxes cannot be sterilized in
this manner, they will have to be disinfected separately with a 10 percent
Clorox solution in which they are soaked for 30 minutes, rinsed, and then
filled with treated soil.

Boiling water treatment. Many growers find pouring boiling water
over pots filled with small amounts of soil and provided with drainage a
satisfactory treatment for the growing of fern spores. For a given amount
of soil pour at least twice as much (or more) boiling water through it. By
placing a clean paper towel over the moist soil before pouring, much of the
lighter material in the mix may be kept from floating up to the surface.

Direct boiling treatment. Though boiling soil in a cooking pot directly
over heat kills the undesirable organisms, this method is not recommended.
Direct boiling reduces the soil to a soggy mush which takes a long time to
drain and upon drying lacks aeration.

Steam sterilization. Complete or full sterilization will kill all organisms including their spores. Except in scientific work, such as growing
ferns in agar, full sterilization is not required. In this process the material
to be sterilized is placed in an autoclave at 15 pounds pressure for 15

minutes or longer (depending on the size of the mass) at a temperature of 250–254°F. Small amounts of soil, pots, dishes, or other items may be sterilized in a home pressure cooker at 15 pounds for 20–30 minutes.

Dry heat sterilization. In dry heat sterilization material to be sterilized is placed in an oven at 320°F for two hours or longer depending upon the mass. The dry heat makes soil very difficult to wet after sterilization. However, this method is useful in sterilizing paper envelopes used to store sterilized spores and other such items. To sterilize thin objects such as envelopes it is necessary to put them in a heavier box before subjecting them to the given oven temperature.

FERTILIZERS

Ferns growing in rich soils are well supplied with mineral nutrients and do not need supplements or fertilizers. But though most gardeners do not have such fertile soils, they want the best-looking plants possible. Ferns which receive ample fertilizers or mineral nutrients grow faster, are bigger, and are more luxuriant. However, it is also well known that ferns are sensitive to improper applications of fertilizers, making the beginning grower hesitant about applying them. It is important therefore to select the proper fertilizers and learn how to apply them correctly.

WHAT FERNS NEED FERTILIZERS?

Ferns that need fertilizers grow slowly, are smaller than normal, and/or produce poor-quality foliage. Ferns that are producing healthy green fronds do not need fertilizers. If you do not wish a fern to grow large or quickly, do not fertilize unless it shows poor foliage color. In that case, light applications of fertilizer will improve the color.

CHOOSING A FERTILIZER

Beginners are advised to select fertilizers with a reputation for "low burn." Low-burn fertilizers have a low percentage of highly soluble salts (salts which dissolve quickly in water). Liquid types with a low-burn reputation include fish emulsion, Spoonit, Hyponex, and Blue Whale. Dry types with low-burn properties include fish meal, cottonseed meal, castor bean meal, and activated sewage sludge.

LIQUID VS. DRY FERTILIZERS

Liquid fertilizers are probably safer and easier to use by beginners. A liquid fertilizer may be applied at the same time watering is done; this saves on labor. Also, when fertilizer is diluted for application, there is less likelihood of an accidental overdose. A disadvantage of liquid fertilizer is that some of it quickly passes beyond the root zone and is wasted. That which remains leaches out of the soil easily and will need to be replenished sooner than dry forms.

Dry fertilizers last longer in the soil. You must spread the powder or granules thinly and evenly over the surface of the soil. If the dry fertilizer contains much soluble salt and is accidentally concentrated in one spot, the soluble salts will surely injure the plant.

New fertilizers have been developed which stay in the soil for three to nine months and slowly release soluble salts. Some of these fertilizers release salts upon watering, so that every time the plant is watered some of the salts are released. Since ferns require more frequent watering than other plants, be careful in using these fertilizers lest overfertilization occur. Dry and slow-release fertilizers are not recommended for staghorn ferns, as granules caught behind the base fronds may injure the tissue.

ORGANIC VS. INORGANIC FERTILIZERS

Organic fertilizers are derived from organic substances, while inorganic fertilizers are mostly derived from chemicals or mining processes. Fertilizers such as fish emulsion, bone meal, or castor bean meal are organic types, while those like ammonium sulfate and superphosphate are inorganic types.

Beginners are advised to use organic fertilizers with low-burn reputations and defer use of inorganic types unless they also have a low-burn reputation. Generally, organic types contain fewer soluble salts than inorganic types and result in less burn. They also release their nutrients more slowly than inorganic types and last longer in the soil. However, inorganic fertilizers produce quicker plant responses. Exceptions occur in both fertilizers in regard to their soluble salt content. Blood meal (an organic fertilizer) contains a high amount of soluble salt and may readily burn plants if applied carelessly. Some inorganic fertilizers have salts which do not dissolve quickly in water, hence would not burn the plants as readily. Do not use manures in soils where warmth and high humidity prevail, as in greenhouses. Their usage will encourage bacteria and molds.

COMPLETE OR INCOMPLETE FERTILIZERS

Beginners are advised to use complete fertilizers. Complete fertilizers contain the three most important elements needed by the plant. They are nitrogen, phosphorus, and potassium. Complete fertilizers are generally preferred over incomplete ones, though results may vary according to the plant, soil, or cultural conditions. Incomplete fertilizers may have only one or two of these important elements.

The percentage of each of these three elements contained in the fertilizer is cited on each fertilizer package. The percentages appear as 5-2-2 for most fish emulsions or 15-0-0 for hoof and horn. The first number indicates the percentage of nitrogen, the second the percentage of phosphorus, and the third the percentage of potassium. Fish emulsion is a balanced fertilizer, whereas hoof and horn is not.

There are a number of elements needed by the plant, but nitrogen is the nutrient most needed by ferns. Trace elements, those needed by plants in very small amounts, are usually present in sufficient amounts in the soil or in fertilizers as impurities.

APPLICATION OF FERTILIZERS

Follow the manufacturer's directions for application. Never give more than the recommended dosage. There is no harm in giving less, particularly if you are uncertain about the fern's tolerance to the fertilizer. Some growers regularly reduce the amount applied for ferns to half the recommended dosage. It is more beneficial to give smaller amounts over several spaced applications than the full dosage all at once. Though more work is involved in this method, the plant makes better use of the fertilizer.

Fertilizers which must be diluted should be diluted accurately. Dissolve as much of the fertilizer as possible before application. For watering large numbers of plants, a range of mechanical devices may be purchased. Those which mix the fertilizer with the water as it flows through the water line are great time savers. Those which operate only with a strong stream of water are not desirable, as the force of the water may damage the fronds and wash the soil from the roots.

Powders or granular forms must be sprinkled evenly and thinly over the moist soil surface. Do not till the soil to work these fertilizers into the ground. The fern roots are fine and fibrous. They grow close to the surface and will be injured by tilling. Water thoroughly immediately after application. Any fertilizer accidentally spilled on the foliage should be washed off immediately. If too much fertilizer has been accidentally applied to one spot, particularly near the crown of the fern, remove it or spread it out thinly. Not only will this reduce the possibility of burning the fern; it will also reduce the concentration of mold growth. Although organic fertilizers must have microorganisms to decompose and release the nutrients, a very high concentration of mold may damage the fern.

FREQUENCY OF APPLICATIONS

The frequency of fertilizations depends on the manufacturer's recommendations. On the average one application every three weeks is needed for liquid fertilizers and longer intervals for dry fertilizers. Fertilize infrequently if you do not wish the fern to grow too large. Ferns which do not enter any noticeable rest period but continue to grow actively the year around benefit from fertilizers the year around, unless you do not wish to encourage new growth prior to winter for fear of frost damage. Ferns which are inclined toward a rest period or dormancy should not be fertilized during this time, as there is little intake of nutrients then. Where there is heavy watering or frequent rainfall on very porous soils, the water will leach out the fertilizer. Ferns growing in such areas will have to be fertilized more frequently. On the other hand, soils which do not drain readily retain fertilizer and need not be frequently fertilized.

TREATING OVERFERTILIZED FERNS

If you have accidentally overfertilized, immediately remove all fertilizer that might be on the surface and see that the plant is well drained. Then water heavily to leach out any remaining fertilizer. After this liberal watering, water sparingly so the soil will be well aerated. Increase the humidity and remove badly burned and wilted fronds which have not recovered. Recovery of the plant usually depends on the amount of root and rhizome damage. Ferns which are young or lack fleshy rhizomes are more difficult to save than older ferns or those with fleshy rhizomes.

Damage from overfertilization is caused by the release of too much soluble salt. The excess salts dehydrate the fern roots and kill them. Without living roots the foliage wilts. If only parts of the roots are injured there may be a partial wilting of the foliage and/or the characteristic leaf scorch or burn appearance. Fertilizer salts on the leaf may also dehydrate and burn the leaf tissue. The partial loss of roots or foliage sets the plant back, and it may be stunted for some time. Successful fertilization works on the principle that a little soluble salt is good but too much is bad.

FERNS AND PLANT HORMONES

The effects of plant hormones (auxin, gibberellic acid, etc.) on ferns (sporophytes) are not well known. Gibberellic acid seems to increase the growth rate of young walking ferns (*Camptosorus rhizophyllus*). The effects of plant hormones on germination of spores and the early stages of prothallial development are complex and technical. Studies indicate that hormones, quality of light, and various chemicals have an effect on the germination and prothallial development of some ferns.

6. THROUGH THE YEAR WITH FERNS

YEAR-ROUND NEEDS

Where ferns are actively growing the year around, watering, fertilizing, and grooming will be required the year around. If maximum growth is desired, fertilize more frequently during the growing seasons and less or none during the cool months. Watch for slugs and snails as well as other pests and for sudden damaging changes in the weather.

Remove old or badly damaged fronds from vigorously growing plants. Cut them off at the base of the stipe. Removal of these fronds maintains a neat appearance and reduces hiding places for pests. If the plant is not growing well and has only a few fronds, avoid removing any fronds except those that are totally brown or yellow. Sometimes only the tip or margin of an otherwise lovely frond is disfigured. Rather than cut the whole frond off, the disfigurement may be trimmed away with scissors and the remaining part cut into a shape that is close to the natural one.

Ferns benefit from an occasional fine spray to remove dust, dirt, and lurking insects. Fronds with hairy surfaces tend to catch debris which does not wash off easily; use a soft brush.

Water spots on the foliage left by salts in the water cause no harm if there aren't too many of them. If spots are conspicuous and objectionable they can be removed by misting them gently with a liberal amount of water, to dissolve the salts and wash them off. About half a tablespoon of mild household detergent added to a quart of water will dissolve the salt faster. Spots may be avoided if tap water is not applied to the fronds or if distilled, rain, or deionized water is used. Remember that applications of liquid fertilizers which settle on the leaves will also produce water spots. Commercial leaf polishes may be used on thick leathery ferns to remove spots and give a shine, but the shine is not necessary for the welfare of the plant.

WINTER CARE

If you live in a temperate area, the outdoor ferns are mostly dormant and will require little care other than to see that their protective coverings or shelters are not disrupted. Outdoor ferns in subtropical climates are slow in their growth. Aside from removing withered fronds, watering, and fertilizing once or twice a month during the winter or not at all, there is little else that needs to be done. Winter is the low point in an outdoor subtropical fern garden, but if the fronds were well taken care of in late summer and fall, they will grace the garden through the winter. Do watch for early spring growth and remove old fronds before the emerging fiddleheads become hopelessly entangled in the old fronds. Indoor ferns, greenhouse ferns, and those in tropical gardens will require their usual program of care unless certain species show a natural rest period, in which case water and fertilize these plants less.

SPRING CARE

In temperate and subtropical areas ferns, like most other plants, produce a surge of growth in spring. New fiddleheads will be pushing up and uncoiling. In temperate areas remove the mulch and winter shelters. In all areas remove dead and old fronds before the fiddleheads have elongated. This will minimize the injury to the new fiddleheads and provide room for their development. Aphids most commonly appear on the ferns in early spring, so watch for them as well as other pests. If the winter and spring rains have washed some of the soil away from the roots, replace this soil or mulch the soil. Resume fertilizing every two or three weeks if maximum growth is desired. Spring is a good time to divide, transplant, or repot ferns; try to do this before the fiddleheads uncoil. Some ferns will shed all or most of their fronds just before putting on new fronds. The squirrel's-foot fern (*Davallia trichomanoides*) drops its fronds in late winter or early spring; the Canary Island davallia (*D. canariensis*) drops its fronds in spring or early summer. The Knight's polypody drops its fronds in late spring. These ferns look forlorn with their withered fronds, but new fronds soon appear to clothe the basket again. Remove any lingering old fronds to make way for the new. All ferns must be protected from unseasonable heat waves, particularly since new fronds are still developing and uncoiling; they are very soft and dehydrate easily.

SUMMER CARE

Most ferns will continue growing new fronds into summer. Old fronds that yellow and brown should be removed. Fertilization should be continued for maximum growth. Watering and keeping the air humid will be the major problem in some areas, especially for hanging baskets and pots. Watch for thrip and scale, which frequently appear at this time. Snails, slugs, and other biting pests will also be very active. In many parts of the country where there is a long growing season, it is still possible to divide, replant, and repot. Trim back the more robust species of ferns when they threaten to shade the smaller and slower-growing species. Be ready to mist when the weather gets too hot. Avoid overwatering the soil when increasing the humidity. Sprinkle the walkways instead of saturating the soil. Fern spores are most frequently formed at this time and in the fall.

FALL CARE

From late summer into fall, the growth wanes. Less water will be required. Fertilization should be reduced or withheld. Deciduous ferns will yellow and brown, and new growth will stop until spring. Leave the old fronds on the plant to protect them through the winter in areas where frost and freezes occur. Some ferns will need mulches and even screens or frames built over them in very cold climates. It is important to mark or remember where deciduous species are located in the warmer garden so they will not be accidentally dug up or injured during winter garden activities.

In subtropical gardens where there is a longer growing period, the ferns will still need to be groomed and watered. Where there is danger of frost, do not remove green fronds even if they are tattered, for to do so may encourage new growth which may be damaged by frost. Defer the urge to trim until the danger from frost has passed. Also reduce fertilizers to avoid encouragement of new growth before winter. As the weather cools, the ferns will not be using as much fertilizer or water. Most of the fronds that remain on the plant in late summer and fall will stay on the plant through the winter, though if the temperatures are mild, some ferns will continue to produce a few, smaller fronds in the months ahead. If the temperature cools very much, the fronds will yellow.

7. PLANTING

PLANTING TIME

Spring is generally the best time to plant, replant, transplant, or propagate ferns. This allows for a long growing period so the fern may establish itself before cool weather. Ferns which form only one set of fronds a year —for instance, *Osmundas* and others—are best moved in early spring before the new fronds have appeared, or in fall after the old ones have died. If they must be moved while in leaf, try to preserve as much of the foliage as possible to ensure good growth the following year. Ferns which produce new fronds throughout the growing season can more safely be moved while in leaf.

BEDS, POTS, OR BASKETS?

Deciding whether to plant ferns in the ground, in pots, or in hanging containers is determined by the fern, climate, setting, and personal preference. Ferns planted in the ground usually require less care than those in pots or baskets. They don't dry out as fast, and the soil acts as a buffer to absorb extra moisture, excess fertilizer, high or low temperatures, and other unfavorable conditions. Also, ferns planted in the ground do not have to be replanted as frequently as those grown in pots. However, hanging containers show cascading or drooping fronds to their best advantage.

If you desire to move your plants about for decorative purposes or winter protection, plant them in containers. If you want to keep a natural effect with potted plants, sink the pots into the ground to hide them. Many ferns which grow naturally in the ground (terrestrial ferns) may be planted in baskets directly or planted in a pot which is then placed in a basket. They will need to be kept sufficiently moist. Ferns which naturally grow in trees or rocks (epiphytic ferns) are generally planted in pots or baskets with a loose soil mix, but may be planted in the ground if very good drainage is provided.

Terrestrial or epiphytic ferns with long creeping rhizomes and fronds which grow far apart are generally not attractive in pots, but most are suitable for hanging baskets. In pots, these creeping ferns soon grow to the edge of the pot and may die because of drier conditions or salt accumulation on the pot. Some may grow over the edge of the pot and dry, or grow down into the pot and become trapped. This leaves the old rhizome in full view while the new growth has dried, grown out of the pot, or buried itself. Such ferns are best planted in moss-lined baskets where the rhizomes may root themselves over a broader surface. Very wide creeping ferns are best planted in the ground or where they have ample space to grow and may be free to climb up trees or moss-covered posts, if they are of such habit.

Ferns with closely placed fronds, erect or semierect stems, or short creeping rhizomes are best for planting in pots where they can display their foliage patterns. Ferns native to dry or seasonal climates are best planted in pots or separate places in the garden where their particular watering needs may be more easily met.

PLANTING IN BEDS

SELECTING THE SITE

Before planting in the ground, check the site for proper light, wind exposure, and soil conditions. Anticipate the full size of the fern you wish to plant. Will it fit your landscape needs? It is easier to consider these factors now than later. Start with hardened plants if possible. (Hardened plants are those which have adjusted to exposure.) Greenhouse plants moved immediately outdoors may wilt, especially if they have soft succulent growth. These plants should be gradually exposed to drier air over a week or more.

PREPARING THE BED

Prepare the soil so it is moist and loose (friable). Use soil that has at least half organic matter (see Chapter 5, "Soils"). Soil in the planting bed does not have to be deep because fern roots are not deep. Ten to eighteen inches of soil is sufficient for small to medium ferns. Tree ferns will do better with 24 inches of soil. This does not mean the entire bed of soil needs to be changed to the given depth. If the soil is unsuitable for ferns and you do not wish to change the whole bed, plant the ferns in "pockets" of suitable soil, but provide good drainage, especially in very heavy clay soils, by adding coarse gravel or broken crock to the bottom of the planting hole. The area of suitable soil for ferns should be large enough to fit the anticipated spread of roots. This is roughly one-third to one-half the anticipated spread of the fronds.

Once the soil has been prepared, dig the hole to the depth and width of the container. Gently firm the soil at the bottom of the hole so it will not settle too much after planting. Proceed as follows:

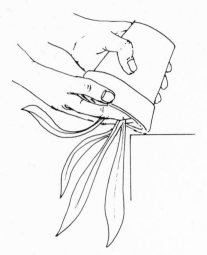

Have the soil moist.

Support the soil with one hand.

Invert the pot and tap it sharply on the edge of a table.

a

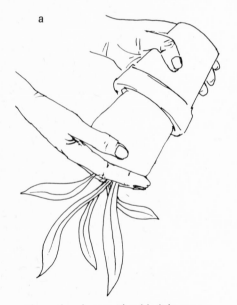

The soil and roots should slide out of the pot intact.

Fig. 7.1   Removing plants from pots.
a. removing from a small pot;
b. removing from a large pot

BASIC PLANTING PROCEDURES

1. Getting the plant out of the container. If the soil in the container is on the dry side, water it. Do this a day before removal, if possible, so the soil won't be muddy. Moist soil will not fall away from the roots as easily as dry soil. If the fern is in a can, have the nurseryman cut the can. Ferns in small pots are easily tapped out. Support the top of the soil with one hand, turn the pot over, and give the edge a sharp tap on the edge of a bench (*Fig. 7.1*). The ball of soil and fern should slide out intact. Lay larger pots on their side, protect pot edges with padding, then tap with a mallet until the ball of soil slides away from the pot. Stubborn soil balls may be floated out by applying water pressure from a hose into the drain hole.

2. Digging ferns out of the ground for transplanting. If a fern must be taken out of the ground and replanted, the best time to do this is in early spring. Water the plant a day or two before transplanting so the soil will not be muddy but moist enough to cling to the roots when the plant is moved. The diameter of the ball of roots and soil should be about half the spread of the fronds. The depth will depend upon the size of the fern.

3. Positioning and planting the fern. Normally, note the soil level of the fern you are moving and replant it at the same level (*Fig. 7.2a*). (If an erect or semierect fern has been toppling over, you may remove old stipe bases and set it deeper into the soil. Do not, however, cover its crown or growing tip [*Fig. 7.2b*].) Measure the height of the soil ball. Add or remove soil from the hole (or pot) so as to bring the crown to the proper level when it is set in place. For pots the level of the soil should be half an inch

b

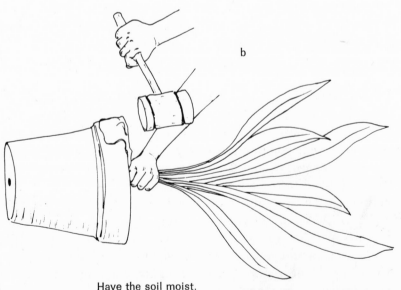

Have the soil moist.

Place the pot on its side.   Tap edges with a mallet.

Protect the edges   Soil and roots should slide
of the pot with padding.   out intact.

or more below the top edge to provide a catch basin for water (*Fig. 7.3*).

If the soil attached to the roots is particularly poor, gently shake most of it loose before replanting. Remove dead, old, and inactive roots. Cut old broken fronds and stipe bases back to the rhizome. If the fern is badly root-bound, gently loosen some of the surface roots and spread them out. In positioning creeping ferns, turn the growing tip of the rhizome in the direction you wish it to grow. (In a pot, place the tip as far from the edge of the pot as possible. This may place the fern at the edge of the pot instead of the center, but maximum growing room is provided [*Fig. 7.4*].)

Once the plant is positioned, fill in the spaces around the roots. Gently firm the soil into place as it is added until you reach the desired level. Do not cover the crown or growing point if it was growing exposed before. If surface-creeping rhizomes refuse to stay in place after planting, anchor them with pieces of bent wire or some small rocks. Water the plant well with a gentle sprinkle of water. A strong stream of water may flatten your plants or wash the soil away from the roots, destroying the soft, well-aerated soil structure. Vitamin B_1 preparations sold for stimulating root growth and recommended by some for transplanting, generally have no effect on intact plants. The leaves make sufficient amounts of B_1 which can be stored in the stem or passed to the roots. Within the first few days after planting, some of the softer fronds may wilt and die. Remove them. New fronds should soon grow out to replace those that were lost.

SPECIAL CARE

Remove dead and damaged fronds. Keep leaves raked away from the crowns, particularly if slugs and snails are a problem. Keep alert about trimming back faster-growing plants which may shade the slower-growing ferns. Promptly replace soil which may have been washed away by rain or watering. Apply mulches (see Chapter 5, "Mulches") if desired. Some beds may need to be reworked every few years. Slower growth and packed soil are indications that change is needed.

PLANTING IN POTS

SELECTING THE POT

Some thought and care in the selection of pots will be helpful in giving the fern the best growing conditions possible as well as displaying the plant to its best advantage.

Pot size. The pot size will depend on the fern. In general, the diameter of the pot should be about one-third the height of the fern (measured from the soil level). Repotting will generally require the next size up. For looks as well as for growing, avoid the temptation to put plants in pots that are too big. Many ferns, especially the maidenhair ferns, do not grow well when "overpotted." This is because the larger amount of soil holds too much moisture in proportion to the active roots. The roots cannot use up enough of the surrounding moisture to keep the soil well aerated.

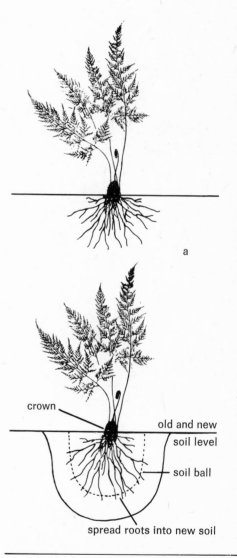

crown

old and new
soil level

soil ball

spread roots into new soil

Fig. 7.2   Replanting.
a. transplanting
an established plant

Clay vs. plastic pots. If proper adjustments are made, ferns do equally well in plastic or clay pots. Remember that plastic or glazed pots retain more moisture than porous clay pots or wooden tubs and will need less water and more aeration than clay pots. Water less or use a coarser, quicker-draining soil mix than you would with clay pots. If the soil in a plastic pot has dried and pulled away from the sides, take special care to wet the soil thoroughly lest the water merely trickle between the soil and the pot and never penetrate to the roots. Plastic pots are usually not as likely to support algae or become heavily encrusted with salt as clay pots. Plastic pots do have the advantage of being light in weight, and holes are easily made with a hot ice pick for extra drainage.

Pots without drain holes. Beginners should avoid pots without drain holes. However, there are two ways to provide drainage for the plant in pots without holes. Place one to two inches of drainage material at the bottom of the pot before planting. Water the plant with distilled water. Water only to keep the soil moist, not wet. Do not overwater. The other method is to find a clay or plastic pot with a drain hole that will fit into the undrained pot. Plant the fern in the pot with the drain hole. The fern can be removed as needed for watering, permitted to drain, and then easily slipped back into the holeless pot. Some gravel or drainage material may be placed at the bottom of the holeless pot to prevent the fern from standing in water that may have accumulated at the bottom.

Shape of pot. When purchasing pots, look inside to see that the drain hole is large enough and either flush with the bottom surface or depressed to allow the water to flow out freely. Some novelty containers have such a small capacity that very frequent watering may be necessary to keep the plant from wilting and roots may fill the space much too soon. If drainage, aeration, and room for soil are adequate, the shape of the pot should not affect the growth of the plant. However, do consider the aesthetic aspects of the pot. The pot should show off the plant, not detract from it. Bright colors and bold designs will draw attention to the pot, not to the plant.

The majority of ferns do well in standard pot shapes, particularly the stouter pots known in the trade as fern or bulb pots. Nonstandard pots with very broad flat bottoms do not drain well. Add extra amounts of gravel or other drainage material if larger holes or more holes cannot be added.

PLANTING IN THE POT

Providing drainage. Very small pots (2½-inch diameter) do not need anything over the drain hole. Larger pots (4- to 8-inch diameter) need at least a piece of broken clay pot, gravel, or coarse moss over the drain hole. This permits the water to drain but keeps the soil in the pot. Deep pots and very large pots (10-inch diameter and up) need a layer of drainage material at the bottom of the pot. Pieces of broken flower pot, gravel, or perlite may be used. The amount of drainage material will depend on the pot size, the frequency of watering, and the soil mix. Hanging pots which do not drain well in spite of sufficient drainage material may be induced to drain by

b

remove old
stipe bases
crown
new soil level
old soil level
soil ball
spread roots into new soil

Fig. 7.2 b. replanting a plant
which has toppled:
remove old stipe bases,
plant deeper,
but do not cover
the crown

Place coarse gravel or broken pieces of clay
flower pots over the drain hole.

Fig. 7.3   Repotting

Add fresh soil. Depending on the size of the pot,
the soil ball should rest ½ to 3 inches
below the top edge of the pot.

Loosen and spread out dense or compacted roots.

Center the plant. Add more soil around the soil ball.
Firm soil in place.

Bring the soil level to the level of the soil ball
unless the roots are exposed,
in which case raise the soil level slightly.

Remove old or broken fronds.

Water gently but thoroughly.

inserting a cotton wick through the drain hole. Pots should be clean. Used clay pots should be scrubbed thoroughly before use.

Basic planting procedures. After providing for drainage, follow the "Basic Planting Procedures" listed under "Planting in Beds" in this chapter.

SPECIAL CARE

Potted plants will need to be carefully watched for drying or for excessive water.

Poor drainage. Never let pots stand continually in water unless the fern happens to be one of the rarely cultivated swamp varieties or aquatic ferns. If water accumulates in a saucer, empty it or keep the pot raised on pebbles above the water level in it. If your plant wilts without standing in water, it probably needs repotting.

Poor drainage in small to medium-size pots may be detected by tapping the soil ball out of the pot a day or two after watering. Examine the soil to see whether it is waterlogged. Replace the soil ball, and examine it again the next day. If the soil is still soggy and the plant has not been growing

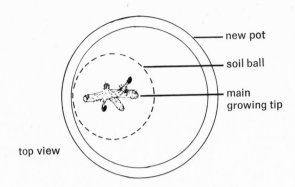

top view

new pot

soil ball

main
growing tip

Place plants with creeping rhizomes
in new pots so they will have
maximum growing room.

Place the growing tips as far
from the edge of the pot as possible

Fig. 7.4   Potting ferns with
creeping rhizomes

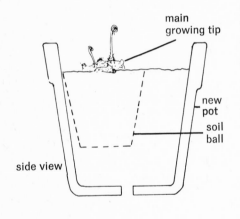

main
growing tip

new
pot
soil
ball

side view

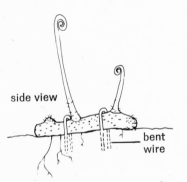

side view

bent
wire

If the rhizomes do not stay in place,
anchor with bent wire.

well, water it less frequently or improve the drainage. The presence of soft decaying roots and a strong odor of decaying vegetation are positive indication that drainage is poor (see Chapter 4, "Watering"). In flower beds or very large containers it may be necessary to check the drainage by digging a narrow hole into the soil to determine whether the soil is waterlogged.

Root-bound ferns. A fern that is too big for its pot and becomes root bound will need frequent watering, grow slowly, produce small fronds, and have lower leaves which yellow rapidly. If the fern's rhizome branches or clumps, the center section may be inactive or dead while the younger parts may be growing over each other at the periphery of the pot. Such a plant may be kept growing for a time with careful watering and fertilizing, but it will eventually decline in vigor.

Root-bound ferns should either be replanted or be divided and replanted. If you wish to increase the size of the plant, trim off the dead parts and replant it into a next larger size pot. If you wish to keep the plant in the same size pot and it is a fern that can be divided (has many growing tips), thin it to size by removing the smaller and weaker rhizome branches and other dead parts. Keep several large and husky rhizomes with their growing tips intact, and replant in the same size pot. Root-bound tree ferns and ferns with unbranched rhizomes cannot be divided and usually must go into larger pots. However, if there are many old and inactive roots that can be trimmed away, the root ball may be reduced sufficiently to be replanted in the same pot.

Salt crust on pots. The whitish salt crust on pots is unsightly, does not dissolve away readily, and may injure the plants. Change the pot if you can, or soak and wash the pot. Physan (Consan) added to the soak water makes cleaning easier. For badly encrusted pots, chip or scrape off as much of the crust as possible, then soak and flush the rest off with water. Discard very badly encrusted pots. Vinegar will dissolve some of the salt crust, but avoid getting vinegar on the soil or the plant. Reduce the salt build-up on pots by watering thoroughly once a week or by using plastic pots or cans instead of clay pots (see Chapter 4, "Water Quality and Salt Injury").

PLANTING IN BASKETS

Ferns which in their native habitat grow on trees are called epiphytes. Since soil is absent, they secure nutrients by sending their roots into the bark, debris of leaves, moss, lichen, and other substances. These ferns are adapted to rapid drainage and drier air than terrestrial ferns. Most ferns used in hanging containers are epiphytes, though certain terrestrial ferns do grow well in baskets. Ferns with drooping or cascading fronds are particularly suited for baskets.

SELECTING THE BASKET

To simulate the native conditions of epiphytic ferns, plant them in baskets that are open in structure, to provide good drainage and openings for creeping rhizomes to root. Terrestrial ferns may be planted in open-structured baskets but do better in more tightly woven ones that do not drain as rapidly. Baskets may be made of wire, wood, pieces of tree ferns, ceramic, or other substances. Although ordinary clay or plastic pots may be used, they will have to be planted with a looser soil mix or watered less frequently.

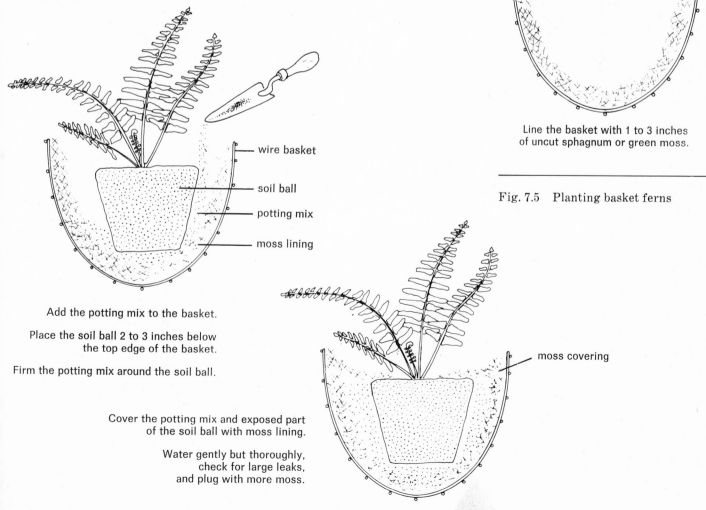

wire basket   moss lining

Line the basket with 1 to 3 inches of uncut sphagnum or green moss.

Fig. 7.5   Planting basket ferns

wire basket

soil ball

potting mix

moss lining

Add the potting mix to the basket.

Place the soil ball 2 to 3 inches below the top edge of the basket.

Firm the potting mix around the soil ball.

moss covering

Cover the potting mix and exposed part of the soil ball with moss lining.

Water gently but thoroughly, check for large leaks, and plug with more moss.

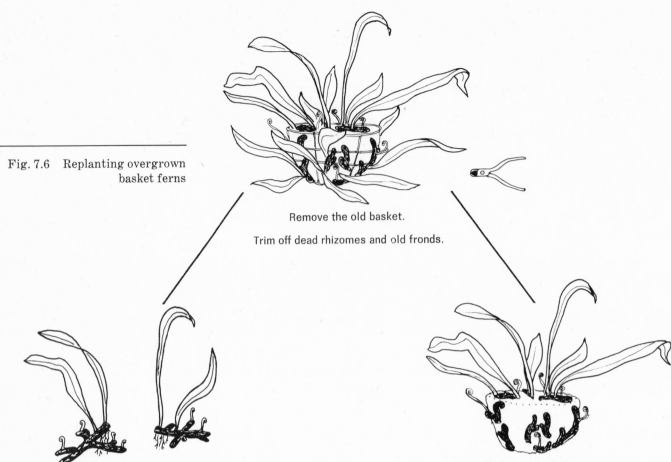

Fig. 7.6   Replanting overgrown
basket ferns

Remove the old basket.

Trim off dead rhizomes and old fronds.

Separate rhizomes into smaller clumps.

Select the healthiest clumps with
the most growing tips.

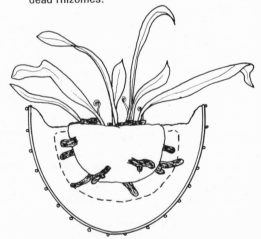

Trim off all the fronds from
the sides of the basket.

Loosen and spread out the rhizomes.

Remove and discard old and
dead rhizomes.

Replant the clumps into a new basket
(see Fig. 7.5)

Extra rhizomes of suitable length may
be thrust into the sides of the basket.

Water gently but thoroughly.

Replant into a new basket
(see Fig. 7.5)

Spread the loosened rhizomes into
the fresh potting mix and moss lining.

Water gently but thoroughly.

Wire baskets. Commercially made wire baskets are inexpensive and readily available. However, their very open structure requires much lining material, and the wire does rust away in a relatively short time. Epiphytes with long creeping rhizomes that have a tendency to grow down the sides of a container do best in wire baskets which provide numerous places for the rhizomes to root. Do not make wire baskets from copper wire: copper is toxic to plants.

Wood baskets. Redwood baskets are most favored because of their resistance to rotting. Wood baskets come in many designs and are generally less open in structure and therefore require less lining material. Epiphytes which like moister conditions and have short creeping or clumping rhizomes do best in wood baskets.

Tree fern fiber baskets. Baskets made from tree fern fibers are very good for epiphytes because they drain well yet retain sufficient moisture and do not require lining material. Baskets made from Central American tree ferns are more durable than those from the Hawaiian Islands.

Ceramic baskets. Ceramic baskets or containers can be very attractive and come in a variety of styles. Open-structured ones are particularly well suited to long creeping rhizomes and provide the best drainage.

PLANTING THE BASKET

Baskets with openings or meshes are lined with a moist two inches of coarse or uncut moss (green moss or sphagnum moss) or coarsely shredded tree fern fiber (Hapu). Shredded redwood bark is a particularly good lining but has not been recently marketed. If the fern is an epiphyte, it is then planted in the cavity with uncut or shredded sphagnum moss or a very friable potting mix high in organic matter. For terrestrial species, use an ordinary potting mix in the cavity (see "Basic Planting Procedure," above). Press the soil firmly in place and then cover it with an inch of the lining material, so that subsequent watering will not dislodge the loose soil mix (*Fig. 7.5*). Extra pieces of rhizomes may be poked through the sides of the basket into the moss. Rhizomes that will not stay in place may be anchored down with bent wires. Water newly planted baskets with a gentle spray or soak them in a tub for a few minutes.

REPLANTING BASKET FERNS

Basket ferns need to be replanted when the basket rusts or rots away or when the rhizomes begin to grow over one another and become weak and thin (*Fig. 7.6*).

A fern that is growing only out of the top of the baskets (and not out of the sides or bottom) is merely freed from the old basket, its dead tissue and old soil removed, and then replanted into a new basket as mentioned above.

There are various ways of replanting a basket when the fern is growing

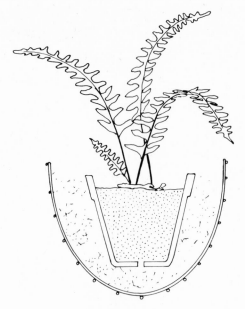

Plant potted fern in basket
lined with moss.

Fig. 7.7   Keeping basket
ferns moist

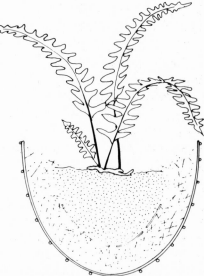

Place a piece of plastic sheet
over the moss lining before planting.

Punch holes in the plastic
for drainage.

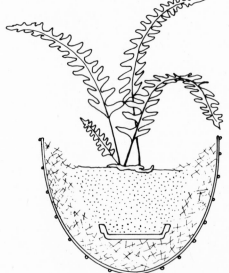

Place a clay saucer over
the moss lining before planting.

out of the top sides, and bottom of the basket. (1) Cut away the basket and remove the fern rhizomes in big pieces. Replant the biggest and best pieces in a new basket as previously described. (2) Cut the fronds off the sides and bottom of the basket, lift out the plant, and drop it into a new basket lined with fresh moss. Fill any intervening spaces with loose planting mix or moss. New rhizomes will grow through the new moss layer in time. (3) Another way to revitalize an old basket fern covered with rhizomes is to cut out the center of the basket from the top. Do not disturb the growth at the sides and bottom. Fill the hole with fresh potting mix and then cover with uncut sphagnum or green moss. If the outer part of the wire basket has rusted away, reinforce it with more wire or fashion a wire sling to support the basket. (4) Build a new basket around the old one. This requires suitable wire, much patience, and care to minimize the damage to fronds and rhizomes on the sides and bottom of the basket. Cut galvanized wire of suitable strength to form the rings of the new basket. Join each of the rings around the old basket. To hold the rings in place, tie them with cross-wires or solder on cross-wires. Moss is then stuffed into the space between the old and the new baskets.

SPECIAL CARE

Once properly planted, basket ferns will last for a number of years. If the fern is an epiphyte, be certain the drainage is very good. Terrestrial ferns planted in baskets may dry too quickly in their elevated position or their fronds may show low-humidity damage, particularly if indoors. These plants should be substituted with more adaptable plants or rotated with fresh plants. If you keep them in pots they can be lifted out of the moss-lined baskets and easily replaced.

In arid climates such as that of southern California, hanging baskets dry very quickly and are sometimes difficult to wet again without soaking. To prevent such drying, a small sheet of plastic placed over the moss lining at the time of planting helps to retard rapid water loss. A shallow clay saucer has also been used, but holes may be punched more easily into the plastic for more drainage (*Fig. 7.7*). At the top of the basket, to one side of the fern, flower pots may be sunk into the basket to act as catch basins for water. The rim of the basket may be built up to act as a catch basin as well. Keep alert for wires which are weak or rusting and replace them immediately. As moss or lining material decays or falls away, replace it by stuffing fresh lining material into the cavities.

8. PROPAGATION

Ferns reproduce in two basic ways: from pieces of the parent plant or from spores. The first method is called vegetative propagation, and the offspring produced are genetically the same as the parent. The second method, by spore, is called sexual propagation, and the offspring produced may vary. Before discussing how the grower may employ these methods in propagation, it is necessary to understand some basic facts about the life cycles of the ferns.

TYPICAL LIFE CYCLE

Fern spores grow into new ferns indirectly (*Fig. 8.1*). If a spore lands on a moist place with sufficient light, it will germinate. In several days the spore will send out a slender cell (a rhizoid) which secures the spore in place. The spore then produces a green cell which divides into a thread of cells. In about three months the tip of this thread has typically grown into a flat, heart-shaped piece of tissue about a quarter-inch wide. This small plant is called the prothallium or gametophyte. On the underside of this tiny plant are male structures (antheridia) bearing sperms and female structures (archegonia) each bearing an egg. When sperms are released from their structure they find their way to an egg. The sperm may swim to an egg on the same or a different prothallium. A film of water must be present on the prothallium to allow the sperm to swim to the egg. The need for this film of water explains why ferns are particularly abundant in moist climates.

The union of a sperm with an egg is known as fertilization. Fertilization marks the start of the sporophyte—the familiar fern which eventually bears the spores. The fertilized egg (zygote) divides and forms an embryo or young sporophyte which develops roots, stems, and leaves. As the roots grow out and establish themselves in the soil, the prothallium disintegrates, leaving the sporophyte on its own. If fertilization does not occur, the prothallium may continue to live for years.

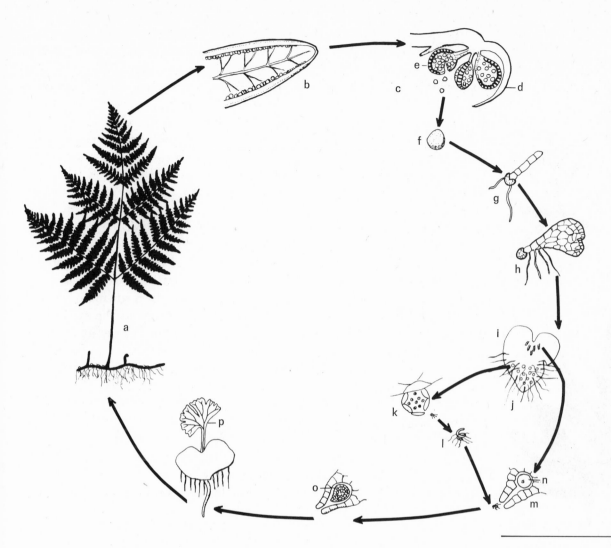

Fig. 8.1   Fern life cycle.
a. familiar fern plant or sporophyte;
b. pinna bearing sori;
c. sorus enlarged; d. indusium;
e. sporangia; f. spore;
g. spore germinating;
h. young prothallium or gametophyte;
i. mature prothallium or
gametophyte; j. rhizoids;
k. antheridium; l. sperm;
m. archegonium; n. egg;
o. embryo; p. young sporophyte

The first series of leaves produced by the young sporophyte usually do not resemble those of the adult plant. The successive leaves that are produced will eventually take on the typical adult leaf form (*Fig. 8.2*). In about five months to a year after the spores have been planted, a small but well-established fern is developed. Some ferns grow faster than others and may produce spore-bearing fronds in six or seven months. However, most ferns take about two years to complete the full life cycle—that is, to grow from spore and produce spore-bearing fronds—although staghorn ferns and tree ferns take several years. Normally, spore-bearing fronds are produced yearly thereafter. Once spores are produced and shed from the frond, the life cycle begins again.

OTHER LIFE CYCLES

There are other ways in which ferns may reproduce. New ferns may reproduce directly from parts of the sporophyte. Parts of the root, rhizome, or frond may produce new plants. Branches taken from the rhizome are common means of propagation. On some ferns special clumps of tissue

known as buds or bulblets may form and grow into new plants. These buds normally develop on the roots, blade, vein, or midrib of the blade or pinnae of certain species (*Fig. 8.3*). Less commonly, pieces of the stipe base may be induced to form buds (e.g., *Cystopteris* sp., *Dryopteris filix-mas, D. spinulosa, Matteuccia struthiopteris, Phyllitis scolopendrium, Pteridium aquilinum*), as well as pieces of the stipules if present (*Angiopteris evecta, Marattia* spp.). Fronds from young plants of some ferns may also be induced to form buds. In rare cases prothallia may also grow directly from fronds of young sporophytes (*Fig. 8.4; Osmunda regalis* cv. Cristata, *Polystichum setiferum* var. Pulcherrimum, and others). This means of reproduction is known as apospory (without spores) and forgoes the need to produce spore-bearing fronds.

In numerous species new plants (sporophytes) may be produced from the surface of the prothallium instead of through the union of egg and sperm (*Fig. 8.5*). This process, called apogamy (without sex cells), produces ferns faster than by the usual sexual method. In a sowing of spores, the sporophytes of apogamous prothallia tend to appear at the same time, whereas the sporophytes of nonapogamous prothallia appear at different times. Ferns developing apogamously also tend to produce leaves before the roots, whereas ferns going through the sexual life cycle tend to produce roots before the leaves. Ferns which reproduce only apogamously include *Pteris cretica, Cyrtomium falcatum*, and *Dryopteris atrata*. Some ferns may reproduce by both apogamous and sexual means.

The prothallium itself may also be able to reproduce more prothallia. New prothallia may form from the margins and in this way perpetuate the growth of the prothallium generation (*Fig. 8.6*). If conditions are favorable, growth goes on for years unless fertilization occurs. Then the

Fig. 8.2   Age variation in fronds, showing fronds produced from progressively older plant of *Doryopteris nobilis*

Fig. 8.3   Proliferous buds. a. root bud and a young plant established from a root bud on *Asplenium auritum* roots; b. leaf bud on the underside of a frond of *Woodwardia radicans*

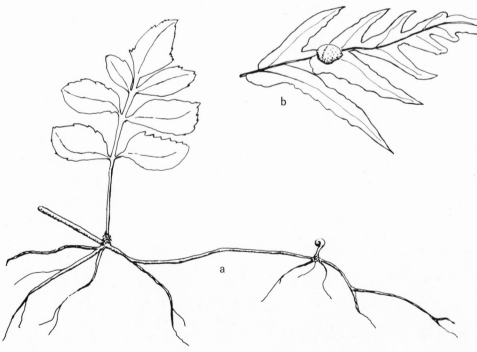

prothallium dies as the sporophyte develops. In filmy ferns, shoestring ferns, grammitids, and some polypodiums new prothallia are produced from bits of spindle-shaped or rod-shaped tissue (gemmae) borne on short stalks arising from the prothallia.

VEGETATIVE PROPAGATION

Plant parts that may reproduce new plants are the rhizome, root, and frond. The branching rhizome is most frequently used in vegetative propagation. Ferns which do not have branching rhizomes or do not form new buds from roots or fronds (as with most tree ferns) generally cannot be vegetatively propagated and must be grown from spore. Success in vegetative propagation is greatest when a moist soil and sufficient humidity are maintained with as little watering as possible.

DIVISIONS

Rhizomes may branch and spread or form clumps. Pieces of these rhizomes may grow into new plants. To make a division, look for the growing tips where new fronds arise. Side buds may be stimulated to form on a thick rhizome by partly cutting through it and waiting for the buds to develop before making the division. Before you remove a tip or a clump of tips for a division, be certain that there are enough left on the parent plant to keep it growing. Look for a joint or naturally weak spot to make the cut from the parent plant (*Fig. 8.7a*). The larger the rhizome or clump taken, the better the chances of a successful division. Use a clean, sharp knife to make the cut. With a trowel, dig up the division. Avoid injuring the grow-

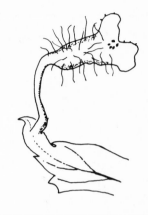

Fig. 8.4 Apospory. Prothallium developing from the tip of a pinnule in *Polystichum setiferum* var. *Pulcherrimum*. After Bower, *The Ferns (Filicales)*

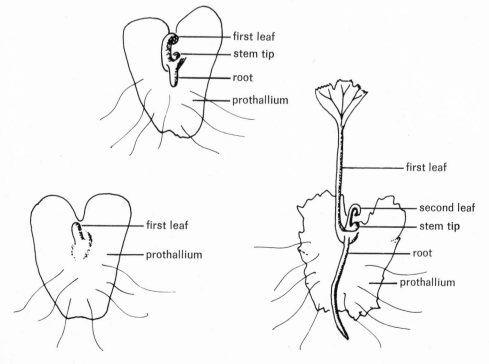

Fig. 8.5 Apogamy. Various stages of ferns developing apogamously. On each prothallium note the appearance of a new fern directly from the surface of the prothallium rather than from within an archegonium. Schematic

ing tips, and keep as much of the soil around the roots of the division as possible. Cut off old or broken fronds. Cut the withered stipes as close to the rhizome as possible and remove any old or broken roots. Replant the division to its former soil level, unless the roots were previously exposed. In that case, set the division slightly deeper in the soil, so that the roots are covered. Firm the soil in place and water well. Keep the plant lightly shaded for a few days. Apply inorganic fertilizer two to three weeks after division.

Smaller rhizome pieces or rootless pieces need to be kept in more protected moist places until new roots form. With these pieces, remove parts of the larger fronds to reduce the water loss, particularly if the humidity is dry. Dust the cut ends of the rhizome with a fungicide such as Captan. Plant in a well-drained rooting medium; a mixture of one part peat moss and one part perlite will do. Provide the box, flat, or pot with very good drainage. Avoid using soil, manures, compost, or other substances which may have bacteria and fungi in large amounts. Creeping rhizome pieces without roots will need to be firmly secured to the rooting medium to keep them from drying out. Plant these pieces at half their thickness into the medium and hold them in place with pieces of bent wire (*Fig. 8.7b*). Or if the pieces are a few inches long, their cut ends can be thrust diagonally into the soil to about one-third their length (*Fig. 8.7c*). Do not cover the growing tip with soil, but keep it exposed. Keep the planting humid, shaded, and warm until rhizomes are rooted enough to be transplanted. Avoid overwatering. If mold or decay develops, increase ventilation, cease overhead watering, and use a fungicide drench.

Fig. 8.6 Prothallium proliferation. Proliferation of an old prothallium into 8 new prothallia and a long, tapered cylindrical process bearing another new prothallium at its tip. *Platycerium quadridichotomum*

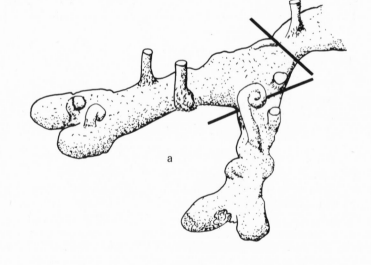

Fig. 8.7 Dividing and planting the rhizome divisions.
a. dividing the rhizome, roots not shown (*Polypodium*);
b. planting the rhizome at half its thickness (*Davallia*);
c. planting the rhizome diagonally (*Davallia*)

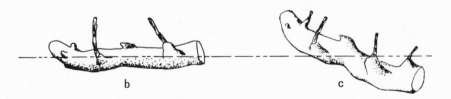

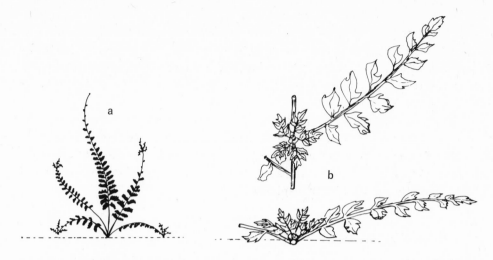

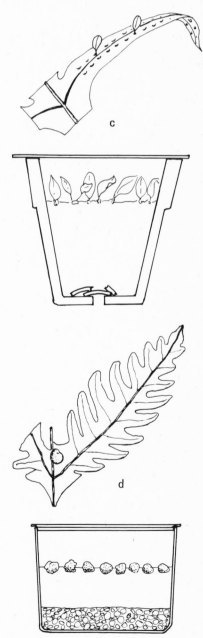

Fig. 8.8   Planting buds.
a. layering or rooting a bud still
attached to the mother plant
(*Adiantum caudatum*) ;
b. rooting a bud attached to
a section of a frond,
top and side view (*Polystichum*
setiferum cv. *Proliferum*) ;
c. rooting detached buds in a pot
(*Woodwardia orientalis*) ;
d. rooting detached buds in a
plastic container (*Tectaria gemmifera*)

Propagation by air layering is easily done if the rhizomes are long and tend to grow away from basket or soil. Wrap damp sphagnum moss around the rhizome. Tie the moss into place with string or strips of plastic. The moss may also be wrapped with a small sheet of plastic before tying.

BUDS

Some ferns produce new plantlets on their fronds and even from their roots. These plantlets develop from knots of tissue called buds. Fronds with buds may be anchored to the soil surface while still attached to the mother plant or the frond, or they may be detached and planted (*Fig. 8.8*). Buds left attached to the mother plant benefit from an adequate supply of water and food during their rooting period. The bud is anchored to the soil with a bit of soil or clean sand. Bud-bearing fronds detached from the mother plant may be planted whole or in pieces. The whole frond or pieces are anchored to the soil surface with a planting mix or clean sand, watered and then covered to provide adequate humidity. Once the buds have rooted sufficiently, cut the mother frond to separate the plantlets.

Buds removed from the fronds for rooting are planted at half their thickness in a rooting medium. Water gently but thoroughly and then cover with a piece of glass or plastic. Keep the air humid, but avoid excess humidity and overwatering. Buds may also be grown conveniently in clear plastic shoe boxes or refrigerator boxes lined on the bottom with an inch of perlite, preferably with holes for drainage. Place the planting medium (usually half sand and half peat) over the perlite, and plant the buds. The lid may need to be opened to control excess humidity. Plants which may be propagated by removing buds include *Asplenium bulbiferum, A. daucifolium, Polystichum setiferum* cv. Proliferum, *Tectaria gemmifera, Woodwardia radicans, W. orientalis,* and many others.

Small pieces of the stipe of *Phyllitis scolopendrium* and other species reportedly form buds from green, plump, healthy pieces sown over the surface of a planting medium. Stipules of *Marattia* and *Angiopteris* also produce buds when detached and planted. Dust cut ends with fungicide and use disease-free planting medium.

In all these cases, a weak solution of inorganic fertilizer may be applied every two to three weeks and the covering over the planting gradually removed as the buds grow. Transplant the larger plants to avoid crowding the others. If mold develops, increase the air circulation and use a fungicide drench.

Root buds develop on the roots of some ferns such as *Ophioglossum*, some *Platycerium*, *Diplazium esculentum*, *Asplenium auritum*, and other species. They are usually not noticed until the new plantlets emerge from the soil. When these plants are several inches tall they may be separated from the mother plant and transplanted.

MERISTEM CULTURE

Meristem culture or tissue culture is a special method which permits the growing of new plants from microscopic bits of tissue usually taken from adult plants. This technique requires sterile conditions, special nutrient solutions, and equipment. At present it is not adapted to general use. Special laboratories are supplying Boston ferns grown from meristem cultures to wholesale growers. The early cultures were supplied to growers as bits of tissue suspended in liquid; these were reported by some growers to succumb readily to disease. Recent cultures are supplied as one-inch-tall ferns rooted in agar or as one- to two-inch-tall ferns rooted in planting medium. These ferns are planted in the same manner as any young fern of comparable size. Since one adult plant can supply tissue to grow many plants, the grower does not need to maintain large beds of propagating material. Also, disease-free, uniform-sized plants are obtained. Other kinds of ferns are being grown on an experimental basis by meristem culture. It seems that meristem culture of ferns would be helpful when a fern in high demand cannot be propagated abundantly by spores or by ordinary vegetative means. Besides the Boston fern, such plants as *Adiantum tracyii*, *Polypodium subauriculatum* cv. Knightiae, *Pteris cretica* cv. Childsii, and other hybrids or cultivars are well suited to this technique. These plants produce no spores or few viable spores and have only a modest growth rate, making them difficult to propagate in large numbers by divisions. They are attractive, robust-growing plants and have an appeal to the general trade. However, *Platycerium superbum* (*P. grande*) and relatives, though exceedingly slow-growing from spore and even slow-growing as adults, may be just as slow if grown from meristem culture. Their size and less robust habit would not make them popular trade items in any case.

SPORE PROPAGATION

Growing ferns from spores, though not difficult, takes patience and time. The space and equipment requirements are minimal. The fascination and pleasure derived from growing ferns from a dust of spores is a hobby in itself. Most trade ferns grown commercially take about six to ten months from sowing until they are large enough to be planted into two-inch-size pots.

COLLECTING SPORES

The spore cases (sporangia) are usually in clusters located on the underside of the frond. These clusters or sori are from one-sixteenth to an eighth of an inch wide and may be round, oblong, or linear. Less frequently, sporangia are scattered over the entire undersurface of the frond or borne on modified portions of the leaf. Some ferns produce spores all year, while others are seasonal.

When the sporangia begin to ripen they will turn from green to light brown and then to a medium or dark shiny brown (*Fig. 8.9*). (In some species, mature sporangia are yellow or orange.) Dull, frayed-looking sporangia have already shed their spores. Pick the fronds just as most of the sporangia are turning light to medium brown. If indusia (the covering over sporangia) are present, they will be intact, will look firm, and will usually —depending on the species—be light brown, gold or nearly black. Green indusia indicate the spores are not ripe. Shed or shriveled indusia indicate that the sporangia may have shed their spores. Ripeness of the spore cases may be precisely determined with a good 8–15X hand lens (see scientific supply companies in Appendix II for source). Plump sporangia without a cracked wall still have their spores, whereas frayed ones or ones with cracks or slits have shed their spores. Shriveled sporangia will not produce viable spores. Pick fronds when most of the sporangia are still plump. Contamination may be reduced by picking clean fronds or by brushing or rinsing any dirt away before collecting the spores. Collecting spores on a cool or dim day reduces loss of spores or contamination from other species.

Place the picked frond in an envelope or over a clean smooth piece of paper with the sporangia side down. Cover the frond to prevent shedding spores from blowing away. Spores will start to shed on the paper in minutes, but to collect the maximum number of spores wait a day or two. Spores will look like dust. Some fronds produce large numbers of spores, and others do not. Spores are often yellowish brown but may be green, yellow, black, or some other color. Along with the spores may be shed whole or fragmented spore cases, bits of hair, scale, or other tissue. Examine with a hand lens to be certain spores are present. Store in envelopes or folded paper. Write the source, the name of the species, and the date on the envelope for later reference.

CLEANING SPORES

Removal of nonspore material will reduce contamination by algae, fungi, and mosses. The larger nonspore material may be picked out with tweezers or brushed away with a fine brush. If pure or nearly pure spores are desired, they may be separated from nonspore material by slightly tilting the paper upon which the spores are collected and tapping it gently. The spore is left behind as the fluffier nonspore material bounces ahead and can be brushed away. The spore may then be stored until use.

Small bottles whose tops have been replaced with a very fine (about .05 millimeters) screened mesh can be used to sow and separate the spore from nonspore material. The finest tea screen available, lens paper, and

Fig. 8.9   Determining when
to collect spores.
a. too young;
b. ripe; c. too old.
Thelypteris augescens

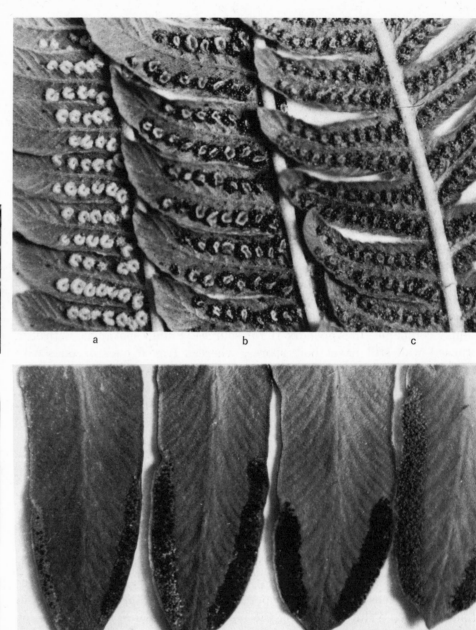

a   b   c

a   b   b   c

ABOVE: enlargements

even cheesecloth have been used as satisfactory screening materials. Check with a hand lens to be sure that the separation is adequate.

"STERILIZING" SPORES

Commercial growers do not sterilize their spores. Most scientific work requires the sterilization (actually only disinfection) of spores. All methods use Clorox (commercial sodium hypochlorite) diluted with water, and most use a wetting agent such as Tween 20, Aerosol OT, or Alconox (see

Appendix II under scientific supply companies for source). It might be possible to use a mild household detergent for a wetting agent instead. The following two sterilization methods are fairly representative of the many kinds used.

Sterilization of spores freed from the sporangia. Sieve the spores to remove the larger nonspore material. Place the spores in a 5 percent Clorox solution (dilute 1 part Clorox with 19 parts water), and add a fraction of a drop of Tween 20 (1 part Tween 20 to 2,000 parts Clorox solution). Soak the spores for 1 minute (5 seconds to 10 minutes have also been used). Collect the spores on filter paper. Rinse two to four times with sterile water. Sow from the water solution or dry and store until needed.

Sterilization of spores still within the sporangia. Select leaflets or fronds with ripe but unopened sporangia. Soak in 5–10 percent Clorox solution to which Tween 20 has been added as above. Remove all air bubbles with a small brush, and keep the leaflets immersed five to ten seconds. Do not rinse. Remove to clean envelopes; place envelopes between layers of clean paper to dry. The spores will be shed from the sporangia within the envelopes. Envelopes and paper may be previously sterilized in a box placed in a hot oven at 320°F for about two hours. Never treat the spores themselves with heat. If you change the absorbing paper between the envelopes, the spores should be shed and dried in two or three days and be ready for storage or use.

VIABILITY OF SPORES

Sow green-colored spores as soon after collecting as possible. They will be found in *Osmunda*, *Todea*, *Onoclea*, *Grammitis*, the filmy ferns, *Equisetum*, and a scattering of other species rarely or not in cultivation. Green-colored spores remain viable for two days to less than one year depending on the species. The fresher the spore the higher the percentage of germination and the quicker the germination. Viability may be extended by refrigeration at 39–40°F for *Osmunda* species and probably others.

Spores that are not green in color may be viable from one to forty-eight years with an isolated record for seventy years (*Plagiogyria*). Storing nongreen spores under cool conditions prolongs their viability. They may be refrigerated. As with green-colored spores, the fresher the spore the higher the germination percentage and the shorter the time required for germination. Variations may exist in the percentage of germination from spores taken at different times from the same plant. The highest percentage of germination is obtained from spores produced during periods of most vigorous growth.

SOWING METHODS

There are many ways to grow fern spores (*Fig. 8.10*), and the most popular systems are listed below. In all cases sterilize or treat the media and pots or containers used (see Chapter 5, "Sterilizing Soils"). Sow the

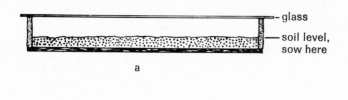

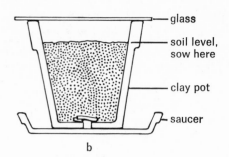

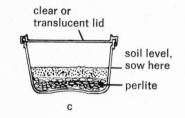

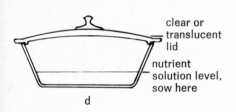

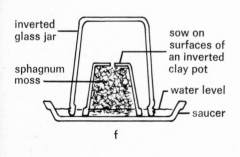

Fig. 8.10   Methods of planting
fern spores. a. flat;
b. pot; c. plastic container;
d. nutrient solution;
e. agar plate;
f. inverted pot method

spores on finely screened moist media. Sow thinly to avoid spindly, tangled prothallia, the tiny intermediate stages from which the ferns proper will grow.

Commercial method. Most commercial growers use a mixture of 1 to 2 parts peat moss and 1 part fine sand (1 part loamy soil may sometimes be added). This mixture is finely screened (use about 1/8-inch mesh) and placed into flats or pots provided with drainage and then treated by steam or by pouring boiling water over and through the soil several times. Plastic boxes may be used after being disinfected with 10 percent Clorox solution and then rinsed before the treated soil is added. Keep the planting medium covered while it is cooling and draining. When cool, dust the spores over the surface. Re-cover the container with clean glass, plastic, or plastic wrap.

Nutrient solution method. Nutrient solutions are occasionally used commercially but are also of interest to amateurs. There are many different solutions. Distilled or tap water or dilute solutions of balanced inorganic fertilizers (at quarter-strength) have been used. The more commonly used nutrient solutions, listed in Table 8.1, are used without dilution. Measures are given in both the metric and the English system to avoid the necessity of special measuring equipment. However, since fractions of ounces or tablespoons are difficult to measure, the formulation makes 25 gallons of solution. The surplus may be used as a liquid fertilizer. If smaller amounts are desired the measurements are given in grams to make 1 liter or approximately one quart of solution. The ingredients are inexpensive and may be obtained from local chemical supply houses, firms selling fertilizers, and drugstores (see scientific supply companies in Appendix II). Prepare the solution by adding the salts to the water in the order given. Impurities in the chemicals and from the water (tap water) will probably provide the trace elements needed. However, if you desire to add trace elements, use the trace element formulation in Table 8.1. If the solution is to be stored for any length of time, add the iron or trace elements just before use.

The pH of these solutions will be about 6 if distilled water is used. This is optimum for germinating most fern species, the range being pH 5–7. Some ferns of limestone habitats may germinate at pH 7–9.

The solution may be sterilized in a pressure cooker (15 minutes at 15 pounds pressure) or boiled for a few minutes. The solution is poured into previously sterilized or clean dishes or plastic containers (boiled or washed with a 10 percent Clorox solution and rinsed). The depth of the solution may vary, but a quarter-inch is sufficient for germination. Cover and cool. Sow the spores and replace the cover. Avoid moving the dish after sowing to keep the spores floating on the surface of the solution. Tilt the lid slightly to prevent condensation from falling on the spores.

Nutrient agar solution. This method provides a solid instead of a liquid media for growing spores in nutrients. It has no advantage over other

TABLE 8.1   NUTRIENT SOLUTIONS

Salts	Formula	Grade of salt	Grams per 1 liter of water	Per 25 gallons of water oz. or tbsp.	
KNOP'S SOLUTION					
Potassium phosphate	KH_2PO_4	Technical	0.2	¾	1½
Potassium nitrate	KNO_3	Fertilizer	0.2	¾	1½
Calcium nitrate	$Ca(NO_3)_2 \cdot 4H_2O$	Fertilizer	0.8	3	7
Magnesium sulfate	$MgSO_4 \cdot 7H_2O$	Technical	0.2	¾	2
Ferric phosphate	$FePO_4$	Technical	Trace		
TURTOX S.L. 30 SOLUTION *(after Turtox 1957)*					
Potassium sulfate	K_2SO_4	Technical	0.3	1	2
Magnesium sulfate	$MgSO_4 \cdot 7H_2O$	Technical	0.4	1½	4
Double superphosphate	40–48% P_2O_5 grade	Fertilizer	0.4	1½	3
Potassium nitrate	KNO_3	Fertilizer	0.6	2	4
Ammonium sulfate	$(NH_4)_2SO_4$	Fertilizer	0.2	¾	1½
Ferric citrate	$FeC_6H_5O_7 \cdot xH_2O$	Technical	0.004	$\frac{1}{48}$	$\frac{1}{24}$
HOAGLAND'S SOLUTION #1 *(after Hoagland and Arnon 1950)*					
Potassium phosphate	KH_2PO_4	Technical	0.14	½	1
Potassium nitrate	KNO_3	Fertilizer	0.51	2	4
Calcium nitrate	$Ca(NO_3)_2 \cdot 4H_2O$	Fertilizer	1.18	4	8
Magnesium sulfate	$MgSO_4 \cdot 7H_2O$	Technical	0.49	1½	4
Ferrous tartrate	$FeC_4H_4O_6$	Technical	0.005	$\frac{1}{48}$	$\frac{1}{24}$
HOAGLAND'S SOLUTION #2 *(after Hoagland and Arnon 1950)*					
Ammonium phosphate	$NH_4H_2PO_4$	Fertilizer	0.12	½	2
Potassium nitrate	KNO_3	Fertilizer	0.62	2½	5
Calcium nitrate	$Ca(NO_3)_2 \cdot 4H_2O$	Fertilizer	0.94	3	6
Magnesium sulfate	$MgSO_4 \cdot 7H_2O$	Technical	0.49	$\frac{1}{12}$	4
Ferrous tartrate	$FeC_4H_4O_6$	Technical	0.005	$\frac{1}{48}$	$\frac{1}{24}$
TRACE ELEMENTS *(after Hoagland and Arnon 1950)*					
Boric acid	H_3BO_3		0.0029		
Manganese chloride	$MnCl_2 \cdot 4H_2O$		0.0018		
Zinc sulfate	$ZnSO_4 \cdot 7H_2O$		0.00022		
Copper sulfate	$CuSO_4 \cdot 5H_2O$		0.00008		
Molybdic acid	$H_2MoO_4 \cdot H_2O$		0.00002		

If tap water is used, addition of trace elements is generally not necessary.

methods, and ferns are reported to grow slower by this method. It is used mainly for scientific purposes or when the spore material is extremely valuable and sterile techniques are necessary to ensure its survival. Agar, the solidifying substance, may be obtained from scientific supply companies.

The medium is made by adding 15 grams of agar (approximately ½ ounce) to 1 liter (approximately 1 quart) of any suitable nutrient solution. Dissolve the agar by heating it in the nutrient solution, stirring occasionally. Then pour the dissolved solution (¼–⅓ inch deep) into shallow dishes, cover loosely, and sterilize immediately in a pressure cooker at 15 pounds pressure for 15 minutes. When the dishes have been removed from the pressure cooker, cooled, and solidified, they are ready to be planted, preferably with disinfected spores. Before and after planting, keep the dishes covered to avoid airborne contamination and to keep the moisture in. Little or no water needs to be added if the dish is kept properly covered.

Inverted pot method. This method is ideal for demonstrating the growth of prothallia and young ferns. It is not efficient for growing ferns commercially, since scraping prothallia off the pot is tedious and awkward.

Fill a small, clean, porous clay flower pot with uncut sphagnum or peat moss, then invert it into a saucer or shallow dish. Sterilize the unit by steam or by pouring boiling water over it, or place the whole unit in boiling water. When drained and cooled, sow with the spores and cover with a larger glass or jar. Replace water in the saucer as needed. There is less likelihood of overwatering by this method, and if the spores are not too densely sown, nicely formed heart-shaped prothallia will develop, free of bits of planting medium. A dilute solution of fertilizer applied in the saucer will hasten growth. Young ferns may be loosened and lifted off the clay pot with tweezers or a flat thin blade and planted in a potting mix.

Miscellaneous methods. Various other methods are used to sow fern spores. These include plaster of paris blocks, broken clay pots, moistened bricks, tree fern trunk fibers, soil, peat moss, sphagnum moss, and so forth. Milled sphagnum is particularly good. Sterilize or treat the soil and container with steam or boiling water as a precautionary measure.

AFTERSOWING CARE

After sowing, place the planting in the proper light and temperature as directed below. The first visible sign of growth is the appearance of a very thin green mat fourteen days or more after the sowing. Germination of the spore usually takes four to fourteen days, but the emerging green cells are too small to be visible in these early stages without magnification.

Light. Place in filtered sunlight of low to medium intensity (150 to 500 foot-candles; see Chapter 4, "Light"). If artificial light ("cool" white fluorescent or Gro-lux) is used, it may be left on continuously or for eight to sixteen hours per day as desired. Research indicates different cellular responses with blue, red and far-red light, but these responses are not of importance to the general growing of ferns from spores. Several weeks of darkness are required for spores of *Botrychium dissectum* before they will germinate.

Temperature. The optimal temperature for spores to germinate and grow is between 68 and 86°F. Most growers keep the temperature near 77°F and lower it as the plants become older. Uniform temperatures will reduce water condensation problems.

Watering. Water will not be necessary for some time after sowing if the medium was thoroughly moistened before sowing and the planting covered. Edges of the containers may be sealed with Vaseline to retain moisture. If water must be added, set pots in a saucer of water. Flats and plastic boxes may be watered with a fine mist or spray. Distilled or cooled boiled water is preferred during these early stages.

Fertilizers. Weak solutions of fertilizer (half strength or less) are used to fertilize plantings every two to three weeks after the appearance of the green mat (except when using nutrient solutions and agar). Although researchers have applied sugar ($2\frac{1}{2}$ percent sucrose) under sterile conditions to hasten growth, this is not recommended for nonresearch purposes, since mold and damage to the culture are very likely to develop.

Transplanting. When the green mat of prothallia form, transplanting may start. Some growers transplant at a very early stage, starting when the mat is thick enough to lift off. Small pieces $\frac{1}{8}$ to $\frac{1}{4}$ inch across are lifted off with tweezers (or the tip of a spoon if using a liquid medium). Waiting longer with liquid media may mean tangled growth and difficulty getting the prothallia to drop off the tweezers or the spoon during transplanting.

The clumps of prothallia are spaced about $\frac{1}{2}$ inch apart and firmed into a moist, finely screened potting mix of half peat and sand or whatever mix is desired. Be certain the clumps are in good contact with the planting medium lest they dry out. The planting mix should be sterilized, disinfected, or treated with a fungicide drench before use. However, this varies with the individual grower and the planting mix used. After the prothallia are planted, water them with a fine spray of water, preferably distilled. Keep the planting covered with glass or plastic. As the prothallia enlarge or the young ferns appear, the clumps are divided and again spaced apart on a second transplant. Gradually lessen the protection from the glass or plastic covering. When the ferns are about $\frac{1}{2}$ to 1 inch tall, they are potted into $2\frac{1}{2}$-inch pots. Fully developed ferns in $2\frac{1}{2}$-inch pots will still need considerable protection and should not be planted outdoors unless adequate protection can be provided. They may be gradually hardened off under lath or in frames.

SPECIAL CARE

Molds may develop in spite of all precautions. Stop any overhead watering. See that water is not dripping from overhead condensation.

Remove the mold and at least ½ inch of the plant tissue beyond the mold area. Do this as soon as the mold is noticed. Drench the area with fungicide (see "Fungi and Bacteria" in Chapter 11). Water molds (*Phythium* and *Phytophthora*) usually cause the prothallia to turn a water-soaked dark color and subsequently collapse. Gray mold (*Botrytis*) will be seen as gray tufts on the prothallia and foliage. It flourishes under cool moist conditions, so increase the temperature and decrease the humidity. *Rhizoctonia* will appear as spaced-out threads. An alga (*Oscillatoria*) may also form a blackish to grayish moldlike growth, but the threads form dense mats and do not directly damage the prothallium tissue (see Chapter 11, "Algae"). If persistent mold or alga infection occurs even with the sterilization of materials and equipment, and proper cultural conditions, the sporing room may need to be washed down or drenched with a disinfectant such as formaldehyde, Clorox, or Physan (Consan). Keep air movement from the outside to a minimum in sporing rooms and growing rooms—it may carry in fungus spores.

Fungus gnat larvae may damage the prothallia extensively (see Chapter 11). Spray or keep the adult flies out of the prothallium cultures by tightly sealing the containers with plastic wrap, Vaseline, or cotton batting placed between the pot and glass covering. Foliar nematodes have also appeared on prothallia (see Chapter 11).

Failure of mature prothallia to produce young fern plants after a reasonable length of time may mean the sperm is not getting to the egg. Flood the prothallia with a fine film of water and leave it on for a few hours. This will provide a medium for the sperm to swim to the egg.

Crowding of tree fern prothallia produces poor growth but may not affect other ferns, such as *Pteris*, unless excessive. Limestone-loving ferns —for example, *Pellaea* and some *Adiantum*—may show poor growth in peat-moss mixtures (see Chapter 5, "Acid and Base Soils"). Mosses and algae tend to be more troublesome in slow-growing cultures (see Chapter 11).

COMING TRUE FROM SPORES

Depending on the species and its cultivars, spore-grown offspring may breed true or be variable. The variations may range from subtle to very conspicuous (see Chapter 12, "Variations Within Species"). Commonly cultivated species which are known to produce variable offspring frequently include *Adiantum raddianum* and some of its cultivars, *Asplenium bulbiferum* (the narrow segment form), *Athyrium filix-femina* and its cultivars, *Polypodium aureum* and some of its cultivars, *Phyllitis scolopendrium* and cultivars, *Polystichum setiferum* and some of its cultivars, and others. From these species, obtaining plants with the qualities of the parents by spore propagation will require culling to remove undesirable forms. However, there may always be the reward of finding a superior offspring.

The majority of ferns produce rather uniform offspring, but occasional sporelings appear that are different. These different offspring are mostly due to mutations or new hereditary combinations and may or may not come true from spore. Rarely are they due to hybridization of different species.

HYBRIDIZING FERNS

Natural fern hybrids have been found, and hybrids have been produced in laboratories. North American and European *Asplenium* have produced several hybrids, as well as *Thelypteris* and other species. Hybrids between *Asplenium, Phyllitis, Camptosorus, Ceterach,* and *Pleurosorus* have also been found or artificially produced. Most hybrids are intermediate in appearance to their parents. But if parents differ widely in certain structures, these structures tend to be irregular in the hybrid though bearing characteristics of both parents. Such irregularities occur in vein patterns, sorus shape, and most conspicuously in the frond shape. Hybrids made at different times from the same parent are not always identical.

Fern hybrids do not necessarily produce plants superior to their parents. However, *Adiantum tracyii* has some physiological qualities superior to both its parents (*Adiantum jordanii* and *A. pedatum*). In cultivation it grows more robustly than either parent and remains green and active most of the year in California. An undesirable feature of this hybrid and many others is that they are sterile and may be reproduced only by rhizome divisions.

The simplest method used to hybridize ferns is to sow the spores of the two parents together and hope that the sperm of one will fertilize the egg of the other (*Fig. 8.11a*). The main disadvantage of this method is that all the resulting plants will have to be grown to locate the hybrid, if any are

a

Fig. 8.11   Hybridizing ferns.
a. plant spores
or young prothallia of both
parents together;
b. grow parents separately,
then combine parts of
them together and grow

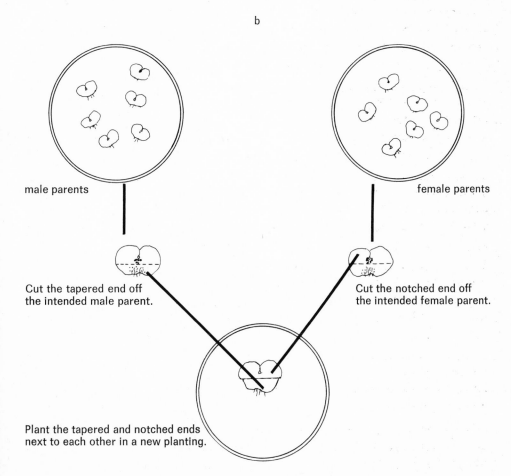

b

male parents

female parents

Cut the tapered end off
the intended male parent.

Cut the notched end off
the intended female parent.

Plant the tapered and notched ends
next to each other in a new planting.

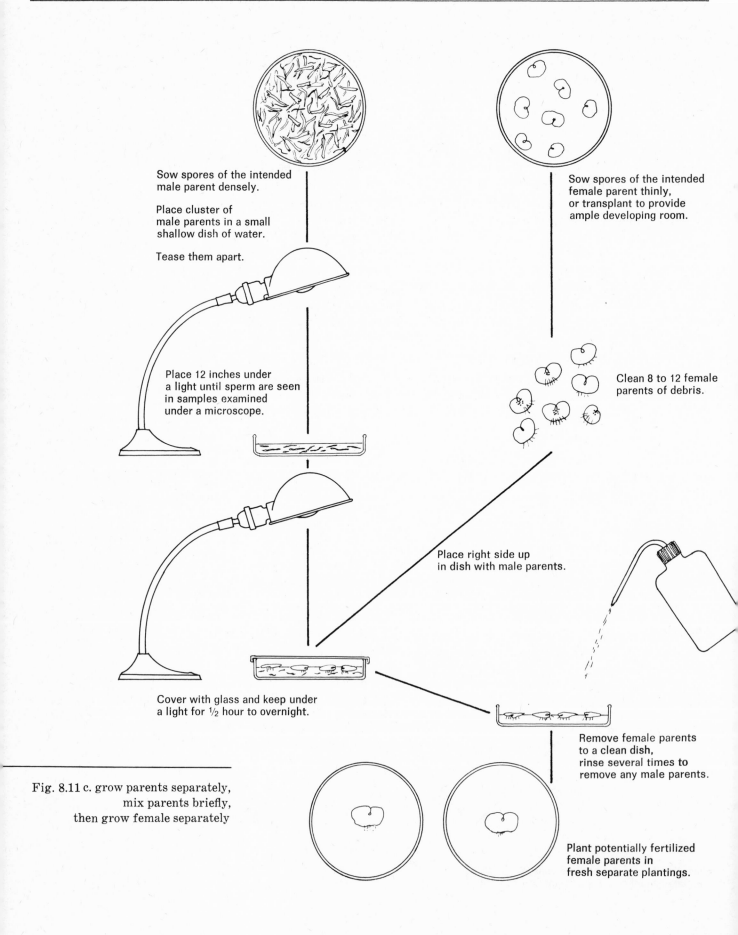

Sow spores of the intended
male parent densely.

Place cluster of
male parents in a small
shallow dish of water.

Tease them apart.

Place 12 inches under
a light until sperm are seen
in samples examined
under a microscope.

Sow spores of the intended
female parent thinly,
or transplant to provide
ample developing room.

Clean 8 to 12 female
parents of debris.

Place right side up
in dish with male parents.

Cover with glass and keep under
a light for ½ hour to overnight.

Remove female parents
to a clean dish,
rinse several times to
remove any male parents.

Fig. 8.11 c. grow parents separately,
mix parents briefly,
then grow female separately

Plant potentially fertilized
female parents in
fresh separate plantings.

formed. This wastes time and material. If you know what the young sporeling of both parents looks like, it is easier to recognize the hybrid sporeling, which will usually be intermediate in appearance to the parents.

Another method is to sow the spores of the parents separately and then transplant the prothallia close to each other and hope a hybrid may develop. With this method you are certain that spores of both parents have germinated and produced prothallia.

Hybrids may be produced by planting different parts of two prothallia close together at the proper stage of maturity (*Fig. 8.11b*). The notched end of the prothallium bears most of the archegonia which contain the eggs. The remaining part of the prothallium or tapered end bears most of the antheridia which contain the sperm. By cutting a third of the prothallium at the notched end of one parent and a third at the tapered end of the second parent and planting these ends together, it is possible to obtain a hybrid. Sporophytes growing from such a treatment are not necessarily hybrids, since self-fertilization may have occurred before the separation, or even after the separation from antheridia which might be present on the notched end or from new new proliferations of the prothallium. Similar problems may exist in the following method, but the chances of producing a hybrid are much better (see Lovis 1968).

Hybridization can also be effected by concentrating the sperm of one parent in water and subsequently adding prothallia of the other parent. The prothallia intended to be the male parent are densely sown to encourage more antheridia to form (*Fig. 8.11c*). Prothallia to be used as the female parent are sown thinly or are spaced apart by transplanting to produce more archegonia. The prothallium cultures are sparingly and carefully watered by soaking the soil from below, so as to prevent a film of water from developing between the soil and prothallia. This film of water may cause self-fertilization or premature dispersal of the sperm. Care is also taken to prevent water droplets condensing on the cover from falling on the prothallia. Since antheridia develop before archegonia, sow the prothallia of the female parent four to six weeks earlier so both parents will be at the proper stage of development for hybridization. As it is difficult to predict when the two parents are at the optimum stage of development for hybridization, have several cultures of both sown on different dates. Prothallia with antheridia suitable for hybridization usually develop three to four months after sowing, while archegonia will develop one to two months after the antheridia are ready. Because unwanted self-fertilization may occur in the archegonia before they are used in hybridization, the archegonia must be examined carefully for signs of sporophyte development before use. This is done best under a high-powered dissecting microscope.

The hybridization technique consists of placing about a quarter-inch square of the small young prothallia bearing the antheridia in a dish (a watch glass) with a small amount of warm water (77–95°F) and teasing the antheridia apart. The dish is then placed 12 inches beneath a 40-watt light bulb or in sunlight. At twenty-minute intervals the water is checked under a microscope for any active sperm. Once these have been found, eight to twelve prothallia of the female parent which have been cleaned of debris and examined for the absence of sporophytes are immediately placed, right side up (archegonia down), on the water containing the sperm. The dish is covered with glass to prevent drying and returned to the light. It is left undisturbed for a half hour to overnight.

At the end of this time the female prothallia are removed, washed several times in fresh water to remove any of the small male prothallia, and planted in fresh soil. Hybrid sporophytes usually appear from a month to a month and a half after fertilization. Sporophytes appearing before this time will most likely be products of self-fertilization. Around 80 percent success has been reported with this technique in producing hybrids between closely related and compatible strains.

Generally only closely related ferns will produce hybrids. Other abnormal plants are sometimes confused with hybrids. Abnormal fronds are caused by injury, mutation, or unusual gene recombinations. If a suspected hybrid can be replicated by a hybridization process, then it probably is a true hybrid. Indirect proof is to compare a suspected hybrid with its parents and look for intermediate features. In all cases keep records of the parents and the methods used, as this information is of importance to botany. It is known that sperm of ferns are attracted to malic acid (.01 percent) and citric acid, and this may be of use in hybridization work.

FERNS EASY TO GROW FROM SPORES

The following ferns are easy and quick to grow from spores and are recommended to the beginner.

Adiantum capillus-veneris
Adiantum hispidulum
Adiantum raddianum
Anogramma chaerophylla
Asplenium platyneuron
Athyrium filix-femina
Cyrtomium falcatum (apogamous)
Hypolepis punctata
Osmunda, all species; fresh spore may germinate in one day.
Pityrogramma calomelanos
Polypodium aureum
Pteris cretica (apogamous)
Pteris multifida
Pteris tremula
Pteris vittata
Thelypteris dentata
Thelypteris parasitica
Thelypteris torresiana

9. LANDSCAPING

When landscaping with ferns, as with any plants, be sure that they will receive enough warmth, sunlight, humidity, wind protection, and proper soil conditions. Keep in mind their future size and any special problems that may arise in their upkeep. Attention to these considerations will avoid later disappointment. The planting design you have in mind should also be visualized in relationship to its surroundings. Will the fern and its surrounding elements harmonize? Are there too many elements in the design which may create a sense of confusion? Sometimes things that are different provide a refreshing sense of contrast, but again they may be jarring or disturbing if not carefully selected. The placement of the plants in relationship to the surroundings should provide a restful sense of balance; if unbalanced it may be sharply or vaguely disturbing to the eye's sense of equilibrium. These considerations are basic landscape design principles which when correctly applied will provide the most pleasing aesthetic arrangement to your garden whether it be a formal English type, or informal woodland type, or some other type of garden.

SOLVING PARTICULAR LANDSCAPING PROBLEMS

Besides using ferns in general landscaping and in blending or contrasting with other plants, ferns may be used to solve particular problems.

CENTER OF INTEREST

Plants used to create center points of interest are called accent plants. The most effective accent plants either have strong, bold, well-defined patterns to their foliage or, at the other extreme, are soft, fine, and delicate. Accent ferns should not be too small or be crowded among other plants. The general outline of the plant should have an interesting pattern rather than just an uninteresting blob of pretty foliage.

Fig. 9.1   Using ferns
in landscaping and decorating

75

Illusion of distance.

Hiding distracting views.

CREATING THE ILLUSION OF DISTANCE

Use fine-textured, airy-looking plants with soft lines to give the feeling of distance. Coarse-textured plants give the feeling of closeness. Generally dull-colored foliage gives the sense of distance while bright colors give the sense of closeness.

HIDING DISTRACTING VIEWS

By the proper placement of plants it is possible to hide distracting views effectively. Hanging baskets are very good at blocking off the top parts of a distracting view. The lower parts of such views that are still in sight can be hidden with medium-sized ferns planted in back or in front of the hanging baskets.

MAKING A CURTAIN OF FERNS

By carefully hanging baskets at different heights it is possible to produce a curtain of foliage across the side of a patio or outside a window. The climbing ferns (*Lygodium* spp.) are well suited to producing a screen of foliage if they are provided with several wires for support.

Curtain of ferns.

Adding height to walls.

ADDING HEIGHT TO WALLS

Basket ferns may be placed on top of walls to give added height or to hide distracting views (such as the neighbor's clothes line). Wire fencing (2-by-1-inch mesh) can be cut, bent, and formed into a basket that will fit nicely across the top of a concrete block fence. The lower front and back edge of the basket should be extended to form a lip to secure the basket on the wall. The basket in effect straddles the wall.

PROVIDING FOLIAGE ABOVE EYE LEVEL

Sometimes the effect of a small palm or tree is needed in a small area, but there is not enough room to place a large container on the floor. Hanging a basket fern from the ceiling will achieve the same effect and keep the floor space open.

ADDING INTEREST TO A BARE WALL

Ferns in wall-hang-type baskets or containers, or staghorn ferns mounted on boards, add interest to walls. A small piece of wood or a wad of aluminum foil wedged between the basket and the wall will minimize water stains on the wall.

SOFTENING ROCK SURFACES

Certain ferns creep over rock and soften the hard lines. Provide pockets of soil in the rock to get these ferns started. *Polypodium*, *Davallia*, and *Humata* are admirably suited for this use. See listing under "Rock Garden and Wall Ferns," below.

BORDER AND FOUNDATION PLANTINGS

Border ferns are particularly useful in softening the hard lines of a concrete walk. For most walks use small to medium-sized plants that will not quickly grow out of bounds. Many *Adiantums* are the right size for this use and will like growing along the concrete. *Blechnum occidentale* is good for warmer, arid climates. To break the monotony of a bare foundation or wall, plant ferns along the base. Maintenance is less troublesome if short creeping species are used.

GROUND COVER

Where conditions are shady, ferns do well as a ground cover. They may also prevent erosion. See listing under "Ground Covers," below.

FERNS FOR PARTICULAR LANDSCAPE USES

OUTDOOR FERNS

The ferns listed are selected because they are easy to grow, attractive, and relatively easy to obtain in areas where they are popular. Ten are chosen for each section of the United States, but many more are equally good.

Northeastern States. Hardy ferns are the only ones suitable in this area, which may have prolonged cold periods.

Adiantum pedatum
Athyrium thelypterioides
Dryopteris erythrosora
Dryopteris goldiana
Dryopteris marginalis
Matteuccia struthiopteris
Onoclea sensibilis
Osmunda claytoniana
Osmunda regalis
Polystichum acrostichoides

Foliage above eye level.

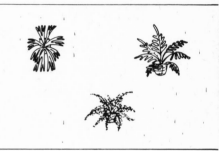

Decorating on bare walls.

Softening rock surfaces.

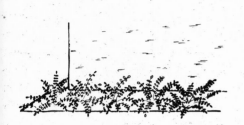

Borders.

Ground covers.

Southeastern States. Depending upon the locality, ferns for this area may be hardy to semitender species. For cooler areas, see listing for Northeastern States and for milder areas see listing for southern Florida, coastal, central, and southern California.

Southern Florida and Hawaii. A wide range of ferns grows in this area with the exception of some hardy species. The species listed are semitender or tender and like the mild winters and humid summers.

Adiantum trapeziforme
Aglaomorpha coronans
Asplenium nidus
Ctenitis sloanei
Davallia fejeensis
Nephrolepis biserrata cv. Furcans
Polypodium polycarpon cv. Grandiceps
Polypodium scolopendria
Polypodium subauriculatum cv. Knightii
Pteris ensiformis var. victoriae

Central States. In the northern part of this area only very hardy ferns are suitable; see listing for Northeastern States. For the southern area see listing for Southwestern States.

Northwestern States. In the coastal areas some semihardy ferns will grow, but the hardy species listed here will be more reliable on the coast and in the inland areas.

Adiantum pedatum
Athyrium filix-femina
Athyrium niponicum cv. Pictum (*A. goeringianum* cv. Pictum)
Blechnum spicant
Dryopteris dilatata
Dryopteris filix-mas
Phyllitis scolopendrium
Polypodium scouleri
Polystichum andersonii
Polystichum munitum

Southwestern States. In the inland areas mostly hardy or semihardy ferns will do best. A few areas will be mild enough to grow semitender species. Aridity and summer heat will be a problem in most cases. Suitable hardy to semihardy species are:

Adiantum capillus-veneris
Asplenium platyneuron
Athyrium filix-femina
Dryopteris filix-mas
Onoclea sensibilis
Osmunda cinnamomea
Pellaea atropurpurea

Polystichum acrostichoides
Woodsia obtusa
Woodwardia virginica

Coastal Central and Southern California. Semihardy or semitender species do best in this area.

Adiantum raddianum (*A. cuneatum* cv. Pacific Maid)
Asplenium bulbiferum
Cyrtomium falcatum
Davallia trichomanoides
Dicksonia antarctica
Microlepia strigosa
Polystichum polyblepharum (*P. setosum* of trade)
Pteris cretica
Rumohra adiantiformis (*Polystichum adiantiforme*)
Sphaeropteris cooperi (*Alsophila cooperi, A. australis* of trade)

SHADE-TOLERANT FERNS

The following ferns will grow in areas that are shadier than usual, but they still must have a certain level of light. Provide more light if the climate is frequently overcast. These ferns are not restricted to the more densely shaded areas, and most will grow in brighter light intensities but may be less luxuriant.

Adiantum capillus-veneris
Adiantum pedatum
Adiantum raddianum
Arachniodes standishii (*Polystichum standishii*)
Asplenium bulbiferum
Athyrium filix-femina
Blechnum spicant
Dennstaedtia punctilobula
Dryopteris dilatata
Dryopteris erythrosora
Dryopteris filix-mas
Dryopteris goldiana
Dryopteris marginalis
Nephrolepis biserrata
Nephrolepis cordifolia
Osmunda cinnamomea
Osmunda claytoniana
Osmunda regalis
Phyllitis scolopendrium
Polypodium polycarpon
Polystichum acrostichoides
Polystichum munitum
Polystichum setiferum
Thelypteris normalis
Thelypteris phegopteris

SUN-TOLERANT FERNS

Ferns seldom look their best growing in direct sun if they grow at all. The following ferns maintain a reasonably good appearance with direct morning and late afternoon sun. Some may tolerate full exposure to sun if the skies are often overcast. Elsewhere they will need filtered light during the hottest part of the day. Those marked with an asterisk will tolerate full sun if soil moisture and humidity are adequate and the light is not too intense.

Aglaomorpha coronans
Anemia phyllitidis
Athyrium filix-femina
*Blechnum occidentale
*Cibotium glaucum
Cyrtomium falcatum
Davallia trichomanoides
*Dennstaedtia punctilobula
*Dicksonia antarctica
Diplazium esculentum
Doodia media
Dryopteris erythrosora
*Dryopteris noveboracensis
Lastreopsis microsora (*Ctenitis microsora*)
Lygodium japonicum
Microlepia platyphylla
Microlepia strigosa
Nephrolepis cordifolia
*Onoclea sensibilis
Onychium japonicum
*Osmunda, all species
Pellaea, most species
Pityrogramma, most species
Platycerium, most species
Polypodium aureum (*Phlebodium aureum*)
Polypodium subauriculatum cv. Knightii
Polystichum polyblepharum
*Pteridium aquilinum
Pteris cretica
Pteris vittata
Rumohra adiantiformis
*Sphaeropteris cooperi
Thelypteris augescens
Todea barbara
Woodwardia, most species

WET-SOIL FERNS

The following ferns will grow in wet or boggy areas.

Acrostichum aureum
Acrostichum daneaefolium

Blechnum serrulatum
Ceratopteris, all species, aquatic
Dryopteris cristata
Matteuccia struthiopteris
Onoclea sensibilis
Osmunda regalis
Thelypteris thelypterioides (*T. palustris*)

DRIER-SOIL FERNS

The following ferns will tolerate drier, more exposed areas than most ferns but will still need moisture. They will need regular watering and protection until they are well established. These are not xerophytic ferns, which are discussed in Chapter 10.

Aglaomorpha coronans
Blechnum occidentale
Cyrtomium falcatum
Davallia trichomanoides
Dennstaedtia punctilobula
Microlepia strigosa
Nephrolepis cordifolia
Polypodium aureum
Pteridium aquilinum
Pteris cretica
Pteris vittata
Rumohra adiantiformis
Sphaeropteris cooperi
Woodwardia fimbriata

RAPID-GROWING FERNS

If temperature, light, and mineral requirements are optimum the following species tend to grow relatively rapidly.

Adiantum raddianum
Anogramma chaerophylla
Athyrium filix-femina
Cibotium schiedei
Dennstaedtia punctilobula
Hypolepis, most species
Matteuccia struthiopteris
Microlepia platyphylla
Microlepia strigosa
Nephrolepis biserrata
Nephrolepis cordifolia
Onoclea sensibilis
Polypodium subauriculatum
Pteridium aquilinum
Pteris cretica
Pteris tremula

Pteris tripartita
Pteris vittata
Selaginella kraussiana
Sphaeropteris cooperi
Sphaeropteris cooperi cv. Brentwood
Thelypteris augescens
Thelypteris dentata
Thelypteris normalis
Thelypteris parastica
Thelpyteris phegopteris
Thelypteris thelypterioides
Thelypteris torresiana
Woodwardia radicans
Woodwardia virginica

SLOW-GROWING FERNS

The following greenhouse or subtropical ferns are slow-growing.

Aglaomorpha, all cultivated species
Angiopteris, all species
Cibotium glaucum
Dicksonia antarctica
Dicksonia fibrosa
Drynaria, all species
Marattia, all species
Nephrolepis exaltata, certain cultivars
Platycerium, all species
Polypodium polycarpon
Pyrrosia lingua

COLOR IN FERN FRONDS

The new fronds of many species of *Adiantum* and *Blechnum* are red when they emerge and then turn green. Other ferns are naturally white or yellow on the underside. Variegated ferns, those with stripes or blotches of white, yellow, red, or other colors on their fronds, are mostly cultivars or forms of green species and are generally more difficult to grow.

Adiantum hispidulum	young fronds red
Adiantum macrophyllum	young fronds red
Adiantum raddianum cv. Variegatum	variegated white
Alsophila tricolor (*Cyathea dealbata*)	underside white
Arachniodes aristatum (*Polystichum aristatum*) cv. Variegatum	variegated white and yellow
Athyrium niponicum cv. Pictum	variegated grayish and purple

A lovely example of a species requiring special culture— a filmy fern.

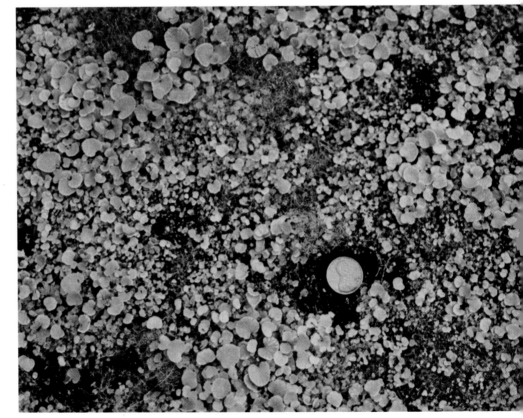

Above, closeup of a
bird's-nest fern,
Asplenium nidus, from
New Caledonia.
Right, tiny green prothalli
grown from spores,
four or five months old.

Above, top, young staghorn ferns,
Platycerium superbum.
Left, *Selaginella uncinata.*
Above, a late stage in spore culture—a tiny fern
sprouts from a prothallus.

Top left, *Polypodium subauriculatum* cv. Knightii.
Both *Blechnum brasiliense* cv. Crispum, left,
and *Blechnum orientale*, above,
are ferns displaying decided color in their foliage.

Top left, a fern of
the desert:
Parry cloak fern
(*Notholaena parryi*).
Top right, holly fern
(*Polystichum lonchitus*),
an alpine species.

Bottom left,
another colored fern—
Japanese painted fern,
Athyrium niponicum
cv. Pictum.
Bottom right, two species
in a Michigan rock garden:
maidenhair spleenwort
(*Asplenium trichomanes*)
and walking fern
(*Camptosorus rhizophyllus*).

Above, the spectacular goldback fern, *Pityrogramma hybrida*, in a Los Angeles garden. Below, a rock garden collection of hardy ferns: lady fern, hart's-tongue fern and others.

Blechnum brasiliense	young fronds red
Blechnum occidentale	young fronds red
Microlepia platyphylla	bluish green foliage
Pityrogramma argentea	underside yellow or white
Pityrogramma calomelanos	underside white or yellow
Pityrogramma chrysophylla	underside white or yellow
Pityrogramma x *hybrida*	underside yellow
Pityrogramma triangularis	underside white or yellow
Polypodium aureum cv. Glaucum	bluish green foliage
Polypodium aureum cv. Mandianum	bluish green foliage
Polypodium aureum cv. Mexican Tasseled	bluish green foliage
Polypodium aureum cv. Variegatum	variegated yellow
Pteris argyrea (*P. quadriaurita* var. argyrea)	variegated white
Pteris cretica cv. Albo-lineata	variegated white
Pteris cretica cv. Alexandrae	variegated white
Pteris ensiformis cv. Evergemiensis	variegated white
Pteris ensiformis var. victoriae	variegated white
Pteris quadriaurita a variegated form	variegated red
Pyrrosia lingua a variegated form	variegated yellow
Selaginella several species	red, gold, blue; some metallic, iridescent, or variegated

EVERGREEN AND DECIDUOUS FERNS

Ferns which stay evergreen even if the temperatures stay below freezing for days are indicated in Chapter 13 after the species listing by the code number 3. Ferns which are fully deciduous regardless of the temperatures are indicated in Chapter 13 by the code number 4. These ferns may, however, vary in their period of dormancy. Dormancy periods of *Davallia* species and *Polypodium subauriculatum* cv. Knightii are so very short in southern California and Florida that new fronds may be emerging before the old ones have fully withered.

Most ferns are somewhere between a fully evergreen and a deciduous condition. Oftentimes the extent to which they wither and brown is determined by the temperature. If the temperature is cool, yellowing, subsequent browning, and withering are more pronounced. If the temperature is mild, greener conditions will prevail. New leaves will appear continuously over a period of time and not all at once as with truly deciduous species.

ACCENT FERNS

Accent ferns have distinctive lines, shapes, textures, or patterns. They are plants used as center points of interest in landscaping. The following are suitable accent ferns:

Aglaomorpha coronans
Asplenium bulbiferum
Asplenium nidus
Blechnum brasiliense
Cyrtomium falcatum
Matteucia struthiopteris
Nephrolepis biserrata
Osmunda, all species
Platycerium, all species
Polypodium aureum and cultivars
Polypodium polycarpon cv. Grandiceps
Tree ferns, all species

BORDER AND FOUNDATION FERNS

These are ferns which spread sparingly or keep their general shape when planted along a flower border or walk, or against the foundation of a building. Ferns which are short creeping or clumping or with erect rootstocks are good for this use. Ferns which spread by long creeping rhizomes are not suitable because they outgrow their boundaries too quickly; such ferns are better used as ground covers.

Adiantum hispidulum
Adiantum pedatum
Adiantum raddianum
Athyrium filix-femina
Athyrium niponicum cv. Pictum
Dryopteris erythrosora
Microlepia strigosa
Pellaea rotundifolia
Phyllitis scolopendrium
Polystichum acrostichoides
Pteris cretica and cultivars
Pteris multifida and cultivars

GROUND-COVER FERNS

Ferns useful as ground covers will grow to cover the soil. They may spread by rhizomes or stolons, though short creeping ferns bearing clusters of arching fronds may produce the same effect. The following ferns spread by rhizomes or stolons:

Blechnum occidentale
Blechnum penna-marina
Davallia trichomanoides
Dennstaedtia, all species

Gymnocarpium dryopteris
Humata tyermannii
Hypolepis, all species
Nephrolepis cordifolia and other species
Onoclea sensibilis
Selaginella, several species
Thelypteris acuminata
Thelypteris hexagonoptera
Thelypteris phegopteris
Thelypteris thelypterioides

BASKET FERNS

Ferns in baskets or hanging containers are much used in today's house and garden décor. Epiphytes and terrestrial ferns are both used in hanging displays. Species with fronds cascading over the edges of the container are particularly attractive. General directions on the selection, planting, and care of basket ferns are given in Chapter 7; details on growing specific groups of ferns are given in Chapter 10. Some of the more popular basket ferns are as follows:

Adiantum capillus-veneris
Adiantum raddianum
Aglaomorpha, all species
Athyrium filix-femina
Davallia, all species
Humata, all species
Nephrolepis, all species
Phyllitis scolopendrium
Platycerium, all species
Polypodium aureum
Polypodium scouleri
Polypodium subauriculatum cv. Knightii
Polypodium vulgare
Pyrrosia lingua
Rumohra adiantiformis
Scyphularia pentaphylla

ROCK GARDEN AND WALL FERNS

Many ferns may be grown among rocks, but traditionally rock walls or rock gardens have been planted with small to medium-small ferns. The elevation of the rocks permits these ferns to be more easily seen, enjoyed, and safely tucked away from misplaced feet or rapidly growing plants. Ideally, some of the rocks used should be of limestone so that lime-loving ferns may be accommodated. If limestone rocks cannot be obtained, add lime to the soil mixes (see Chapter 5). Planting spaces between the rocks are usually a few inches wide and deep and must be provided with drainage. Ferns are firmly planted with a loam or potting mix. Some ferns will need additions of coarse sand. Small rocks added while planting the fern will help secure the fern and soil in place. Protect the surface soil from erosion by firming it and placing a few small stones on top of it. Generally temperate species of rock ferns adapt poorly to warm-climate gardens. Where rainfall is not heavy, xerophytic ferns do well in rock plantings (see Chapter 10, "Xerophytic Ferns"). Also see Kaye (1968) for more details on planting hardy ferns in rock gardens. Some ferns suitable for rock gardens are as follows:

Adiantum capillus-veneris
Adiantum hispidulum
Adiantum pedatum cv. Imbricatum
Adiantum raddianum cv. Pacottii
Adiantum venustum
Asplenium pinnatifidum
Asplenium platyneuron
Asplenium trichomanes
Athyrium filix-femina, small cultivars
Camptosorus rhizophyllus
Camptosorus sibericus
Ceterach aureum
Cheilanthes, all species
Cryptogramma crispa
Cyrtomium falcatum
Cystopteris bulbifera
Cystopteris fragilis
Davallia trichomanoides
Doodia media
Gymnocarpium dryopteris
Humata tyermannii
Lemmaphyllum microphyllum
Nephrolepis cordifolia cv. Duffii
Notholaena, all species
Pellaea, all species
Phyllitis scolopendrium
Pityrogramma, all species
Polypodium hesperium
Polypodium polypodioides
Polypodium scouleri
Polystichum lemmonii
Polystichum tsus-simense
Pteris cretica and cultivars
Pteris multifida and cultivars
Pyrrosia, all species
Selaginella, many species
Woodsia obtusa
Woodsia oregana

TREE FERNS

See Chapter 10, "Tree Ferns."

10. GROWING SPECIAL FERNS

HOUSE FERNS

Ferns add a touch of grace to a room, and if the room is not too dry and has adequate light, a variety of species are suitable for permanent decorations. Light and humidity often may be improved to an extent, but if not, it is best to have several ferns and use them in rotation. Replace a plant with a fresh one when it shows poor growth. Plants removed from display will recover if given sufficient light, humidity, and care. Since the most humid rooms in the house are the kitchen and bathroom, those are good places to grow ferns if the light is adequate.

Generally, robust ferns with leathery fronds like those of the house holly fern (*Cyrtomium falcatum*) and the leather fern (*Rumohra adianti-formis*) grow well indoors. Also good are most davallias. Some are very attractive for their finer-cut foliage (*D. fejeensis* and *D. trichomanoides*, the finer form). Most frequently used indoors are the Boston ferns, which come in a variety of textures.

If possible, start with medium-size ferns which have been accustomed to drier humidity. These "hardened" plants will adjust far better to the drier atmosphere in the house than those recently out of a humid green-house. Avoid selecting plants which appear unduly soft and green for their species.

When to water will depend upon the climatic conditions of the room, size of the fern, type of soil, and kind of pot. Most indoor ferns will require thorough watering twice a week—more if the climate is dry, less if it is cool.

When watering, water until the water runs out of the drain hole. This will wash out salts which tend to accumulate in the soil. Do not permit pots to sit continually in saucers of water. If you are watering them by setting them in saucers, remove them as soon as the soil is moistened through. If there are no drain holes in the pot, use distilled water or rain water to avoid salt accumulations and be careful not to overwater. Be sure that a layer of coarser drainage material such as gravel, broken pots, or perlite is at the bottom of the pot. Charcoal added to the soil mixture will help absorb noxious chemicals produced by microorganisms which are encouraged by the wetness. However, it is better to avoid overwatering than to rely on the charcoal's absorptive power. Always remember that the soil should feel moist, not soggy wet!

Every two weeks or so apply a fine spray of water to the foliage to wash off dust and insects. Watch for scales, mealybugs, and aphids. Once these appear they spread quickly, since they have few natural enemies indoors. Indoors, the young insects are not washed off by rain or overhead watering as they are outdoors.

The main problems in growing ferns indoors is to provide enough humidity and light. Otherwise the culture of indoor ferns is similar to fern culture elsewhere.

SOME FAVORITE HOUSE FERNS

Adiantum hispidulum. Rough maidenhair. Compact growth, reddish tint to the young fronds, small fern.

Asplenium bulbiferum. Mother fern. Light green, fine-textured medium-size fern.

Asplenium daucifolium (*A. viviparum*). Dark green, smaller than above.

Asplenium nidus. Bird's-nest fern. Broad, undivided fronds borne in a rosette, may grow large in time.

Cibotium schiedei. Mexican tree fern. Large finely divided, drooping fronds, quick-growing, large fern.

Cyrtomium falcatum and cultivars. House holly fern. Dark glossy green pinnae, endures drier humidity than most ferns, medium-size fern.

Davallia fejeensis. Finely divided triangular fronds, the rhizomes creeping, medium-size fern.

Davallia trichomanoides. Squirrel's-foot fern. Medium-fine-textured fern, the rhizomes creeping, medium-small fern.

Nephrolepis exaltata and cultivars. Boston ferns. Coarse to finely divided forms, large to small forms.

Pellaea rotundifolia. Dark green round leaflets, medium-small fern. Do not water until soil is nearly dry.

Platycerium bifurcatum. Staghorn fern. Provide with bright light but not direct sun, medium-size fern. Keep on dry side.

Polypodium aureum. Rabbit's-foot fern or golden polypody. Fronds deeply lobed into narrow segments, the fronds coarse wide-spreading, medium to large ferns. *Polypodium scolopendria* is a similar plant and may be used indoors.

Polypodium polycarpon cv. Grandiceps. Climbing bird's-nest fern. Clusters of strap-shaped leaves ruffled, fringed, or forked near or at their tips, slow-growing, medium-size fern.

Pteris cretica and cultivars. Cretan brake. Clusters of fronds divided into ribbonlike segments, medium-small ferns.

Pteris tremula. Australian brake. Medium-textured fronds, rapid-growing, short-lived, large fern.

Rumohra adiantiformis. Leather fern. Medium-textured glossy fronds, medium-size fern.

TERRARIUMS OR BOTTLE GARDENS

Ferns are well suited for terrariums or planting in bottles because they like humidity and can grow indoors in lower light intensities.

SELECTING THE CONTAINER

Suitable containers come in many shapes and sizes. Avoid thick, dark-colored glass containers which reduce the light. Very shallow containers without covers are not suitable for most ferns, as they dry too quickly. If such containers are used, place them in a protected, humid place and frequently check for sufficient moisture. It is best to select containers deep enough to provide for a few inches of soil and head room for the plants. Large brandy snifters or containers with similar shapes are very satisfactory. Some ferns will require less humidity than others and will do well in containers with large openings. A container with a large opening makes planting and maintaining the terrarium much easier. Large openings can always be made smaller with the plastic wrap Stretch 'n Seal. This brand adheres to the edges of the glass even when the excess is trimmed to the very edge.

Plastic containers designed for terrariums are very utilitarian. They are light in weight, less apt to break, can be opened for easy access, are provided with a ventilation hole, and are shaped to accommodate plants. However, they scratch easily and may be unsuitable for certain décors.

SELECTING THE PLANTS

Small-growing plants in two- to four-inch-size pots are best for terrariums. Young plants of large-growing species are easiest to obtain but will outgrow the container in a short time. Some slower-growing large species may be suitable if other species are not available. Always start with healthy plants. Do not mix moisture-loving plants with those that like drier conditions. The following plants are suggested because they are small to medium-small species adapted for terrariums. Because some of them are slow growers and tender, they are not common nursery items and must be purchased in specialty shops or nurseries.

TERRARIUM FERNS

Adiantum capillus-veneris. Southern maidenhair. Rapid grower.
Adiantum hispidulum. Rough maidenhair. Tolerates less humidity than other maidenhairs.
Adiantum raddianum. Delta maidenhair. Use the smaller or finer-textured cultivars such as cv. Gracillimum, cv. Micropinnulum, cv. Pacific Maid, or cv. Pacottii.

Anogramma chaerophylla. Short-lived but rapid grower. Respores itself readily in terrariums.

Asplenium daucifolium (A. viviparum). Like the mother fern (*Asplenium bulbiferum*). Easy to start buds in terrarium.

Asplenium formosum.

Asplenium oligophlebium.

Asplenium trichomanes. Maidenhair spleenwort. A small fern.

Cystoperis fragilis. Delicate-appearing but easy to grow.

Diplazium lanceum var. crenatum (*Diplazium tomataroanum*).

Doodia media. Hacksaw fern. Does not like very moist soil.

Lemmaphyllum microphyllum. Small, fleshy, oval leaves, slow-growing, creeping.

Mecodium demissum (Hymenophyllum demissum). A small filmy fern, likes humidity, creeping.

Nephrolepis exaltata. Boston fern. Use the smaller cultivars such as cv. Childsii, and cv. Mini-ruffles.

Polypodium vacciniifolium. Small oval leaves, slow-growing, creeping.

Polystichum tsus-simense. Tsussima holly fern. Dark green. Does not like very moist soil.

Pteris cretica. Cretan brake. Rapid-growing, use only the smaller cultivars such as cv. Wilsonii, cv. Albo-lineata.

Pteris ensiformis var. victoriae. Victorian brake.

Pteris multifida. Spider brake. Rapid-growing, does not like very moist soil.

Trichomanes radicans. A small filmy fern, high humidity required.

Also see listing under "Xerophytic Ferns," below.

PLANTING THE TERRARIUM

For a one- to two-gallon container, place a quarter-inch to one inch of perlite at the bottom of the container for drainage. If you have charcoal granules, mix some into the perlite. Place one to two inches of good moist potting soil over this. Unless the potting soil is already disinfected, it should be treated to rid it of any troublesome algae, bacteria, or fungi. This should be done a few days before use. Boiling water, a soak in Physan (Consan) for half an hour, or some other method is usually adequate to disinfect the soil (see Chapter 5, "Sterilizing Soils"). Permit the soil to drain well. Do not use very dry or very soggy wet soil at planting. Use evenly moistened soil, and keep it that way for best growth.

Plant the fern to the same level it was before. If necessary, remove some of the soil around the roots or from the terrarium to accommodate the roots of the new fern. Taller ferns should be in the center or the back with the smaller ferns, selaginellas, or mosses around them or in front of them. Firm the soil around the roots with a blunt-tipped tool. Long sticks and tongs may be needed to plant ferns in narrow-mouth jars. Wire tools made from bent coat hangers are very serviceable. Long tweezers are useful for picking off dead fronds. Carefully moisten the planting with distilled water; moisten thoroughly but avoid overwatering. The terrarium may need to be covered, partly covered, or uncovered, depending on the humidity and water needs of the plants, the size of the opening, the amount of soil moisture, and the extent of damage to the roots during the planting. If *much* condensation appears on the sides of a covered or partially covered container, keep it uncovered or enlarge the opening in the plastic wrap to allow some of the moisture to evaporate. Replace the cover after a day. If condensation again appears, repeat the procedure. For the first few days after planting, keep the terrarium in a well-shaded place.

CARE OF PLANTED TERRARIUMS

Terrariums planted with ferns need ample light but never direct sunlight. Long, thin growth indicates a lack of light. Growth which leans to one side is due to the plant's tendency to grow toward light. Turn the terrarium occasionally to eliminate this problem. Growth will be faster in warm rooms and slower in cold ones. Never place terrariums in very warm or hot places, such as on the top of a television set.

As long as the soil stays moist, the terrarium will not need extra water. Much of the water in a closed or nearly closed terrarium will evaporate from the soil and foliage, condense on the glass, and fall back to the soil. Expect some condensation on the glass. This recycling of water often provides sufficient moisture for the plants, and extra water may not have to be added for six weeks or more. However, it is far safer to check the water needs at least weekly. Open terrariums will need to be watered more frequently, about once a week. Water with distilled water when the soil starts to feel slightly less than moist. Never let the soil dry beyond this point for ferns. Apply water as a gentle sprinkle. Very fine-textured ferns and most xerophytes should not be watered on the foliage. If you should accidentally overwater, carefully tilt the terrarium and blot up the excess with strips of paper towels or other absorbent material. Or push a long eyedropper to the bottom and suck up the excess water. Keep the cover off the terrarium to assist in the evaporation of the excess water.

There is no need to fertilize if the plants are growing well. If they become off color, fertilize sparingly with a dilute solution (half strength or less) of liquid fertilizer. Don't fertilize too much—it will cause the plants to grow too large for the terrarium, in which case they will need to be trimmed back or replaced.

MAIDENHAIR FERNS

Maidenhair ferns (*Adiantum*) have a fine billowy texture and attractive black stalks which, since they resemble hair, have given the group its name. They are found in many parts of the world but are most abundant in the American tropics. Most of the cultivated varieties are finely divided, and many have ruffles, fringes, cresting, and other types of fancy foliage.

The common kinds are not difficult to cultivate; they need only moist soil, good drainage, and humidity. Let them go to the dry side of moist before rewatering, but not to the point of wilting. They are more suitably grown outdoors or in greenhouses than in homes unless a humid place like the kitchen or bathroom is available. Shriveling of new fronds is usually a sign of low humidity, especially if the soil is moist. The other common cause of shriveling is poor root development, possibly the result of overwatering or lack of nutrients. These plants are particularly sensitive to being planted in pots too big for them. In oversized pots the roots are poorly aerated. Most maidenhairs slow their growth by fall and take a rest period until spring. Water them lightly during this inactive period lest the rhizomes rot.

Dividing, transplanting, or repotting is best done in spring, prior to active growth. A soil mix consisting of one part sand and one to two parts peat moss or leaf mold is suitable. A handful or two of coarser material (ground bark or perlite) may be added to a six- to eight-inch pot for better drainage. The Delta maidenhair, Venus' hair, and *A. tenerum* like calcium-rich soils; however, the use of balanced fertilizers usually satisfies the requirement. If not, additions of lime, limestone, oyster shell, and the like may be added. Fish emulsion or other suitable fertilizers are applied every three weeks to ferns planted in sand and peat moss alone.

To keep the plants attractive, cut the old or discolored fronds off as they appear during the growing season. With species that form dense clumps of fronds (as *A. capillus-veneris* and *A. raddianum* and its many garden forms), the center of an old clump may die. To avoid complete replanting, cut out the dead part and fill the space with fresh soil. In frost-free climates all the spent and unsightly fronds may be trimmed off between fall and spring. In areas with frost, wait until spring to remove them. In all cases, avoid damaging new growth by trimming off all the old fronds in spring just before the new growth uncoils. Though the plant looks bare after this process, its alternative—having to remove the old fronds carefully without injuring the new ones—is far more tedious.

Slugs and snails are a constant problem in some areas and must be persistently controlled. Sowbugs and pillbugs may also damage ferns. Aphids usually appear in spring. Use care in selecting and applying the proper insecticide, since most will burn maidenhairs. With doubtful insecticides use only a quarter to half the recommended dosage on a few test plants.

The well-known American or five-finger maidenhair (*A. pedatum*) of the northern woods is easy to grow in cold temperate climates but not in warm ones. The Venus' hair (*A. capillus-veneris*) and the hairy maidenhair (*A. hispidulum*) are good for warm, temperate, and subtropical climates. The Delta maidenhair (*A. raddianum*) is more tender than Venus' hair but is favored for its wide selection of garden varieties. The Delta maidenhair and Venus' hair are sometimes slow to establish themselves, but once established grow rapidly, particularly among cement sidewalks and foundations where presumably more calcium is present. For tropical areas or in greenhouses, *A. tenerum* and the coarser-leaflet forms such as the silver dollar (*A. peruvianum*), diamond maidenhair (*A. trapeziforme*), *A. anaceps*, and *A. macrophyllum* may be grown. The rough maidenhair (*A. hispidulum*) can tolerate lower humidity than most maidenhairs and is suitable as a house plant.

Special maidenhairs include *A. tracyii*, which is semihardy and evergreen, but because it reproduces only from divisions it is rare. The kidney-shaped fronds of *A. reniforme* are handsome, but the plant is tender and difficult to grow. The trailing maidenhair (*A. caudatum*) is interesting for its long frond bearing a new plantlet at its tip. It is easy to grow if kept very well drained and in a warm greenhouse. Large elegant fronds are produced by *A. formosanum*, but because of its wide creeping habit it is not grown in pots, and few people have greenhouses with beds to accommodate it. It will grow outdoors in warmer subtropical gardens. An old favorite is *A.* 'Farleyense' (*A. tenerum* cv. Farleyense), with its gracefully arching fronds and many ruffly segments. However, it requires warm greenhouses with day temperatures near 70°F to look its best. Smaller but just as lovely is green petticoats (*A. capillus-veneris* cv. Imbricatum). It is not an easy fern for beginners but does require less heat than *A.* 'Farleyense.' Pacific Maid (*A. raddianum* cv. Pacific Maid) has overlapping broad segments and gives the light fluffy look of the preceding two species, but it is more erect and a stiffer plant. However, it is a good one for beginners to grow and is readily available in the trade.

With a greenhouse or some means of keeping the temperature warm and the air sufficiently humid, many of the subtropical and tropical species can be grown throughout the United States without difficulty. Keep in mind their particular needs for adequate humidity and consistently moist but well-aerated soil (see Hoshizaki 1970 for more details).

STAGHORN FERNS

Staghorn ferns are prized for their striking appearance and their usefulness as a decoration on walls or tree trunks (*Fig. 10.1*). They require minimum care once established. In subtropical climates, the common ones are grown outdoors year-round. Since these ferns require only moderate humidity they are suitable for indoor plantings. However, they must have plenty of filtered light. Plants which are established and properly mounted need only be hung in place, watered, and fertilized occasionally.

If plants are watered with a hose, water them thoroughly. Plants which are small enough may be soaked in water for 10 or 15 minutes. Do not be tempted to water or sprinkle staghorns every time you water other ferns—they need less water. On the average, water the plant once or twice a week during the summer months, once every week or two during the winter months. More water will be required if there is a hot spell, less if the weather is cool and cloudy.

It is easy for beginners to overwater staghorns. The outer surfaces of the base fronds often may feel dry while the spongy inner layers are completely saturated with water. Press your fingers firmly against the brown base fronds to determine if they are too wet. If they are, water will seep out. If they feel moist and no water oozes out, the plant is moist enough and should not be watered. Do not press against the freshly developed green base fronds, lest they be damaged. Some growers wait until the moss at the bottom of the planting is dry and crumbly before watering. Others wait until the fertile fronds start to become limp. The weight of

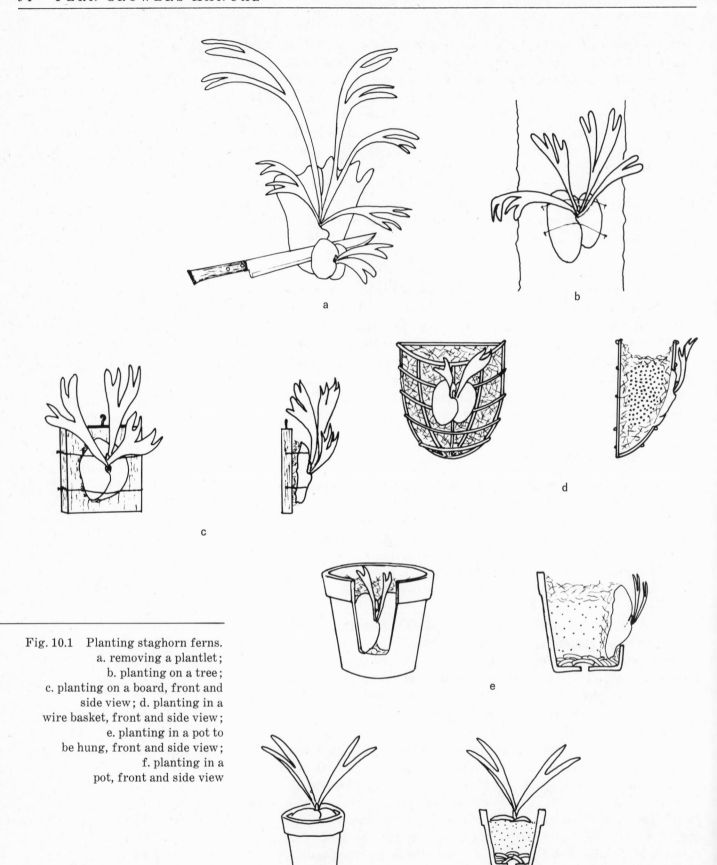

Fig. 10.1   Planting staghorn ferns.
a. removing a plantlet;
b. planting on a tree;
c. planting on a board, front and
side view; d. planting in a
wire basket, front and side view;
e. planting in a pot to
be hung, front and side view;
f. planting in a
pot, front and side view

the plant also indicates relative wetness and dryness. If the plant is not too large to lift, you should learn to judge whether a plant needs watering by its weight.

In placing the plant be sure that it will not receive a constant drip of water from overhanging baskets, eaves, or condensation from the roof. Symptoms of overwatering of staghorns include no or very poor growth, absence of new base fronds, soggy base fronds, algae developing on the moss, and at worst, purplish to blackish spots of decay on the base fronds.

Inadequate watering over a period of time also results in slowed or no growth. A sudden and severe lack of water causes the very young fronds to shrivel and wilt and the older foliage fronds to become limp and take on a grayish cast. The inner layers of base fronds will be dry.

Beginners are advised to start with the easy-to-grow species of staghorns and their many cultivars. The easiest to grow are *Platycerium bifurcatum, P. hillii,* and *P. veitchii.* Needing slightly warmer conditions are *P. willinckii* and *P. vassei (P. alcicorne).*

These species often form buds or young plantlets from their roots and sometimes from their rhizomes. These are called "pups" by some gardeners (*Fig. 10.1*). When these pups are big enough they may be separated from the mother plant. There is a greater chance of success if the pups are not removed from the mother plant until they have several shield fronds. Spring is a good time to make the separation, or just before fresh shield fronds grow out. Use a garden fork or knife to pry or cut beneath and around the oldest shield frond of the pup (*Fig. 10.1a*). If possible, take a little of the base fronds from the mother plant. Slip your fingers into the cut and lift the pup from the mother plant. Plant the pup with the growing tip on the upper side.

If the total thickness of the base fronds is more than an inch, the pup may be mounted directly on to a board and secured with wire (not copper) or stout strips of plastic (*Fig. 10.1c*). If the thickness of the base fronds is less than an inch, place a one- to two-inch pad of sphagnum moss between the shield fronds and the board.

If you are going to mount the fern on a tree, do not wrap wire around the trunk of the tree: you may damage it by girdling the trunk. Use plastic strips or discarded women's hosiery or string to tie the plant on the tree. Or use small nails to which the wire may be secured (*Fig. 10.1b*).

If you wish to grow a larger plant that will not need remounting for some time, it may be placed in a broken clay pot, wire basket, or shallow box filled with a loose humusy soil mix and covered or lined with sphagnum moss to keep the mixture from falling out (*Fig. 10.1d, e, f*). To keep the moss in place in the box, cover with chicken wire in which a hole has been cut for the plantlet. The surface of the plant, particularly the buds, should be level with or slightly above the surface of the sphagnum moss. Plants so mounted will have much more rooting media, but they are also easily overwatered. Keep recently mounted pups moist but well drained. When foliage no longer appears wilted, plants may be placed in more exposed places. The wires or strips of plastic will soon be covered with new base fronds. Remounting established plants is the same as for mounting pups, except that very old base fronds may need to be trimmed away. If you wish to grow large symmetrical staghorns, keep one plant, and remove all the pups that appear.

Fertilize plants about every three weeks, less during cooler months. Use liquid fertilizers. Solid fertilizers, whether granules, powder, or pearl types, do not dissolve readily and if caught between the base fronds may cause fertilizer burn or start a mold infection.

Once infection of fungus or bacteria starts, it will be difficult to control. Control means are varied and are not always effective. Some growers report some success by cutting the decaying spot out before it spreads. Cut at least half an inch beyond the decay area. Others try soaking the plant in fungicides (see Chapter 11, "Fungi and Bacteria"). Others reduce the watering drastically in hopes of killing the infection before killing the plant. Prevention is better than an uncertain cure. Do not overwater, and fertilize with only thoroughly dissolved material.

Aside from giving staghorns a bright airy place to grow and watering them correctly, the common species of this group pose no special problems and will reward you with their interesting growth. The less commonly cultivated species are more difficult. Most of them are large plants which will require much more space. But if you have gained experience from the common species and have a place for the uncommon, they are worth trying out. See Franks 1969 for more details.

DAVALLIA AND RELATIVES

The commonly cultivated squirrel's-foot fern (*Davallia trichomanoides*) is the most frequently seen davallia. Its finely divided triangular fronds borne on chaffy rhizomes may cover the entire basket, and its decorative nature is sure to attract attention. Though davallias are usually grown in hanging baskets or pots, they are also suitable as ground cover or over rocks if given enough soil to secure a footing. They are suitable in the house if there is enough light. As epiphytes of firm texture, they can withstand slightly drier air than most other ferns. They should not be kept too moist. If fertilized a few times during the growing season they will multiply readily from their creeping rhizomes. Davallias and their relatives mentioned here are deciduous and shed their fronds sometime between fall and spring. The exact time when they shed their fronds and the length of time before new ones appear varies with the species and climatic conditions. Fronds linger longer on luxuriantly growing plants. In southern California and Florida, the deciduous nature of davallias is hardly noticeable, because new fronds appear before the old ones have withered. The fronds may turn a beautiful yellow before they wither and drop. If old fronds have not fallen by the time new ones appear, remove them to provide developing room for the new ones.

Baskets which become covered with layers of rhizomes should be replanted. In mild climates, fall or spring is a suitable time. Tear the clumps apart. Save the clumps with the most growing tips, but remove and discard the dead or very old parts of the rhizome. Line the new basket with two or three inches of coarse sphagnum moss. Fill the center with a humusy, loose planting mix (see Chapter 5). Plant the larger clumps of rhizomes in this "nest." Tuck a one-inch layer of sphagnum moss around the rhizome and over the soil mix, but keep the tips above the soil. Push any leftover, shorter sections of rhizome into the sphagnum moss at the sides of the basket. Water the basket well immediately after planting. Watch for soil leaks through the moss, and plug them with more sphagnum. Keep the basket moist but well drained and in a humid place until the plants are established. (See Chapter 7 for further details on planting basket ferns.)

All the cultivated species of *Davallia* are easy to grow, though some are tender and others are slow growers. The most tender species include *D. solida* and the finely divided *D. fejeensis*. Both may be grown outdoors in southern Florida. Larger fronds, thicker rhizomes, and slower growth characterize *D. canariensis* and *D. embolstegia*. They can be grown outdoors in southern California and are probably able to withstand short periods of below-freezing temperatures. *Davallia trichomanoides*, the most popular species, tolerates temperatures below freezing for a number of days, though the foliage dies back. There is a finer form of *D. trichomanoides* that grows faster and sheds its fronds earlier than the coarser form. Less commonly encountered is the Japanese ball fern (*D. mariesii*), which withstands freezing temperatures but likes humid climates.

Related to the davallias is *Scyphularia pentaphylla* (*D. pentaphylla*), which has medium-small, coarsely cut fronds. Because it is tender, it is used as a potted house plant. The bear's-foot fern (*Humata tyermannii*) looks very much like *D. trichomanoides* but has whitish rhizome scales and is slower-growing. It is grown outdoors in southern California and southern Florida but may withstand cooler temperatures.

BOSTON FERNS AND RELATIVES

Boston ferns and their relatives belong to the genus *Nephrolepis*. *Nephrolepis* includes some of the most popular home and garden ferns. They are particularly favored as pot or basket specimens indoors or outdoors in warm climates. They are epiphytes and prefer bright airy places and good soil aeration. They do not like soil saturated with water, so keep them on the drier side of moist, especially when they are not actively growing, as in cool weather. The fronds are more lush with ample humidity and fertilization.

The commonest causes of poor growth are underwatering or overwatering and low humidity. Some of the fancy forms of Boston ferns are quick to show the effects of poor cultural conditions and may soon yellow and shed their leaflets. However, even with proper cultural conditions a few of the lower leaflets and older fronds will yellow. Trim these off as they appear. *Nephrolepis* plants also produce long, slender, scaly, hairlike stems, or stolons. These may be trimmed off or wound around the plant and tucked inside the pot to keep a tidy look.

When repotting these ferns set the older, longer rootstocks deeper into the soil than they were before, but do not bury their tips. Be sure to trim away most of the old leaf bases on the rootstock. Avoid planting them in oversized pots—they don't mind being somewhat root bound. Use an epiphytic soil mix or a mixture of half sand and half peat moss. (See Chapter 5, "Soil for Potting.") Most *Nephrolepis* ferns may be propagated by spores (except the Boston fern and derivatives), by divisions, or more commonly by stolons. Stolons produce new plants when they touch the soil. Planting *Nephrolepis* in benches or shallow broad containers gives the stolons room to spread in all directions and take root. The resulting plants may be separated and potted when they have two or more fronds. Boston ferns and their many variants generally do not produce spores and must be propagated vegetatively by rooting the stolons or by meristem culture. Provide bright airy places for their culture. Commercial greenhouses use as much as 1,000 foot-candles of light (see Chapter 8 for more details on propagation).

The Boston fern (*N. exaltata* var. bostoniensis) comes in an amazing variety of sizes, shapes, and textures. There are some that will produce fronds as long as five feet. Some have broad fronds; others are narrow. The finely divided and other fancy-foliage forms are often slow-growing. Fine forms or those congested with foliage should not have water applied directly to their foliage. Water mats and breaks the fronds and, if it stands on the leaves for long, causes the leaflets to become water-soaked. This may result in loss, disfigurement, or yellowing of the foliage. If water should mat the foliage, gently shake the water off or blot it up. Varieties which form dense masses of foliage will need to be groomed regularly by removing the dead or declining fronds and unwanted stolons. This will allow more air and light to reach the younger growth. It will also make the plant more attractive.

The tuber sword fern (*N. cordifolia*) is a very easy fern to grow. It is perhaps the most cold-tolerant of all, being able to withstand short periods of cold near 32°F. In southern California and Florida it is commonly seen as an outdoor border plant with stiff erect fronds. It has produced a number of cultivars, the most popular being *N.* 'Tesselata' (*N.* 'Plumosa'), which has divided leaflets. It is a slower grower than its parent. Even slower is the cultivar 'Duffii,' which has rounded leaflets and is best if grown under glass except in warm, humid climates.

The scurfy sword fern (*N. hirsutula*) is rank and generally unattractive except in warm, humid places. It does not like nights lower than 55–60°F and has no particular advantage over the other types except that it is very easy to grow from spores.

Nephrolepis species with long drooping fronds are difficult to obtain commercially because growers dislike having to grow and ship them. They must be displayed in baskets or elevated to be attractive. Some of the long frond types which may be secured from specialty nurseries include *N. biserrata* (*N. ensifolium*), *N. pendula*, *N. exaltata*, and its cultivars 'Gretnae,' 'Piersoni,' and 'Roosevelti.'

POLYPODIUM AND RELATIVES

Polypodiums are a large and diverse group of ferns which vary greatly in their cultural requirements. Most of the species in cultivation are epiphytes and grow best in baskets or hanging containers that provide good drainage and aeration. Some polypodiums may be grown in the ground if they are provided with good drainage and not overwatered.

Aside from our native species most of the polypodiums in cultivation are semitender or tender. They are therefore restricted to greenhouses or to indoor use in most parts of the United States. Place most species in good light but not direct sun. Plant in a loose humusy soil mix. Those with creeping rhizomes will need to be replanted when the rhizomes have crept out of the pot or tub or have grown down into the interior of the pot. Creeping types are best planted in a moss-lined basket so they may root into the moss as they grow along, thus avoiding frequent replanting. To replant rhizomes, separate the actively growing ones and their roots from the old or inactive part of the rhizome. Discard the old parts. As a precautionary measure before replanting, dust the cut ends with a fungicide such as Captan. Replant these divisions to their old level or slightly deeper if the roots are exposed. Do not cover the rhizomes completely. If necessary anchor the rhizomes to the soil surface with pieces of bent wire. Small pieces of rhizomes without roots may be induced to grow into new plants by following the directions above and then going on to plant the pieces in a clean, well-aerated planting mix that will retain its moisture without need for frequent rewatering. A mixture of half peat and half perlite will do.

Among some of the more popular cultivated polypodiums grown in the United States is the rabbit's-foot fern or golden polypody (*P. aureum*). It comes in many varieties, some of which are bluish gray in color and very attractive. Given plenty of light they grow rapidly once established. Water them when the soil is nearly dry. Some are more cold-tolerant than others. Variants with the broader, thinner lobes and sori in two or more rows on each side of the segment seem to need warmer temperatures than those with the narrower, firm lobes and sori in a single row on each side of the segment. The bluish green Manda polypody (*P. aureum* cv. Mandianum) has thin, ruffled lobes. It does best indoors or in very sheltered places if unblemished fronds are desired.

The Knight's polypody (*P. subauriculatum* cv. Knightii) is a favorite basket fern for people who have room to grow it. The long pinnate fronds are fringed along the margin and droop to form a beautiful hanging plant. It is tolerant of some neglectful watering once it is established. Outdoors in southern California and Florida and along coastal areas up to central California the old fronds are shed in spring but are soon replaced with new ones. The cut fronds last for a long time in flower arrangements.

Polypodium diversifolium is not as widely known or used as it should be. English literature lists this as a hardy fern, and it should be tried in cooler areas of the United States. It is a medium-size fern with its blade deeply divided into the lobe that looks somewhat like the golden polypody (*P. aureum*) or the East Indian polypody (*Polypodium scolopendria*).

The so-called climbing bird's-nest fern (*P. polycarpon* cv. Grandiceps) makes a handsome house plant. Its thick, glossy green leaves, ruffled and irregularly forked or notched, withstand the drier air of the house admirably well. Because it is a slow grower it seldom needs repotting attention.

A course, large, but durable fern is *Aglaomorpha coronans* (formerly

P. coronans). Though it is a slow grower, once established it tolerates periods of dryness and aridity. Remove the old fronds as they start to decline; otherwise the individual leaflets will drop and scatter about.

Most of the small polypodiums with simple entire fronds are tender species and do best in humid greenhouses or terrariums. Because they are small, they are not particularly showy plants and are therefore seldom seen in fern collections. The colorful *P. squamulosum* has red-tinged veins.

The temperate species of polypodiums are variable in their cultural needs. In gardens the more common ones are planted in baskets or among rocks. The licorice fern (*P. glycyrrhiza*) is a frequent volunteer in baskets lined with moss collected in western Canada and United States. A choice species is the leathery polypody (*P. scouleri*), which grows along the coast in the Northwest. Its fronds are small to medium in size, deeply lobed, thick, and glossy green. It is a slow grower, suitable for pots and baskets in cool humid climates. The resurrection fern (*P. polypodioides*) is a small fern interesting for its ability to roll up its leaflets to conserve water during dry periods and unroll them when moist weather returns.

TREE FERNS

Tree ferns, whether used individually or in groups, are sure to be noticed. They may also be used to provide a background for other accent plants. Most ferns bearing fronds in a whorl at the top of a tall erect stem are called tree ferns by gardeners and are found in a scattering of fern genera including *Sadleria*, *Blechnum*, and *Ctenitis* in the *Polypody* family. Almost all the ferns in the *Dicksonia* and *Cyathea* families are treelike and are the tree ferns referred to by most botanists.

Tree ferns of the *Cyathea* and *Dicksonia* families, as well as some in the genus *Blechnum*, are mostly native to cool and constantly moist upland areas of the tropics. About 700 species of the *Cyathea* and *Dicksonia* families are estimated to exist, but probably fewer than 50 have been tried in cultivation in Europe and the United States.

Temperature tolerances of the tree fern are the first consideration in selecting them for cultivation. Some are hardy, others tender. The night temperatures also seem to be important, as many of them prefer cooler night than day temperature. Those ferns which require cooler night temperatures do not do well in southern Florida, where day and night temperatures are nearly the same. Generally the Australian species do better in California, while the West Indian species do best in Florida. Tree ferns should be planted in well-drained soil. Add peat and sand to heavy soils or replace the clay. Sites receiving strong winds must be avoided. Do not permit water from overhead eaves or hanging baskets to drip constantly into the crown. Provide plenty of head room for their development. Though some tree ferns may be lowered by severing their trunks and replanting them, the risks are high. The procedure consists of wrapping the trunks with moss months before cutting and hoping that new roots will grow into the damp moss. Ample humidity and warmth hastens the process. When roots have developed, the trunk is cut below the rooted part and the rooted part is then planted. Do not try this method on tree ferns which do not readily develop roots on their trunk—for example, the Australian tree fern (*Sphaeropteris cooperi*, also known as *Alsophila australis* in the trade). *Cibotium glaucum*, *C. menziesii*, and *Dicksonia antarctica* root relatively easily from the trunk and may be lowered by this method.

The Australian tree fern (*Sphaeropteris cooperi*) is the most frequently grown tree fern. It grows in sun or shade in coastal, central, and southern California, in southern Florida, and in conservatories in cooler areas. It can tolerate frost and short periods of freezing temperatures, but its foliage may die back. On older plants the fronds tend to spread more horizontally than on younger plants and may be 20 feet across. The trunks are relatively slender, and cultivated plants seldom form extensive aerial roots. Since they generally lack buttressing from such roots, the trunks are relatively weak and have been known to snap off in strong wind storms. Therefore they are best grown under tall trees where their crowns have room to spread out yet be protected from wind. The lower fronds will drop once or twice a year in a very conspicuous manner. This is usually accompanied or preceded by a heavy discharge of spores. For the sake of neatness, these drooping fronds are usually removed close to the trunk. If left on the plant they will eventually dry and fall off on their own accord. Under optimum conditions this fern may grow a foot a year when young, and the cultivar known in the trade as *Alsophila* 'Brentwood' (*Sphaeropteris cooperi* cv. 'Brentwood') is even more rapid-growing. The fronds and trunk are covered with many small scales which when brushed on the skin are physically irritating and certainly should be kept from getting into the eyes. Washing the skin removes the scales and itching.

The New Zealand tree fern (*Dicksonia antarctica*) is the second most frequently seen tree fern in cultivation. It is semihardy to semitender and has been reported to endure 20°F or a bit lower for short periods as well as snow on its fronds. However, it prefers a higher average winter temperature, about 48°F. Its fronds are shorter, narrower, stiffer, harsher, and more numerous than those of the Australian tree fern. The crown of foliage reaches about 12 feet across and has a tufted appearance on the stout trunk. It is slower-growing than the Australian tree fern, growing only a third as fast. It prefers areas with ocean influence or cool humid conditions. *Dicksonia fibrosa* and *Dicksonia squarrosa* are seldom seen in cultivation because they are more difficult to grow.

The Hawaiian tree fern (*Cibotium glaucum* or *C. chamissoi* of trade) is seen now and then in outdoor plantings in southern California. Bare-root trunks are imported from the Hawaiian Islands, and trunks may be rooted by planting them about one-third their length in a well-drained soil mix. Spore-grown plants form more symmetrical crowns but are infrequently found in the trade. The Hawaiian tree fern fronds tend to ascend and arch more gracefully than those of the Australian tree fern. Their leaf bases and trunks are covered with silky yellowish tan hairs, unlike the chaffy scales of the Australian tree fern. Occasionally mixed in shipments of imported tree fern trunks are *Cibotium chamissoi* (*C. menziesii* of trade) and *Sadleria cyatheoides*. *Cibotium chamissoi* is called the man fern by the Hawaiians, possibly because its trunk is covered with stiff black hairs. It requires the same cultural conditions as the Hawaiian tree fern. *Sadleria cyatheoides* tends to be more difficult to grow than the other Hawaiian species and is sensitive to having its roots disturbed, at least in cultivation. Its bare-root trunks may be distinguished from others by the presence of scales instead of hairs. *Sadleria* and Hawaiian Cibotiums tend to grow more slowly than the Australian tree fern.

The Mexican tree fern (*Cibotium schiedei*) was once widely sold as a house plant, but it grows too big for the average house. It forms only a short trunk but freely forms offshoots around its trunk base. Its many light-green fronds droop gracefully to give the plant a soft effect. In eastern United States the tall *Cibotium regale* is often used in conservatories.

The silver tree fern (*Alsophila tricolor*, formerly *Cyathea dealbata*) and the black tree fern (*Sphaeropteris medullaris*, formerly *Cyathea medullaris*) need more protection from wind and sun than the other species to look their best.

Tree fern-like species in cultivation include *Blechnum gibbum* and *B. brasiliense*. These ferns are medium in size but form erect stems which are trunklike. They are semitender to tender. The plant sometimes called the American tree fern (*Ctenitis sloanei*, formerly *C. ampla*) is native to south Florida and may form a short erect stem, giving it a tree fern-like appearance. Naturalized in Florida and cultivated there and in California is *Diplazium esculentum*, which in the gardener's sense is a small tree fern forming a slender erect stem. For further details on tree ferns see Chapter 13.

XEROPHYTIC FERNS

Xerophytes are plants which have adapted to dry climates. Many xerophytic ferns grow in the arid climate of southwestern states. In more humid climates they are found on trees or rocks or similarly exposed places.

Many different genera of ferns have xerophytic species. *Actiniopteris*, *Doryopteris*, *Pityrogramma*, *Cheilanthes*, *Notholaena*, *Pellaea*, and *Polypodium* are genera which are noted as being largely composed of xerophytes or having many members that are nearly xerophytes. Many xerophytic ferns are covered with hairs, small scales, or powder to help them retain their moisture. If these coverings are white, silver, or yellow they make the fern especially attractive. Most xerophytic ferns are small and therefore suitable for rock gardens or enclosed containers. Some are a challenge to grow and may require several tries before the proper conditions are found.

In general, the fronds should be kept free of water droplets, though fog does not seem to bother a number of them. Their roots prefer a well-drained soil which is kept on the drier side of moist. Most seem to do best where there is an evenly moist soil or one that does not rapidly fluctuate between a wet and a dry condition. In cultivation they grow best in bright but indirect sunlight except along cloudy coastal areas, where they may be planted in full sun.

Xerophyte fanciers have devised ways of meeting the cultural needs of these ferns. The well-drained soil they prefer consists of one part gravelly sand to one part peat or leaf mold. They are planted among rocks (see Chapter 9, "Rock Garden and Wall Ferns") or in very well drained boxes or beds. It is important to keep them away from plants which need more water; accidental overwatering need occur only a few times to kill xerophytes. If they are planted in clay pots, plant the first pot into a larger pot, using the same soil mix. This double-potting procedure is useful in keeping the soil moisture uniform for longer periods of time. To keep water off the fronds, water early in the morning so that any water that inadvertently settles on the fronds will evaporate during the day.

Xerophytes have been successfully grown in open glass or clear plastic containers. The soil water evaporates more slowly, hence maintaining a fairly constant level of moisture. Water sparingly and carefully to avoid wetting the foliage. The humidity in the container, if not excessive, produces fronds even more attractive than those in nature.

Most of the xerophytic ferns have a summer dormancy in their native habitats. In cultivation the dormancy may or may not appear. Many may show slower growth as cool weather approaches.

FILMY FERNS

Filmy ferns have been grown successfully in various botanical gardens and private collections. They are noted for their very membranous leaves and their need for much humidity. The group consists traditionally of two genera, *Hymenophyllum* and *Trichomanes*; however, these genera have been divided into many smaller genera. Those in cultivation include *Mecodium* (a splinter of *Hymenophyllum*) and *Trichomanes*, and others may be found in specialty collections. The elegant Prince of Wales plume (*Leptopteris superba*), though not a true filmy fern, requires the same cultural conditions as the others. It is in cultivation in England.

Besides high humidity, these ferns prefer moderate temperatures, good drainage, and low indirect light. Climates with such conditions favor the cultivation of these ferns greatly. In less favorable climates, special growing chambers with air conditioners and a means of maintaining the humidity will be required, though some species may be grown in terrariums. Ordinary greenhouses are too arid for their culture. A special enclosure or chamber is usually located in a shady part of the greenhouse. Construct the top and at least one of the sides of glass or plastic. Line the other walls with moss held in place by chicken wire or nylon cord. Do not use copper wire. Plant the ferns in the moss-lined walls, in pots of moss, or on pieces of tree fern trunk. Mist them several times a day or humidify them automatically to keep the humidity near 100 percent. Walls of chambers have also been made out of hollow cement blocks, with the centers filled with moss and opening upward. A pipe on top of the wall drips water into the moss-filled center of the block and keeps the walls moist within the chamber. Ferns are hung in pots against the wall. Provide some means of draining the water away from the enclosure. The quality of tap water may pose problems. If the salt content is high, salt-free water will have to be used. Farrar (1968) achieved good growth of filmy ferns in chambers at 100 percent relative humidity with temperatures between 65 and 75°F and indirect natural light at or below 300 foot-candles.

FERN ALLIES

Fern allies are plants which are of the same evolutionary level as ferns. They include the whisk ferns (which are sometimes considered true ferns), the ground pines, the selaginellas, and the horsetails. All of these plants produce spores as do ferns, but none of them possesses the large leaves characteristic of ferns and seed plants. Fern allies have leaves which are inconspicuous bracts or small scales. Water clovers (*Marsilea*), azollas, and salvinias are ferns which might be confused with fern allies because of their unferny look. For further details on these and the fern allies in cultivation see Chapter 13.

WHISK FERNS

Whisk ferns or *Psilotum* appear as clusters of leafless green branches, but closer examination shows a few small narrow scalelike leaves along the stem. The upper branches may bear roundish three-lobed sporangia or spore cases. These epiphytic plants grow in trees or rock pockets in subtropical or tropical areas. They grow easily in greenhouses with strong light, thriving best in soil with organic matter and with periodic applications of bone meal. Propagation is easy through divisions of the rhizome clump. Volunteer plants appear in greenhouses from spores, but growing plants by intentional sowing of the spores is rarely successful. Plants have been reproduced by spores sown into pots of other greenhouse plants. The gametophytes (comparable to the prothallia of ferns) are about one-eighth inch long, cylindrical in shape, and grow under the soil.

GROUND PINES

Ground pines, club mosses, or running pines are technically known as *Lycopodium*. They have stems ranging from a few inches tall to several feet in length. Stems may be erect, creeping, trailing, or drooping. They are amply covered with scalelike leaves which may bear spore cases at their base. Native lycopodiums are difficult to transplant to gardens, and tropical species are difficult to grow. In all cases simulate the native environment as closely as possible. Tropical species in cultivation are epiphytes and are grown in moss-lined baskets or hanging pots in warm humid greenhouses. They are usually propagated by divisions, since they are difficult to start from cuttings, but a few cuttings may take root. Use only the tip of the stem with sterile leaves (non-sporangia-bearing). Cut the stem tips about three inches long, remove the leaves from the lower inch of the stem, and root in clean potting soil mixed with four to five parts sand.

SELAGINELLA

Selaginellas are more easily cultivated than lycopodiums. They look similar to lycopodiums but are generally softer, mossier, or fernier plants than the stiffer, harder-textured lycopodiums. However, their basic difference is that of spores. *Selaginella* produces two kinds of spores, male and female, whereas *Lycopodium* produces only one kind.

Most of the tropical selaginellas thrive in humid greenhouses, and many grow luxuriantly at temperatures near 70°F. Creeping or prostrate forms (*S. kraussiana* types) are used as ground covers, while the taller forms (e.g., *S. emmeliana*) are used as taller ground covers or in pots. Some may be propagated by pegging the foliage to the soil to root. All may be propagated by divisions of the clump. Species which root all along the underside of the stem are easily propagated by 1½-inch-long cuttings placed in clean builder's sand and finely misted three or four times a day until rooted. Taller specimens which do not root except near the base of the stem are harder to root by cuttings and may be propagated sexually. Select mature branches which have leaves bearing sporangia. These leaves are often shorter than those lower on the branch. Cut these mature tips into half-inch lengths, and scatter them thinly over a firmed, clean, well-drained mix containing one part garden soil and four to five parts sand. Sprinkle some of this finely screened soil over the cuttings to anchor them down. Cover the container or flat with a piece of glass or plastic wrap and keep at 70°F. In about nine months small plants of *S. emmeliana* appear by this method. It is important to use fully mature branches, since they have well-developed gametophytes growing in the axils of their leaves.

HORSETAILS

Horsetails or *Equisetum* are reedlike plants with jointed stems, ranging from a few inches to 20 feet tall. They are also called scouring rushes because the silica in their stems make them good for scrubbing pots. Horsetails grow in wet areas and are used in wet parts of the garden or as novelties in pots. Some are deciduous. They must be kept moist. *Equisetum hyemale* is grown outdoors in southern California; *E. telmateia* in northern California. If planted in the ground it should be grown in sunken containers to keep the plant from spreading. Equisetums grow best in full sun or bright light. They are propagated by rhizome divisions, though some have been grown by spores which are produced in conelike structures formed at the stem tips. Spores are viable for only a few days and must be sown shortly after collecting. Sow as for ferns. Spores do not grow well if crowded. The gametophytes are disk- or cushioned-shaped, about one-eighth inch in width.

FERNS FOR SHOWS AND EXHIBITS

GROWING SHOW FERNS

The beautiful ferns seen in fern shows and exhibits may be grown by any gardener willing to give a little time on a regular schedule to grow these ferns. It is most important to be consistent and to stay alert for sudden changes in weather or growing conditions. Large show plants need plenty of space to produce symmetrical growth, but small- to medium-size show plants can be grown in limited space. Although large ferns are spectacular show subjects, the smaller ferns are often more interesting and tend to be overlooked by amateurs. Provide the following conditions in particular for show plants:

1. Ample growing space protected from very hot and very cold temperatures and winds. Crowded plants compete for light and are usually lopsided in their production of foliage. Space without adequate protection from the weather is of no avail, for the fronds will be disfigured or damaged.

2. Even distribution of light. Evenly distributed light will help produce symmetrical growth on ferns. If the light is weaker on one side of the fern, turn the fern weekly to encourage symmetrical growth. Attaching a swivel to the wire-hang makes the job of turning large baskets easier.

3. Frequent dilute applications of fertilizers. Make frequent applications of one-fourth-strength fertilizer solutions rather than monthly applications of full strength. Apply weak solutions every one to two weeks during periods of active growth. If water spots (salt deposits) appear on the leaves, take care to apply the fertilizer solution to the soil and not on the foliage.

4. Groom plants as necessary. Grooming encourages the development of perfect fronds. Remove yellowed, damaged, or misshapen fronds and those which are crowding or will crowd perfectly formed and positioned fronds.

5. Produce one large plant. Most show entries are based on one plant per container or entry, unless you enter under a multiple-plants category. Offshoots produced in close proximity to the crown of the main plant should be removed if one large plant is desired. Cut the rhizome with a sharp knife, but pull the roots of the two plants apart with a fork or your fingers. A tearing action leaves more roots on the offshoot and the parent plant than a cut. Plants which have creeping branched rhizomes and form a mat are considered a single plant and need not be reduced to one creeping rhizome.

6. Be alert to unfavorable growing conditions—to pest damage, sudden dry weather, heavy rain, strong winds, or other unexpected changes. Cope with them immediately. Spots and blemishes are often due to plant stresses which are avoidable. Do not procrastinate!

7. Before the show groom plants very carefully. Remove water spots and dust from the foliage. Commercial polishes may be used on coarse leathery ferns, but they give an artificial shine objectionable to some judges. Before showtime clean the pots of algae and salt. If it is customary to cover the soil in the pot for entry, do so with materials which will not detract from the effect of the plant. To prevent damage in transport wrap the plant in a cone of newspaper. Ferns with spreading fronds may need to have their fronds tied back to avoid damage. Use soft strips of fabric or discarded women's hosiery to tie back the fronds. Do not transport the plants in open vehicles unless the plants are well protected. Do not leave them in a closed vehicle on a hot day. Anchor them securely in place for transport.

8. Register plants carefully. Be certain that you have followed the registration procedures correctly for the show and have entered them in

the proper category. Be certain the exhibitor's ticket is secured to the plants. Before you leave the plants be certain that they have enough water and make arrangements to have them watered during the show, if this is not taken care of by the show authorities.

FORCING FERNS

Where hardy deciduous ferns are to be exhibited out of season, some of them may be forced into early growth for the show. Others—such as *Woodsia glabella* and *Polystichum braunii*—apparently do not take kindly to forcing. Some develop deformed fronds or produce fronds and collapse soon after. Thurston 1939 forced many New England and Middle Atlantic States ferns for a March flower show. Ferns were planted in pots or flats in fall or earlier. They were placed in outdoor frames and covered with lath. As the weather cooled, the ferns were gradually covered with leaves. The ferns were permitted to freeze in November but under the protection of layers of leaves, branches, lath, glass sash, and straw so as to be easy to dig out at the end of December. Plants were then removed from the frames and placed in a dark shed to thaw for four days at temperatures between 40 and 50°F, after which they were moved to a greenhouse and given light and temperatures of 55°F during the day and 40–50°F during the night. After five days the temperature was raised to 70°F during the day and 50°F during the night. In the greenhouse, the water, heat, light, humidity, and ventilation for each species was judiciously adjusted. The water given was at 70°F and was not permitted to touch the foliage of most ferns. Exceptions were *Camptosorus* and others which liked humidity and were misted. The relative humidity was 80 percent. Hardening off of the ferns began in the second week of February, and temperatures were dropped to 55–60°F during the day and 10 degrees less at night. Ferns were ready for the show by the first week of March. Thurston observed that forced ferns produced good growth for the show, but the continued new growth was not as vigorous as in ferns not forced.

Most semihardy and more tender ferns can be kept in show condition by keeping them in warm greenhouses and protecting the fronds from damage. Little is known about forcing tender species which are deciduous.

11. TROUBLES

RECOGNIZING CULTURAL TROUBLES

Check plants periodically for signs of troubles. Early correction produces the best results. If a plant starts to decline, consider the common cultural conditions first. Have you been giving too much or not enough water? Has the weather turned too cool for the fern? Have you forgotten to fertilize, or have you fertilized incorrectly? Is the light sufficient? Is the plant entering its rest period? Most troubles are caused by poor cultural conditions unless you see pests or signs of them. Common symptoms and causes of cultural illnesses are as follows:

1. Slow growth, few new fronds, the fronds yellowish or an abnormal light green.
   - Plant entering its normal rest period or dormancy. Check species for deciduous habit.
   - Overwatering, especially if the lower leaves yellow and the soil is wet most of the time. Decrease water and/or increase drainage. Use coarser soil mixes. Use clay instead of plastic pots. If the plant is overpotted, plant it in a smaller pot.
   - Temperatures too low, especially if cool weather has started. Growth improves when the plant is moved to a warmer place or when the weather warms.
   - Too much light, especially if the plant is getting direct sun or very bright indirect light. Reduce light.
   - Not enough fertilizer. The new leaves are small and slow to grow. Apply fertilizers.
   - Plant root-bound, especially if it wilts between waterings and roots can be seen to have filled the pot. Repot.
2. Fronds partially yellowed, browned, or burned, young growth often shriveled or wilted.
   - Air too dry. Plant may be in draft or wind, especially if damage is

along the edges of the frond and appears after a windy or dry period. Increase humidity or move the plant to a more protected place.

· Temperatures too high. The damaged spots will be where the leaf is most exposed to the heat source. The frond's margins may also be burned. Damage appears after or during a heat wave. Provide more shade and ventilation. Cool greenhouses in particular.

· Soil was or is too dry, especially if plant wilted earlier. Parts of a wilted frond may recover, but other parts may be permanently damaged. Trim off dead parts, water well, then keep moist, not wet.

· Too much light. Reduce light.

· Insecticide, fungicide, or fertilizer burn, especially if treatment has been applied to or around the plant. Water-soaked tissue may also result in brown spots or areas. Do not permit water to sit on fronds. Trim away badly damaged parts.

· Salt damage, especially if a thick white crust accumulates on the flower pot or soil surfaces and the water is known to contain high amounts of salt. Use fertilizers sparingly. Leach the soil thoroughly. Water less frequently but more thoroughly.

· Frost or freeze damage, especially if the weather has been cold. Trim back dead parts.

3. Edges of the frond cupping under.
   · Insufficient humidity when fronds were developing.
   · Earlier insect or insecticide damage.

4. Fronds suddenly wilting, no evidence of burn or injury to the fronds.
   · Root damage caused by drying or overfertilization. Water well, then keep moist but not wet.
   · Root damage caused by overwatering or noxious materials accidentally applied. If roots have deteriorated, trim dead parts away, replant the rhizome into fresh soil, keep moist, not wet, and hope for the best.

5. Fronds skimpy in development, having a stretched-out appearance.
   · Not enough light. Give more light.

6. Fronds with good color, ample in size, but thin and lacking firmness.
   · Too much humidity. Reduce humidity.
   · Too much nitrogen fertilizer. Reduce nitrogen fertilizer.

RECOGNIZING PESTS AND DISEASES

If you can find no fault with the cultural conditions, examine the plant carefully for signs of insects, fungi, bacteria, or other pests. A hand lens will be helpful.

Look carefully on the underside of the frond for specks, dots, or unusual-looking structures. Do not confuse these with the clusters of spore cases or sori. Sori are regularly placed on the underside of the frond; insects are scattered and often favor nestling in the angle of the veins. Sucking insects may cause poor growth, puckering of the foliage, distortion, bleached spots, and discoloration. (Discoloration is also caused by nematodes.) The most common sucking insects on ferns are aphids, scales, mealybugs, and thrips (*Fig. 11.1*). Biting insects and pests will eat parts of the frond away, and some of the commonest of these are grasshoppers, caterpillars, cutworms, pillbugs, sowbugs, slugs, and snails.

Fungal infections usually accompany overwatering or too much humidity. Look for rotting, slimy, or water-soaked tissue, tufts or mats of mold, sooty spots, and circular spots of dead tissue, particularly those with small dots or concentric patterns. They may be anywhere on the plant. Look particularly at the base of the frond stalk near the soil. Sudden wilting of the plant, tip and marginal browning of fronds, and distortion of emerging fronds may be caused by fungi, but are usually difficult to distinguish from culturally caused troubles.

PREVENTING INSECTICIDE AND FUNGICIDE DAMAGE

If insecticides or fungicides must be applied for control, the following cautions should be observed in order to help control the pest or disease more effectively, avoid or reduce damage to plants and reduce the danger to humans, pets, and the environment.

1. Read the manufacturer's directions completely and carefully. Give the follow-up treatments if recommended.
2. New products or brands should be used with care. Test them out on a few plants before wider use. If damage occurs it will appear within two weeks.
3. Use dust or sprays made from wettable powders rather than emulsion sprays if there is a choice. Emulsions contain oil which damages ferns.
4. Proper dosage is given by the manufacturer. However, many fern growers apply as little as an eighth to a fourth of the recommended dosage to avoid burn on sensitive fern foliage. Less sensitive ferns should be given half the recommended dosage. Emulsions of Malathion, Dimethoate (Cygon), Diazinon, Carbaryl (Sevin), and Benelate in particular must be reduced. Dust is generally applied at ¾ pound to 1 pound per 1,000 square feet with satisfactory results.
5. Sprays and dust are most effective when thinly and thoroughly applied to all surfaces of the foliage. Fine mist sprays are best.
6. Aerosols or smoke generators should be used only in greenhouses or in tightly sealed plastic houses.
7. Spray or dust when the leaves are dry to avoid or minimize damage.
8. Spray early in the day so plants may dry rapidly.
9. Spray when the air temperature is below 85°F, and will stay below that temperature for two hours after spraying.
10. Spray when the smog concentration is low.
11. Move house plants outdoors for treatment if possible.
12. The healthier the plant the less the likelihood of spray damage. Plants which are root bound, in need of water, or very young are more easily hurt. If damage occurs it may be only to the foliage, and new growth may appear if the rhizomes have not been harmed.
13. The pesticides mentioned in this chapter are considered the most effective and least toxic of those presently available; however, all pesticides are toxic and should be so treated.

Systemic insecticides or fungicides are those which are taken into the plant tissue and are effective in controlling the insects or fungi from within the plant. Depending on the kind, systemics may be applied as a spray, dry, or as a drench. A drench is a solution applied by sprinkling it over the soil.

INSECTS AND OTHER PESTS

ANTS

Ants spread and protect such harmful lesser insects as scale, aphids, and mealybugs. Ants feed on the honeydew or sugary secretions of these insects.

Control: Place chlordane powder or spray on trails and nest of ants or at the base of the plant. Avoid dusting or spraying the foliage. Chlordane remains active in the soil for a long time.

APHIDS

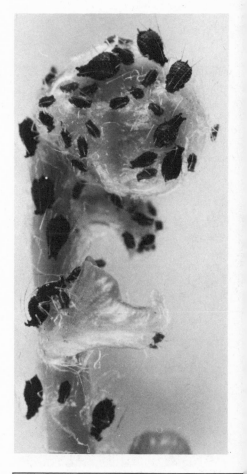

Aphids are small soft-bodied insects which are red, green, yellow, or black. The fern aphid is black with whitish legs. Aphids weaken the plant by feeding on the plant juices, distorting and stunting the foliage. These insects produce a secretion called honeydew which is eaten by ants. Ants encourage and protect the aphids, so ants and aphids must be controlled together. The fern aphid is most common on new growth, particularly in spring (*Fig. 11.1a*).

Control: For mild infestations on a few plants remove the insects with a spray of water, or add half a teaspoon of mild detergent to one gallon of water containing one teaspoon of nicotine sulfate and dip the plants.

Malathion dust or sprays from wettable powders may burn maidenhair ferns; sprays from emulsifiable concentrates burn or severely injure maidenhairs, Boston ferns, pteris ferns, *Polypodium polycarpon*, and perhaps others. Reducing the concentration to a half-teaspoon ger gallon will reduce the injury. Tougher ferns may withstand a stronger solution of one teaspoon per gallon. Heavy infestations will require weekly sprays until controlled.

Carbaryl (Sevin) dust, sprays from wettable powders, and sprays from emulsifiable concentrates are used by growers in California. Emulsions may burn tender foliage or sensitive plants, especially if not applied as a fine spray. Reduce the dosage to half a teaspoon per gallon to minimize burn. This spray may be used around edible plants.

Fig. 11.1 a. aphids, 8X

Diazinon spray from a wettable powder may burn maidenhair ferns. Sprays from emulsifiable concentrates may be injurious to maidenhair and some other ferns. Reduce dosage to a fourth or half to minimize the danger of damage.

Dimethoate (Cygon) spray from an emulsifiable concentrate may burn Boston and maidenhair ferns. This is a systemic insecticide and is effective three weeks after application. It may be applied as a drench to the soil thus minimizing foliage burn.

Meta-Systox-R (Oxydemetonmethyl) spray as an emulsifiable concentrate has been reported safe for maidenhair and other ferns if applied to the soil. It is very toxic to honey bees and fish. This is a systemic insecticide.

Dithio (Sulfotepp, Tetraethyl dithiopyrophosphate) is applied as an aerosol or smoke. It is highly toxic, and local law may regulate its use. Use only in tightly closed greenhouses or plastic houses. Give three or four applications; space application three or four days apart.

Di-syston is a granular concentrate which is applied dry and then watered into the soil. It is a systemic insecticide lasting about six weeks. It apparently is not effective against mealybugs or thrips.

FUNGUS GNATS

The larvae of the fungus gnats are problems in greenhouses and enclosed places. Affected plants grow slowly, lack general vigor, and may die. No visible injury is seen on parts above the ground. When the plant is disturbed small delicate gnats fly up from the soil or base of the plant. The larvae look like small white worms. At the soil or beneath the surface, parts of the plant are destroyed by the larvae. Prothallia are very vulnerable to fungus gnats.

Control: Clean out debris before applying insecticides. Drench, dust, or spray on the plant, on the soil, under the benches, and places where gnats or larvae may be located. Though various insecticides, including Malathion, Chlordane, and Lindane have been used, the following are preferred by fern growers:

Diazinon dust, drench, or spray made from a wettable powder. Use on prothallia and adult plants. Several applications spaced seven to ten days apart may be needed for complete control. See caution under "Aphids," above.

Dimethoate (Cygon) drench or spray from an emulsifiable concentrate used on adult plants. See caution under "Aphids."

Carbaryl (Sevin) drench used at half a teaspoon per gallon.

MEALYBUGS

There are several species of mealybugs which may attack fern foliage or roots. These are small insects characterized by a white mealy look (*Fig. 11.1b*). They weaken the plant by feeding on the juices. Ants are attracted to their honeydew secretions, and fungi may also grow on the honeydew.

Control: Same as for aphids. Control the ants. For root mealybugs use the spray as a drench.

MILLIPEDES

Millipedes generally feed on decaying vegetable material but may eat the tender growth of ferns. They appear wormlike but have many legs, and the garden species, when crushed, emits a pungent odor.

Control: Keep a clean culture; remove debris. Apply Diazinon as a spray or dust. Spray Carbaryl (Sevin) to surfaces where millipedes will

Fig. 11.1 b. mealybugs, 18X

crawl or into cracks where they hide. See caution for these insecticides under "Aphids," above.

NEMAS OR NEMATODES

These microscopic worms cause patchy, blotchy, or wedge-shaped reddish brown or black sections on the foliage between the larger veins. The frond eventually dies. On bird's-nest ferns (*Asplenium nidus*) the discoloration is sharply limited to the area between the parallel veins. In other species and on young ferns the affected area may be more irregular, partly because of irregularly branched veins, but the discoloration is generally limited to areas between the larger veins. These worms feed on the tissue of the plant, may introduce harmful bacteria, and can be spread by the splattering of water. Other ferns susceptible to nematodes include *Pteris cretica, Diplazium proliferum, Rumohra adiantiformis, Nephrolepis cordifolia, Woodwardia radicans, Dryopteris filix-mas, Polystichum munitum,* and *Asplenium pycnocarpon.*

Control: Avoid overhead watering. Keep a clean culture by cutting off and burning infected fronds. Do not discard infected foliage where it may cause reinfection, as the worms live on for some time in debris.

Hot-water treatments are used mainly on bird's-nest ferns but are not very effective. Plants are immersed in water at 110°F for 10 to 15 minutes. This is a drastic treatment. It necessitates enough heat to penetrate the pot to be effective.

Various nemacides are available (sodium selenate and newer products), but they are either too toxic for homegrower use or else fern tolerances are not known. A new product called Vidate seems to be promising.

Preplanting treatments require that the soil be sterilized by steam or other fumigants before planting.

PSOCIDS AND SPRINGTAILS

Psocids or book lice are very small, pale insects that scurry around on damp soil or over decaying vegetation. Springtails have a similar appearance but spring about when disturbed. Neither is harmful to ferns directly, but both may spread fungi and bacteria.

Control: Apply Dimethoate (Cygon) spray, Chlordane powder, or spray to soil, pots, and infested areas. See caution for Dimethoate under "Aphids" and Chlordane under "Ants."

RED SPIDERS

Red spiders are very small reddish mites which can be barely seen. They cause pale or whitish areas on the foliage. They thrive in low humidity, so rarely attack ferns.

Control: Increase the humidity. For plants in general, use Aramite (wettable powder only). Pentac and Kelthane sprays are recommended. Aramite's and Pentac's effect on ferns is not known to me. Kelthane is apparently safe for some ferns. Dithio aerosol is effective, but see caution under "Aphids." Di-syston may be used for red spider on ferns, but use with caution.

SCALES

There are several species of scales that feed on ferns. These are sucking insects which also secrete honeydew and therefore are encouraged by ants. A blackish mold may also grow on the honeydew. The soft brown scale is the most common scale on ferns and is identified by spots of black or brown on its back. Young scales continually emerge from the mother scale for about two months and grow to full size in two more months (*Fig. 11.1c*).

Control: Same as for aphids. Also: control the ants.

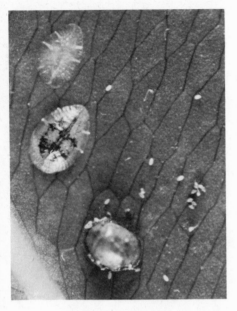

Fig. 11.1 c. scales (note very young scale emerging from old scale on the bottom), 10X

SNAILS AND SLUGS

There are very small- to medium-size snail species that will attack ferns. Slugs and most species of snails leave a shiny slime or mucous track that is the sign they are present. The small fern snail doesn't leave a conspicuous track. It eats the underside of the frond and on maidenhairs leaves strips of damaged tissue. Slugs and snails come out of hiding at night to feed. Slugs do not have a conspicuous shell.

Control: Examine the plants in the late evening to hand-pick and destroy the slugs and snails. Keep a clean culture by removing debris and other hiding places. Apply Metaldehyde dust or bait as directed by manufacturer. Products containing sand in their mix are less unsightly and do not mold. Zectran spray made from an emulsifiable concentrate will burn maidenhair ferns and possibly other ferns, so avoid spraying on foliage.

SOWBUGS AND PILLBUGS

These oval-shaped bugs eat decaying plants and the tender new growth of fronds and rhizomes. Pillbugs roll into a ball when disturbed; sowbugs do not.

Control: Keep a clean culture; remove debris and hiding places. Pour boiling water into hiding places, or attract bugs to one spot with half a potato, pulped on one side and placed pulp side down. Or apply a spray or dust of Malathion, Carbaryl (Sevin), Methoxyclor, or Diazinon into hiding places or surfaces where bugs crawl. See caution for these insecticides under "Aphids," above.

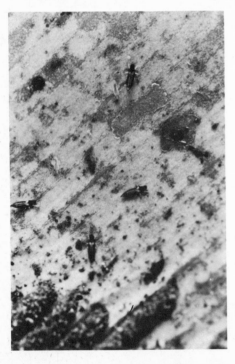

d. thrips (note dots of secretion and bleached leaf tissue), 6X

THRIPS

Thrip damage appears as black, brown, or more often as whitish bleached spots on the frond. Damage is more noticeable during the summer months. Examination of these spots with a hand lens will reveal slender, pale-colored sucking insects, though many of them will have moved to other leaves by the time the spots are noticed. However, tiny dark syrupy spots (honeydew) are left by the thrips, indicating where they have fed (*Fig. 11.1d*).

Control: Remove badly damaged leaves and burn them. Use the same insecticides listed under "Aphids." Begin control as soon as any damage is noticed. It may be necessary to spray weekly until controlled, except with Dimethoate (Cygon), which will last two to three weeks.

WHITE FLIES

These are small white flylike sucking insects which fly out when disturbed. They are not common on ferns.

Control: Malathion, Dimethoate (Cygon), Diazinon sprays, and Dithio (Sulfotepp) aerosols or smoke and Di-syston applied as directed under "Aphids," above.

OTHER INSECT PESTS

Cutworms, caterpillars, other larvae, beetles, crickets, grasshoppers, and cockroaches may also feed on fern foliage or prothallia. Disturbed soil or droppings often indicate their presence. Earthworms and other pests may not be directly damaging to ferns but may churn the soil around prothallia or young sporophytes so as to be damaging.

Control: Control with Chlordane, Carbaryl (Sevin), Zectran, Rotenone, and Pyrethrum sprays or dust. See cautions under "Aphids" and "Snails and Slugs."

FUNGI AND BACTERIA

Generally, cultivated ferns do not have many diseases. Most diseases of ferns appear when the plants have been kept too wet at the roots or on the foliage. Prevention is far better than attempting a cure.

To prevent disease, start with healthy plants. Keep the crown of the plant above the soil, avoid overwatering, water in the earlier part of the day, and space the plants far enough apart so they will have adequate air circulation. Avoid conditions which keep the foliage wet for long periods of time. Fronds, especially finely divided ones which become matted with water, should be gently shaken to remove the excess water. Avoid overhead watering with such ferns. Avoid planting in soils known to be contaminated with disease.

If possible, sterilize the soil, pots, and tools used in planting (see Chapter 5, "Sterilizing Soils"). Captan, Terraclor, or Benelate (Benomyl, Tersan) is sometimes used as a general disease preventative and may be applied as a drench over the soil prior to use. Reports differ on the effectiveness of such treatment. Allow soil treated with Captan to stand a few days before use. Once a disease has appeared it is better to discard the plant. Present-day fungicides merely retard or inhibit the disease; they do not kill it. They are applied to the plant and soil as a spray, dust, or drench. Prevent further contamination of soil, tools, pots, and so forth. Disinfect tools with 1 cup of commercial formaldehyde mixed with 18 cups of water. The tools may be dipped, then rinsed and used immediately. Bench surfaces may be sprinkled with 1 pint of formaldehyde to 6¼ gallons of water (1:50). Use half a gallon of the solution per square foot of surface. Keep the surface moist and provide good air circulation for ten to fourteen days. Do not use until all odor of the chemical is gone. Treatment areas must not be near live plants. Fumes of formaldehyde are very irritating to the eyes and mucous membranes, and there have been rare reports of human allergies to the chemical. A 10 percent Clorox solution may also be used as a disinfectant. Some growers also use Physan (Consan) or Lysol.

ARMILLARIA ROOT ROT

This disease has been reported to kill tree ferns (*Dicksonia antarctica*) in southern California. The plant will decline in general and die. Prying into the stem will reveal the characteristic whitish mold growth.

Control: You may fumigate the soil before planting, but there is no known treatment once the fern is infected. Avoid planting thick-stemmed ferns or woody plants in the area unless they are known to be resistant to the fungus.

BLIGHTS

Blights are various diseases which cause young plants to wither and die, and the tips and margins of older fronds to dry (Boston ferns and others). Blights appear as water-soaked spots on bird's-nest ferns.

Control: Remove and destroy blighted parts, avoid wetting the foliage, reduce humidity, space the plants farther apart to facilitate drying, and improve the air circulation. Benelate or Captan may be effective in control. Also see "Rhizoctonia" and "Water Molds."

DAMPING-OFF

This describes a condition in which very young plants wither and die. See "Blights," "Water Molds," and "Rhizoctonia."

GRAY MOLD

Fine tufts of gray mold seen on dead, injured, or dying fronds are caused by the gray mold (*Botrytis*). Infection usually starts from the upper part of the plant and grows toward the soil. Young ferns may momentarily survive but later produce deformed fronds or cease to grow altogether. The spores of this disease are airborne and common. Cool, moist conditions favor this fungus.

Control: Remove dead and injured leaves. Maintain a warmer, drier environment. Use the systemic fungicide Benelate (Benomyl, Tersan) as a drench on and around the infection. It may burn prothallia. Use only half a teaspoon per gallon of water.

LEAF SPOTS

This disease is not common. It may be caused by several species of fungi that cause various spots and blotches to develop on the leaf.

Control: Control as for blights. However, remember that many other factors may cause spots and blotches on leaves.

RHIZOCTONIA

This fungus disease usually attacks plants near the soil surface. The stem or stipe softens or rots at the point of infection, and the weakened stipe cannot support the frond. Young plants wither or damp off. Older plants grow slowly and produce deformed fronds or stop producing fronds altogether. This condition has been called "hard crown" by some commercial growers. *Rhizoctonia* is often the cause of black-brown spots on the shield fronds of staghorn ferns. If cankers form they often have a wrinkly brown surface.

The decaying parts will have fine individual brownish threads which may be seen with a 10–15X hand lens. These threads are coarse enough to cling to soil particles (other diseases have fine threads which do not cling). Plants which are overwatered or in poorly drained soils are more vulnerable to infection. Infected plants may continue to grow for some time, but they are never robust, and a minor stress may cause them to die.

Control: Keep a sterile culture. Discard infected plants. Do not permit contaminated soil or other equipment to be mixed with clean soil or equipment. Before replanting is done in a contaminated area, the soil should be sterilized. The following drenches will inhibit but not eradicate the disease and are applied to infected plants and soil as a drench.

Arasan (Thiram) may burn the young plants.

Terrachlor (PCNB, Truban, Koban) has a long residual effect; it is known to burn ferns.

Benelate (Beonmyl, Tersan) has systemic qualities but has been reported to burn the prothallia in some instances.

Captan and Semesan have also been used.

ROTS

Many species of fungi and bacteria may cause decay or rots. Cut away rotting spots and treat as for *Rhizoctonia* or water molds. Rots caused by bacteria are much wetter and slimier than fungus-caused rots.

SOOTY MOLDS

This fungus (usually *Fumago*) appears as black smutty patches on the surfaces of the foliage. The fungus grows on the honeydew secretion left by various insects. Though unsightly, these molds do not directly harm the plant. However, their growth shuts off light to the frond.

Control: Control the scale, aphids, mealybugs, and ants. Provide more air circulation.

WATER MOLDS

Water molds (*Pythium* and *Phytophthora*) typically produce a water-soaked appearance to the tissue or cause damping off. The molds start their infection from the tips of the roots instead of at the soil surface as with *Rhizoctonia.* Water molds grow when the soil is kept too wet. The outermost tissue on the root rots and falls away from the center core. When the roots die the plant wilts. Water mold filaments are very fine and do not cling to soil particles.

Control: Use the same measures as listed under "Rhizoctonia," except omit Benelate, which is ineffective against water molds, and Terrachlor, which is ineffective against *Pythium.* The disease may spread by spores, so avoid splashing water. A crystal of potassium permanganate dissolved in a glass of water and used as a drench reportedly inhibits damping off. Dexon, used as a drench or mixed into the soil, is also recommended for control of water molds.

ALGAE, MOSSES, AND LIVERWORTS

These plants do not directly harm the ferns. They do, however, shade and crowd the fern prothallia and young plants and thus reduce their growth.

ALGAE

Of all the algae found in spore pans, the green and blue-green algae (particularly *Oscillatoria*) seem to be the most troublesome. *Oscillatoria* appears as a blackish slime when growing under bright light intensities and as a grayish moldlike mat under high humidity and dimmer light. Though it has been suspected of producing toxic substances that inhibit fern growth, this has not been fully investigated to my knowledge. Nevertheless the mat may grow over the young fern plants and result in diminished growth of the ferns. If fern growth is slow in the spore pans, algae become more of a problem. Hasten growth by providing optimum conditions.

Control: Sterilize the soil before sowing the spores. Use only distilled water; avoid contamination with any possible source of algae—unclean watering cans, old pots, etc. If algae appear, pick out the growth. Drenches of Physan (Consan) require repeated applications, and control is not always certain. Dabbing copper sulfate (bluestone) solution (1 part of copper sulfate to 10 million of water) will inhibit the algae growth somewhat, but avoid getting the solution on ferns. Stronger concentrations of two parts bluestone to 1 million parts of water have also been used to control algae, but I have not tested this on live ferns. Wilson Anti-damp reportedly inhibits *Oscillatoria* but must be reapplied as needed.

MOSSES AND LIVERWORTS

Mosses and liverworts crowd and shade prothallia. If cultures are old and the light bright, mosses and liverworts become more of a problem. Liverworts, particularly *Lunularia*, should not be permitted to become established among prothallia, young ferns, or even older ferns. They spread rapidly and cover the entire soil surface, thus preventing the penetration of water, fertilizer, and air into the soil.

Control: Sterilize the soil before sowing the spores. Water with distilled water. If mosses and liverworts should appear, remove by hand if they are growing over the ferns. Do not fragment liverworts upon removing, as certain small pieces may produce new plants. Grow fern prothallia under slightly lower light intensities to weaken the moss growth. Most species of greenhouse mosses need more light than ferns do to grow robustly. Provide proper temperature and fertilizer to hasten the prothallia to maturity, as old cultures tend to have more moss, liverwort, and algae problems. *Marchantia*, a liverwort, growing around woody nursery stock has been reportedly killed with Physan (Consan) applied at 800 parts per million (2 tablespoons per 2 gallons of water). Regrowth appeared in six weeks (Maire and Elmore 1973). The effect of Physan at this concentration on ferns is not reported.

12. HOW FERNS GET THEIR NAMES

There are an estimated 10,000 species of ferns in the world. Only about thirty species are very commonly seen in cultivation. These ferns are known to most people by their common or popular names. Popular names are easy to remember, often charmingly appropriate or even whimsical. Common names are useful when dealing with a small number of plants and when local usage is uniform. However, when dealing with many different plants and communicating with people in distant areas about them, the common name often results in much confusion. Elsewhere, people may have different names for the same plant, or the same common name may apply to several plants. There is nothing formal or binding as to which common name is correct, and any number may exist. New ones may be made by anyone, but most plants don't even have common names.

Scientific names, on the other hand, are often long, difficult to pronounce, and difficult to remember. But they are understood the world over by people who are acquainted with them, and they do indicate relationships.

Every species or kind of plant known to science has one legitimate scientific name which is used only for that particular plant. However, technical errors, new discoveries, or other problems may result in synonyms or in alternate names for the same species. In these cases, the legitimate name of the plant is usually determined by international rules. People who deal with many different plants or who wish to be precise about their plants will find scientific names worth the time to learn. Understanding them and using them results in less confusion and more accuracy in communication.

NAMING THE SPECIES

The scientific name of a species consists of two words. The first is like the surname of a person (Doe), the second is like the given name (Jane). The first word denotes the genus or larger group to which the plant belongs. The second word denotes the particular plant in the group. For instance, *Asplenium bulbiferum* is the scientific name for the mother fern. The first word, *Asplenium*, is the name of the genus to which the mother fern belongs. The second word, *bulbiferum*, indicates the particular *Asplenium*. There is a similar fern called *Asplenium daucifolium*. It is apparent by the name that the fern is related to the mother fern and belongs in the same genus. It is also clear that the fern is not the same species as the mother fern because it has a different second word (or species epithet). This second fern is different from the mother fern not only in size and color but more significantly in shape of the leaflets and the rhizome scales *(Fig. 12.1)*. *Botryichium virginianum* and *Polypodium virginianum* may have the same species epithet, but there the similarity ends *(Fig. 12.2)*. They belong to two entirely different genera. Having the same species epithet merely means they happened to be named after the state of Virginia.

How do plants get their scientific name? A plant suspected of being new to science is carefully studied by a botanist who will compare it to its relatives. If the new plant does not match any of the known relatives and the botanist believes the plant is not a freak or variant of a known species, he may proceed to give the plant a name according to the rules set forth in the book *International Rules of Botanical Nomenclature*, or the "Botanical Code" for short.

If the plant is very different from known plants, he may decide to give it a genus name all its own. If, on the other hand, he believes the plant belongs to an already established genus, he adds a species epithet to the genus name to complete the species name of the plant. He may name the plant after whatever he wishes; it may be the person who discovered the plant, the place where it was discovered, or a structural feature.

The botanist who names the plant is known as the author of the name. His initials or an abbreviation of his name (the author citation) appears after the scientific name of the plant, though this is often omitted in general use of the name. The scientific name for the bird's-nest fern may therefore appear as *Asplenium nidus* L. The letter L indicates that the species name was given by Linnaeus, the famous Swedish botanist who began the system of giving species two names. This system is called the binomial system and permits a systematic method of arranging species into a filing system.

Fig. 12.1 Closely allied species. a. *Asplenium bulbiferum*, the mother fern, upper half of a frond; b. *Asplenium daucifolium* (*A. viviparum*), a frond

VARIATIONS WITHIN SPECIES

A species may vary. Variations may be in the way the plant is structured or the way it functions. For instance, some variations may have slightly fuller fronds or produce their spores very late in the season. These variations may be due to cultural conditions or they may have a hereditary basis (usually due to special gene combinations or mutations). Variants with a hereditary basis may be given names. Such a name appears after the species name and is preceded by an abbreviation such as cv., var., ssp., or f. These abbreviations stand for, respectively, *cultivar*, *varietas*, *sub-*

species, and *forma*—different kinds of variations which are discussed in the following sections.

CULTIVATED VARIETIES

Cultivated ferns may clearly differ from their parent. If these variations, whether behavioral or structural, are stable and passed on to the offspring through propagation by spores or vegetative means they may be given a name if they are of horticultural interest. Since these variants originate in cultivation, they are designated as cultivated varieties or cultivars. If they originate in the wild, most are properly called forms (*forma*). Some of the common variations appearing among cultivated ferns which are often given cultivar status (*Fig. 12.3*) include:

Changes in the margin, such as fringing, lobing, ruffling, cresting, or forking.
Changes in size of the parts, such as depauperate, narrower, wider, smaller, or larger pinnae or pinnules.
Changes in color, such as variegation.
Changes in overall size of the plant, such as dwarfism or gigantism.
Changes in miscellaneous ways, such as formation of buds, failure to form spores, maintenance of juvenile foliage, apospory, and so forth.

The giving of cultivar names is governed by a set of rules called the "Cultivated Code" (or *International Code of Nomenclature for Cultivated Plants*, 1969; see Appendix II for source). The procedures for giving a name to a cultivar are far simpler than the rules for naming a species. Nurserymen, growers, and horticultural writers should be encouraged to use these rules to reduce some of the confusion in the trade. Giving a cultivar name is not to be confused with obtaining a patent on a plant. One is a botanical matter, and the other is a government matter (see "Obtaining a Plant Patent," below). Cultivar names given to plants after 1959 are in the common language (not Latinized). Cultivar names are preceded by the abbreviation "cv." or by single quotes around the name, but not by both. For instance, the maidenhair fern known as 'Pacific Maid' may appear as *Adiantum raddianum* cv. Pacific Maid or *A. raddianum* 'Pacific Maid' or *A.* 'Pacific Maid.'

Fig. 12.2   Unrelated species.
a. *Botrychium virginianum*,
the rattlesnake fern;
b. *Polypodium virginianum*,
the common polypody

BOTANICAL VARIETIES AND FORMS

Variations of the species which occur naturally and are found in all the individuals in a given geographical area are called botanical varieties or *varietas*. *Varietas* is abbreviated "var." and precedes the name of the variety. For example, the Eastern bracken fern, *Pteridium aquilinum* var. *latiusculum*, is found in the eastern United States, while the western

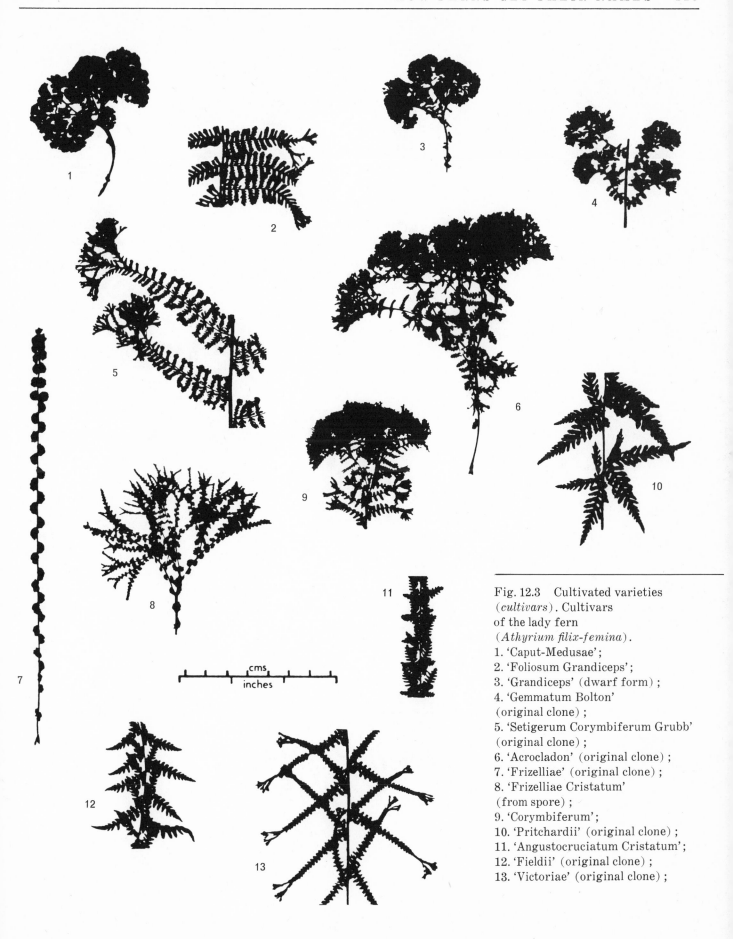

Fig. 12.3   Cultivated varieties
(*cultivars*). Cultivars
of the lady fern
(*Athyrium filix-femina*).
1. 'Caput-Medusae';
2. 'Foliosum Grandiceps';
3. 'Grandiceps' (dwarf form) ;
4. 'Gemmatum Bolton'
(original clone) ;
5. 'Setigerum Corymbiferum Grubb'
(original clone) ;
6. 'Acrocladon' (original clone) ;
7. 'Frizelliae' (original clone) ;
8. 'Frizelliae Cristatum'
(from spore) ;
9. 'Corymbiferum';
10. 'Pritchardii' (original clone) ;
11. 'Angustocruciatum Cristatum';
12. 'Fieldii' (original clone) ;
13. 'Victoriae' (original clone) ;

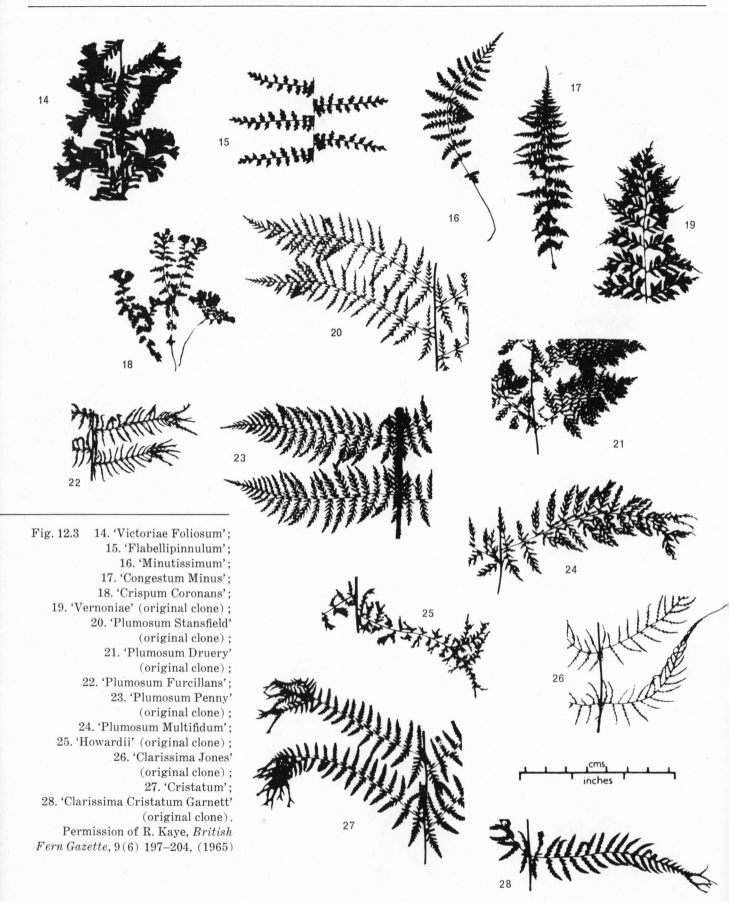

Fig. 12.3   14. 'Victoriae Foliosum';
15. 'Flabellipinnulum';
16. 'Minutissimum';
17. 'Congestum Minus';
18. 'Crispum Coronans';
19. 'Vernoniae' (original clone);
20. 'Plumosum Stansfield'
(original clone);
21. 'Plumosum Druery'
(original clone);
22. 'Plumosum Furcillans';
23. 'Plumosum Penny'
(original clone);
24. 'Plumosum Multifidum';
25. 'Howardii' (original clone);
26. 'Clarissima Jones'
(original clone);
27. 'Cristatum';
28. 'Clarissima Cristatum Garnett'
(original clone).
Permission of R. Kaye, *British Fern Gazette*, 9(6) 197–204, (1965)

Fig. 12.4   Botanical varieties
(*varietas*).
a. *Pteridium aquilinum*
var. *latiusculum*;
b. *Pteridium aquilinum*
var. *pubescens*;
c. *Pteridium aquilinum*
var. *caudatum*

United States has the western bracken fern, *Pteridium aquilinum* var. *pubescens*. *Pteridium aquilinum* var. *caudatum* is found in southern United States and into Latin America. The eastern variety has obliquely placed pinnules and hairless indusia, whereas the western variety has pinnules nearly at right angles to the rachis and hairs on the indusia. The southern variety is narrower in all parts. Early usage of "var." did not distinguish between botanical varieties, cultivated varieties, or forms; hence many plants listed as "var." are in today's definition properly cultivated varieties (cv.) or forms (f.). The abbreviation "ssp." stands for *subspecies* and is used in roughly the same manner as botanical varieties.

Forms are variations appearing sporadically among individuals of a population growing in nature. Form or *forma* is abbreviated "f." An example of its use is in *Blechnum spicant* f. *bipinnatum* (*Fig. 12.5*). This deer fern has deeply lobed pinnae and was found among normal plants growing in nature. The naming of botanical varieties, subspecies, or forms is governed by the "Botanical Code," and the names are always in Latin form.

HYBRIDS

The naming of hybrids, whether originating in the wild or produced in cultivation, is governed by the "Botanical Code." Hybrids may be between species of the same genus or species of different genera. They may be designated by a formula or name. The cross between *Adiantum jordanii* and *A. pedatum* is designated by the formula *Adiantum jordanii* x *pedatum* or its equivalent name, *Adiantum* x *tracyi* (*Fig. 12.6*).

Hybrids between species of different genera are designated by combining parts of the generic names of the parents. The cross between *Asplenium adiantum-nigrum* and *Phyllitis scolopendrium* is *Asplenophyllitis jacksonii* (*Fig. 12.7*). The botanist is free to choose the second word of the name.

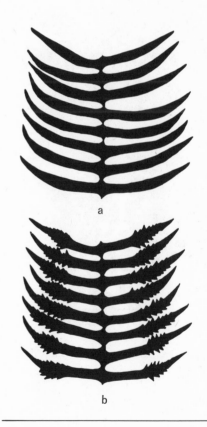

Fig. 12.5   Botanical forms (*forma*).
Comparison of typical
pinnae of the deer fern to a form.
a. typical *Blechnum spicant*;
b. a form, *Blechnum
spicant* f. *bipinnatum*

x

a

b

c

Fig. 12.6   Hybrid between species
of the same genus.
a. parent *Adiantum jordanii*;
b. parent *Adiantum pedatum*;
c. hybrid offspring
Adiantum tracyi.
After B. J. Hoshizaki, *Baileya*,
17(4), 179 (1970)

WHY FERN NAMES CHANGE

There are many reasons why fern names must be changed. Name changes are an annoyance to growers and even to many botanists. But without name changes the new knowledge on ferns would be difficult to assimilate and organize. Keeping familiar names would be like keeping a static file. Newly discovered plants would have to be added to the existing categories in the file. Some categories would contain such large numbers of plants that they would be unwieldy to work with and difficult to understand. Unrelated plants would be inadvertently placed together, while related ones could be scattered in separate categories. It would be like trying to classify vehicles of 1970 into file categories made for the vehicles of 1900.

To accommodate our increasing knowledge of plants and to organize it into a meaningful relationship, files may be expanded and reorganized. New categories are added to the files. Old categories may be combined with other categories or divided up into smaller categories. As a result, there will be name changes. But more important and of broader interest is the fact that the new knowledge on plants and their relationships is incorporated into the file, and the way the plants are organized in the file will reflect our updated knowledge. There are still many gaps in our knowledge of plant relationships, and until these plants are thoroughly studied and understood, name changes are sure to continue.

OBTAINING A PLANT PATENT

Plant patents are obtained through the Patent Office, U.S. Department of Commerce, and information may be obtained through any of their field offices scattered around the country. A patent gives the originator the right to exclude all others from making, using, or selling the patented plant. The patent, if granted, will last for seventeen years.

Among the requirements to apply for a United States patent are: the filing of a Plant Patent application, an initial fee of $65, submission in duplicate of a suitable painting or photograph of the plant, detailed description of the plant, and an explanation of how it differs from others of its kind. The application requires the signing of an oath declaring among other things that the petitioner is the original and sole inventor of the plant, that it has been asexually reproduced by the petitioner, that it is a new and distinct variety (cultivated spore, mutant, hybrid, seedling), and that to his knowledge the plant was not known or used before his invention. If the application is allowed by the Patent Office an issue fee of $100 is required plus other charges. In obtaining a patent, the government recommends that the services of a patent lawyer be obtained. A list of patent attorneys is available from the U.S. Patent Office.

LEARNING THE FERN GENERA

When looking at the variety of cultivated ferns we somehow know that a particular fern is a staghorn fern or a maidenhair fern. Some ferns are so distinct that we have no difficulty recognizing them. With these and some other ferns the overall appearance and aspects are enough to tell us its fern group. Other ferns require closer observations. For instance the maidenhair spleenwort (*Asplenium trichomanes*) and the bird's-nest fern (*A. nidus*) appear very different, yet they both are *Asplenium* (*Fig. 12.8*). The sori and indusia of both species are long and narrow, and though longer in the bird's-nest fern, they are basically the same in both species. The indusium in both species is attached to the upper fork of a vein branch, and the rhizome scales are latticed or look like a stained-glass window (clathrate) through a hand lens. It is this set of features that is important in recognizing *Asplenium* and not the shape of the frond in this case.

The fern student interested in learning to recognize ferns in general should start by studying the genera. Examples of genera are the spleenworts, the staghorns, the maidenhairs, and the polypodys. Start with a fern that you know, such as the maidenhair fern. Select a fertile frond, go to the index, and look up the scientific name. Under the scientific name in Chapter 13 will be a few of the more conspicuous features that distinguish this genus from others. On your fern locate the features mentioned; check your observations with the illustrations of the genus. A hand lens of about 8–15X magnification will assist you greatly. Once you are satisfied that you have seen the features mentioned, keep them in mind, and the next time you see another kind of maidenhair fern, look for them again. In a short time you will be able to associate maidenhairs with a certain set of features. You will also recognize features that do not belong with the maidenhairs. Start with other fern genera that you casually know and repeat the process, that is: (1) look up its scientific name; (2) locate the distinguishing features on your plant; (3) check your observations with the diagrams; (4) examine other members of the same genus for the same features to reinforce your observations. If you happen to be able to recognize the different species of a genus at this time, that is fine, but do not be concerned with their technical differences. Concentrate on the features of the genus. The features used to distinguish a genus are generally less diversified and less confusing than those used for distinguishing species. Besides, the species will be easier to recognize once you have become familiar with the genera. Most of the generic features you will be examining are associated with the position, shape, and type of the sorus and indusium. Also important in distinguishing many genera is the rhizome, which may be short and erect or long and creeping, and it may be hairy or scaly. The pattern of veins and the shape of the frond may also be important. Chapters 2 and 13 and the glossary will discuss or illustrate most of these distinguishing features.

Fig. 12.7   Hybrid between species of supposedly different genera.
a. parent *Asplenium adiantum-nigrum*;
b. parent *Phyllitis scolopendrium*;
c. hybrid offspring *Asplenophyllitis jacksonii*.
After J. D. Lovis and G. Vida, *British Fern Gazette* 10(2), 58 (1969)

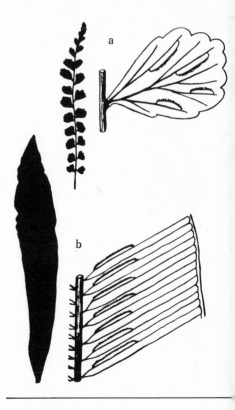

Fig. 12.8   Learning the fern genera (see text for explanation).
a. *Asplenium trichomanes*, the maidenhair spleenwort;
b. *Asplenium nidus*, the bird's-nest fern

13. FERNS AND FERN ALLIES IN CULTIVATION

This chapter lists the species and many of the varieties of ferns and fern allies recently in cultivation in the United States. Pertinent cultural information is given by a system of key words. The list is based on plants found in the trade or circulating among fern gardeners. Ferns found only in very special collections, such as those in botanical gardens, are omitted. Native ferns of the United States are omitted if they are seldom cultivated. Since so many of the botanical varieties or cultivars of ferns are poorly defined and confused, only the better known and defined ones are included. Only the commonly encountered synonyms and common names are given. Most of the entries have been checked against botanical specimens and/or botanical descriptions. However, since so many species are imperfectly known botanically and since so many of the cultivars are confused and poorly documented, the correctness of the names must be considered tentative. For those wishing a classification perspective of the ferns and fern allies in cultivation, a systematic arrangement to the genera is given in Appendix III.

KEY TO FERN STRUCTURE AND CULTURAL REQUIREMENTS
The general form of the fern and its cultural requirements are given by use of tag words after each species name. These requirements are meant to be only guides and may differ greatly with different growers and in different geographical areas. There are also genetic differences in species.

HEIGHT:
Small	Less than 1 foot.
Medium	One to 3 feet.
Large	Over 3 feet.

FORM:
Form 1	Wide creeping or trailing, the fronds mostly spaced about 3 in. or more apart, the rhizome branching.

Form 2 | Short creeping, the fronds mostly spaced about 1 in. apart or less, the rhizome branching.

Form 3 | Clump-forming, the fronds clustered next to each other on the rhizome, the rhizome branching to form dense clumps.

Form 4 | Fronds mostly in a close spiral on a short erect, semi-erect or ascending stem.

Form 5 | Like Form 4 except readily forming offshoots from the stem or rhizome.

Form 6 | Plant spreading by root buds, leaf buds, or stolons.

Form 7 | Tree fern or tree fern–like.

TEMPERATURE:

Hardy | Cold temperature areas, long period below freezing.

Semi-hardy | Warmer temperate areas, short periods below freezing.

Semi-tender | Subtropical areas, with frost or subfreezing temperatures very rare; night temperatures sometimes reaching 50°F.

Tender | Tropical areas, indoors, or in greenhouses not below 60°F at night, 65°F during the day. (Also known as "stove species.")

LIGHT (*filtered or indirect*):

Low light | Lower light intensities, about 200 foot-candles, not under 150 foot-candles.

Low-medium light | Low to medium light intensities, about 200 to 300 foot-candles.

Medium light | Medium light intensities, about 300 to 400 foot-candles.

High-medium light | Medium to higher light intensities, about 400 to 600 foot-candles.

High light | Higher light intensities, about 600 foot-candles or more.

Low to high light | Tolerates light intensities from low to high, about 200 to 600 foot-candles.

SOIL:

Garden soil | Garden soil, preferably humusy loam.

Potting mix | Potting mix.

Drained | Provide with very good drainage, especially for epiphytes.

Acidic | Prefers acidic condition.

Basic | Prefers basic condition.

WATER (*give generally less during cool weather*):

Wet | Keep wet.

Moist-wet | Moist but on the wet side.

Moist | Moist.

Moist-dry | Moist but on the dry side.

Dry | Permit nearly to dry before watering again (mostly xerophytes).

MISCELLANEOUS :

Easy	Particularly easy to grow.
Difficult	Particularly difficult to grow.
Evergreen	Evergreen even in freezing climates.
Deciduous	Fully deciduous even in warm climates.

GENERA AND SPECIES IN CULTIVATION

ACROSTICHUM.   Leather fern. Infrequently grown, very large ferns to 12 feet, native to swampy or brackish places. Grow in pots standing in water or kept very wet. Subject to scales and slugs.

Fronds erect, very large, 1 pinnate, the veins closely and uniformly netted, the sporangia covering the entire undersurface of the frond or tip of the fronds, not protected. Pantropics, mostly in mangroves, 3 species.

A. AUREUM. Leather fern.   Large / Form 4 / Tender / High-medium light / Potting mix / Wet

A. DANEAEFOLIUM. Giant fern.   Large / Form 4 / Tender / High-medium light / Potting mix / Wet

Acrostichum daneaefolium habit

(left) fertile pinna
(right) sterile pinna

Actiniopteris semiflabellata
habit

ACTINIOPTERIS.   Terrestrial small ferns of arid areas, interesting for its fan-palm-like fronds, avoid overwatering, especially during periods of inactive growth. See Chapter 10, "Xerophytic Ferns."

Fronds in a cluster, small fanlike, 3-parted, each part evenly forked into linear ultimate segments, the sori linear, submarginal, covered by a continuous reflexed leaf margin indusium. Tropical Africa and arid parts of tropical Asia, 5 species.

A. SEMIFLABELLATA *(A. australis).*   Small / Form 3 / Tender / High light / Drained potting mix / Moist-dry / Difficult

sori and indusia

ADIANTUM.   Maidenhair fern. Mostly terrestrial, small to medium ferns grown for their fine billowy foliage and black polished stalks. Most like humidity but not wetness at the roots, keep well drained, do not overpot. Some hardy, but most are tender species. See Chapter 10, "Maidenhair Ferns." For a fuller account of the species and many cultivars in cultivation see Hoshizaki 1970.

Stipe mostly black, polished, the leaflets without midribs, the veins evenly forked, the sori marginal, protected by a reflexed leaf margin indusium. Worldwide, centers in American tropics, 200 species.

A. AETHIOPICUM not in cultivation; trade material by this name closest to *A. raddianum* cv. Triumph.

A. ALEUTICUM: see A. PEDATUM f. IMBRICATUM

A. ANCEPS   Medium / Form 3 / Tender / Low-medium light   Potting mix / Moist

A. BELLUM. Bermuda maidenhair. Some trade material by this name is *A. raddianum* cv. Pacottii.   Small / Form 3 / Semi-tender / Low-medium light / Potting mix / Moist

A. CAPILLUS-VENERIS (*A. chilense* of trade). Southern maidenhair, Venus' hair.   Small / Form 3 / Hardy to Semi-hardy / Low-medium light / Potting mix, Basic / Moist

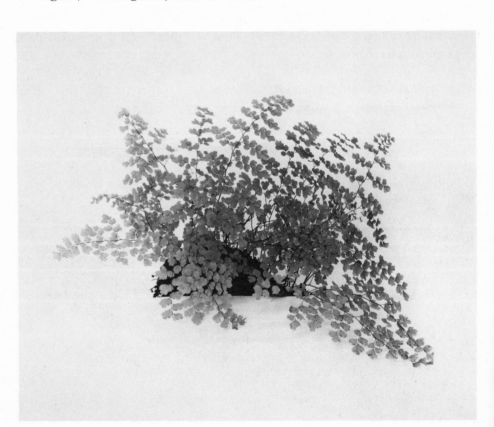

Adiantum capillus-veneris
habit

A. CAPILLUS-VENERIS cv. Imbricatum. Green petticoats.   Small / Form 3 / Semi-hardy to Semi-tender / Low medium light / Potting mix, Basic / Moist / Difficult

A. CAPILLUS-VENERIS cv. Mairisii.   Small-medium / Form 3 / Semi-hardy / Low-medium light / Potting mix / Moist

A. CAUDATUM. Trailing maidenhair.   Small / Form 4-6 / Tender / Low-medium light / Potting mix / Moist

A. CHILENSE: see A. CAPILLUS-VENERIS

A. CONCINNUM. Brittle maidenhair.   Small / Form 3 / Tender / Low-medium light / Potting mix / Moist / Difficult

A. CULTRATUM   Medium / Form 2 / Tender / High-medium light / Potting mix / Moist

A. CURVATUM: see A. RADDIANUM cv. Lady Geneva

A. DECORUM: see A. RADDIANUM

A. DIAPHANUM. Filmy maidenhair.   Small / Form 3 / Semi-tender / Low-medium light / Potting mix / Moist

A. EXCISUM. Chilean maidenhair.   Small / Form 3 / Tender / Low-medium light / Potting mix / Moist / Difficult

Adiantum capillus-veneris frond

A. FORMOSUM. Australian maidenhair.   Medium / Form 1 / Semi-tender / Low-medium light / Potting mix / Moist

A. FRUCTUOSUM   Medium / Form 2 / Tender / Low-medium light / Potting mix / Moist

A. HISPIDULUM. Rosy maidenhair, Rough maidenhair.   Small / Form 3 / Semi-hardy to Semi-tender / Low to high light / Potting mix / Moist / Easy

A. JORDANII   Medium / Form 3 / Hardy / High light / Garden soil or Potting mix / Moist-dry / Difficult

A. LATIFOLIUM   Medium / Form 3 / Tender / Low-medium light / Potting mix / Moist

A. MACROPHYLLUM   Small / Form 3 / Tender / Low-medium light / Potting mix / Moist

A. MONOCHLAMYS   Small / Form 3 / Hardy / Low-medium light / Potting mix / Moist

leaflets with indusia

A. PATENS   Small / Form 3 / Tender / Medium light / Potting mix / Moist

A. PEDATUM. American maidenhair, Five-finger fern.   Small / Form 3 / Hardy / Low-medium light / Potting mix / Moist

A. PEDATUM f. IMBRICATUM (*A. aleuticum* of trade).   Small-medium / Form 3 / Hardy / Low-medium light / Potting mix / Moist

A. PENTADACTYLON cv. Sanctae Catharinae. St. Catharine maidenhair. Medium / Form 3 / Tender / Low-medium light / Potting mix / Moist

A. PERUVIANUM. Silver dollar.   Medium / Form 3 / Tender / Low-medium light / Potting mix / Moist

A. POLYPHYLLUM. Giant maidenhair.   Large / Form 3 / Tender / Low to high light / Potting mix / Moist

A. RADDIANUM (*A. cuneatum, A. decorum*). Delta maidenhair.   Small-medium / Form 3 / Semi-tender / Low to high light / Potting mix / Moist

A. RADDIANUM cv. Croweanum. Crowe maidenhair.   Medium / Form 3 / Semi-tender / Low-medium light / Potting mix / Moist

A. RADDIANUM cv. Fritz Luth. Fritz Luth maidenhair.   Small-medium / Form 3 / Semi-tender / Low-medium light / Potting mix / Moist

A. RADDIANUM cv. Gracillimum.   Small-medium / Form 3 / Semi-tender / Low-medium light / Potting mix / Moist

A. RADDIANUM cv. Grandiceps.   Small-medium / Form 3 / Semi-tender / Low-medium light / Potting mix / Moist

A. RADDIANUM cv. Lady Geneva (*A. curvatum* of trade).   Small / Form 3 / Semi-hardy to Semi-tender / Low-medium light / Potting mix / Moist / Difficult

A. RADDIANUM cv. Micropinnulum.   Small / Form 3 / Semi-tender / Low-medium light / Potting mix / Moist / Difficult

A. RADDIANUM cv. Ocean Spray.   Small-medium / Form 3 / Semi-tender / Low-medium light / Potting mix / Moist

A. RADDIANUM cv. Pacific Maid. Pacific Maid.   Small / Form 3 / Semi-hardy to Semi-tender / Low-medium light / Potting mix / Moist

A. RADDIANUM cv. Pacottii (*A. bellum* of trade). Double maidenhair.
Small / Form 3 / Semi-tender / Low-medium light / Potting
mix / Moist

A. RADDIANUM cv. Triumph (*A. aethiopicum* of trade in part). Triumph
maidenhair.   Small-medium / Form 3 / Semi-tender / Low-medium light / Potting mix / Moist

A. RADDIANUM cv. Tuffy-tips.   Small / Form 3 / Semi-tender / Low-
medium light / Potting mix / Moist

A. RADDIANUM cv. Variegatum. Variegated maidenhair.   Small-
medium / Form 3 / Semi-tender / Low-medium light / Potting
mix / Moist

A. RADDIANUM cv. Weigandii.   Small / Form 3 / Semi-tender / Low-
medium light / Potting mix / Moist

A. RENIFORME   Small / Form 3 / Tender / Low-medium light /
Potting mix / Moist / Difficult

A. SEEMANNII   Medium / Form 3 / Tender / Low-medium light /
Potting mix / Moist

A. TENERUM. Brittle maidenhair.   Small-medium / Form 3 /
Tender / Low-medium light / Potting mix, Basic / Moist

A. TENERUM cv. Farleyense. Farleyense maidenhair.   Small-medium /
Form 3 / Tender / Low-medium light / Potting mix or Basic soil /
Moist / Difficult

A. X TRACYI (*A. jordanii* x *pedatum*).   Small / Form 3 / Hardy /
Low-medium light / Potting mix / Moist

A. TRAPEZIFORME. Diamond maidenhair.   Medium / Form 3 /
Tender / Low-medium light / Potting mix / Moist

A. VENUSTUM   Small / Form 3 / Hardy / Low-medium light / Potting mix / Moist

Aglaomorpha coronans
habit

frond base

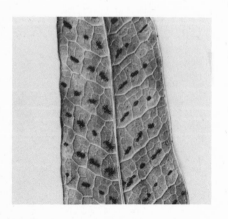

sori

AGLAOMORPHA.   Large, coarse epiphytes forming spreading crowns of foliage in hanging baskets; may be planted in the ground. See Chapter 10, "Polypodium and Relatives," also Joe 1958b.

Rhizome scales brown, the base of the frond often widened and becoming brown and papery, the upper part pinnate, the pinnae broadly attached to the rachis, jointed, dropping when dried, the sori in discrete units on the back of the pinnae, various in shape, not crossing the main veins, no indusium. Formosa to Malaysia, 10 species.

A. CORONANS *(Polypodium coronans).*   Large / Form 2 / Semi-tender / High light / Drained potting mix / Moist-dry

A. HERACLEA *(Polypodium heracleum, Drynaria heraclea).*   Large / Form 2 / Tender / High light / Drained potting mix / Moist-dry

A. MEYENIANA *(Polypodium meyenianum).*   Large / Form 2 / Semi-tender-Tender / High light / Drained potting mix / Moist-dry

A. species, not identified.   Large / Form 2 / Semi-tender / High light / Drained potting mix / Moist-dry

ALCICORNIUM: see PLATYCERIUM

ALSOPHILA.   Tree fern. Large tree ferns, the silver tree fern whitish on the underside, handsomest in wind-protected areas; the creeping tree fern native to cold mountain slopes, sprawling in habit. See Chapter 10, under "Tree Ferns." For more details on classification see Tryon and Tryon 1959, Tryon 1970.

Stems covered with scales, the fronds large, wide-ovate, or triangular, the sori round, dorsal, the indusium absent or present, scalelike to globose. As now defined, consisting only of species with the stipe scales having marginal cells different from cells in the center of the scale in color, shape, orientation, and a stiff hair present on the tip of the scale. Tropics, 230 species.

A. AUSTRALIS: see SPHAEROPTERIS

A. COLENSOI (*Cyathea colensoi*). Creeping tree fern.   Large / Form 7 / Hardy / Medium light / Garden soil or Potting mix / Moist

A. COOPERI: see SPHAEROPTERIS

A. CUNNINGHAMII (*Cyathea cunninghammii*). Gully tree fern.   Large / Form 7 / Semi-hardy / Medium light / Garden soil or Potting mix / Moist

Alsophila tricolor
tip of stipe scale
ending in a stiff bristle

habit

Alsophila tricolor
frond

margin of stipe scale,
marginal cells
different from central cells

A. SMITHII *(Cyathea smithii, Hemitelia smithii)*. Soft tree fern.
Large / Form 7 / Semi-tender / Medium light / Garden soil or
Potting mix / Moist

A. TRICOLOR *(Cyathea dealbata)*. Silver tree fern.   Large / Form 7 /
Semi-tender / Medium light / Garden soil or Potting mix / Moist

ANCHISTEA: see WOODWARDIA

sori,
an indusium visible
on detached sori
upper right

ANEMIA.   Small to medium, terrestrial ferns, interesting for the erect, fertile, branchlike leaflets.

Lower two pinnae each modified into a long stalked branch bearing the sporangia, no indusium. Tropics and subtropics, mostly American, 90 species.

A. ADIANTIFOLIA. Pine fern.   Small / Form 4 / Tender / High-medium light / Garden soil or Potting mix / Moist-dry

A. PHYLLITIDIS   Small / Form 4 / Tender / High-medium light / Garden soil or Potting mix / Moist-dry

Anemia phyllitidis
stalklike fertile pinnae

sporangia

habit

Angiopteris evecta
habit

sporangia

ANGIOPTERIS.   Large, coarse fern with globose stem, seldom grown except in conservatories or outdoors in tropical climates. Avoid damage to the thick fleshy roots. To propagate by stipules, carefully remove stipule, lay at a slant with the inner side up in well-drained planting media. Keep bottom heat at 80°F. Detach buds and pot when 2–3 leaves and roots have appeared.

Stem globose, the stipe swollen where it joins to the stem and flanked on both sides by stipules, the blade to 2 pinnate, the sori submarginal, elongate along the veins, the sporangia large, in a double row, the indusium absent. Old World Tropics, 100 species.

A. EVECTA   Large / Form 4 / Tender / Medium light / Potting
    mix / Moist

pinnae bases

ANISOSORUS: see LONCHITIS

ANOGRAMMA.   Small terrestrial ferns, growing quickly from spore, short-lived, reappearing either from self-sporing or from perennial prothallia. Suitable for terrariums.

Fronds small to 3 pinnate, the pinnules decurrent, membranous, the sporangia following the veins, no indusium. North and South temperate areas, 7 species.

A. CHAEROPHYLLA   Small / Form 3 / Semi-tender / Medium light / Potting mix / Moist

Anogramma chaerophylla sporangia along veins

habit

frond

Arachniodes standishii
frond

Arachniodes standishii
indusia

Arachniodes aristata
habit

ARACHNIODES.   Medium-size terrestrial ferns useful in pots or planting beds.

Rhizome short creeping, the frond broad, anadromous in plan, the sori round, dorsal, the indusium kidney-shaped, attached by an infold. *Polystichum* differs by its peltate indusium; *Dryopteris* differs by its stout rhizome and catadromous frond plan. Tropics and subtropics, 30 species.

A. ARISTATA *(Polystichum aristatum)*. East Indian holly fern.
Medium / Form 2 / Hardy / Medium light / Potting mix / Moist / Evergreen

A. ARISTATA cv. Variegatum.   Medium / Form 2 / Hardy / Medium light / Potting mix / Moist

A. STANDISHII *(Polystichum standishii)*.   Medium / Form 3 / Hardy / Medium light / Garden soil or Potting mix / Moist

Arthropteris tenella
fronds

sori

ARTHROPTERIS.   Rarely grown small creeping epiphytic fern.
Rhizome slender, the stipes jointed, the fronds pinnate, the pinnae jointed, the sori round, dorsal, in a row on both sides of the pinnae midrib, the indusium round, kidney-shaped, or absent. Old World tropics, Australia, New Zealand, 20 species.

A. TENELLA *(Polypodium tenellum)*.   Small / Form 2 / Semi-tender / Low-medium light / Potting mix / Moist

ASPIDIUM: see ATHYRIUM, DRYOPTERIS, NEPHROLEPIS, POLYSTICHUM, TECTARIA, or THELYPTERIS

ASPIDOTIS: see CHEILANTHES

ASPLENIUM.   Spleenwort. Terrestrial or epiphytic ferns of diverse appearance and size. The small species (spleenworts) useful in rock gardens or terrariums. The larger subtropical and tropical species used as pot plants. See Joe 1964a for details on some cultivated species.

Rhizome scales lattice marked (clathrate), the stipe with an X-shaped vascular bundle or 2 bundles bowing toward each other, the fronds simple to several times pinnate, the veins usually forked and typically free, the sorus oblong to linear, dorsal, elongate along the vein, usually borne on the upper fork of a branched vein, the indusium shaped like the sorus, opening toward the midvein. Worldwide, 650 species.

A. ADIANTUM-NIGRUM. Black spleenwort.   Small / Form 4 / Hardy / Medium light / Potting mix / Moist

A. AURITUM. Eared spleenwort.   Small / Form 4 / Tender / Medium light / Potting mix / Moist

A. BELANGERI. Belanger spleenwort.   Medium / Form 4 / Tender / Medium light / Potting mix / Moist

A. BULBIFERUM. Mother fern.   Medium / Form 4-6 / Semi-hardy to Semi-tender / Low light / Potting mix / Moist / Easy

A. DAUCIFOLIUM (A. viviparum). Mauritius spleenwort.   Small / Form 4-6 / Semi-tender / Low light / Potting mix / Moist

A. FALCATUM   Medium / Form 4 / Semi-tender / Medium light / Potting mix / Moist

A. FLACCIDUM (A. mayi and A. majus of trade).   Medium / Form 4 / Semi-hardy to Semi-tender / Medium light / Potting mix / Moist

A. FORMOSUM   Small / Form 4 / Tender / Low light / Potting mix / Moist

A. LUCIDUM. Glossy spleenwort.   Medium / Form 4 / Tender / Medium light / Potting mix / Moist

A. MARINUM. Needs humidity, tolerates sea spray.   Small / Form 4 / Hardy / Medium light / Potting mix / Moist

A. NIDUS. Bird's-nest fern. Several variants in need of study, including plants from Australia, New Caledonia, and Japan.   Medium / Form 4 / Semi-hardy to Semi-tender / Low light / Potting mix / Moist

A. NIDUS cv. Crispafolium (Phyllitis scolopendrium undulatum of some trade use).   Medium / Form 4 / Semi-tender / Low light / Potting mix / Moist / Difficult

Asplenium daucifolium
frond

A. OLIGOPHLEBIUM   Small / Form 4-6 / Semi-hardy / Low light / Potting mix / Moist

A. PLATYNEURON. Ebony spleenwort.   Small-medium / Form 4 / Hardy / Low light / Garden soil or Potting mix, Basic / Moist / Evergreen

A. RUTA-MURARIA. Wall-rue.   Small / Form 3 / Hardy / Low light / Potting mix, Basic / Moist

A. SEPTENTRIONALE. Forked spleenwort.   Small / Form 2 / Hardy / Medium light / Drained potting mix / Moist

A. TRICHOMANES. Maidenhair spleenwort.   Small / Form 4 / Hardy / Low light   / Potting mix, Basic / Moist / Evergreen

A. TRICHOMANES cv. Crested.   Small / Form 4 / Hardy / Low light /Potting mix, Basic / Moist / Evergreen

A. TRICHOMANES cv. Incisum.   Small / Form 4 / Hardy / Low light / Potting mix, Basic / Moist / Evergreen

Asplenium daucifolium
sori and indusia

habit

Athyrium felix-femina
habit, frond

Athyrium australe
fertile pinnules

ATHYRIUM.   Medium to large terrestrial ferns, mostly deciduous with divided, soft foliage. The lady fern comes in numerous garden varieties and botanical forms. These variants may have frond branched, crested, narrow, the pinnae crested, crisscrossed, congested, the pinnules much divided, widened, reduced, rounded, narrowed, jagged, etc. See Fig. 12.3 and Kaye 1965, 1968, for details on variants in cultivation. See *Diplazium* for other species not listed here.

Fronds 1 or more times pinnate, soft, herbaceous, the sori elongate, dorsal, on one or both sides of a free vein, when on both sides the lower sorus shorter, the indusium straight or curved, but at the base of the pinnules or pinnae hooked or U-shaped and crossing the vein. Worldwide, 180 species.

A. AUSTRALE   Medium / Form 3 / Semi-tender / Medium light / Garden soil or Potting mix / Moist / Deciduous

A. DISTENTIFOLIUM. Alpine lady fern.   Medium / Form 5 / Hardy / Medium light / Garden soil or Potting mix / Moist

A. ESCULENTUM : see DIPLAZIUM

A. FILIX-FEMINA. Lady fern.   Medium-large / Form 5 / Hardy / Low to high light / Garden soil or Potting mix / Moist-wet / Easy, Deciduous

A. FILIX-FEMINA cv. Corymbiferum.   Small / Form 5 / Hardy / Low light / Garden soil or Potting mix / Moist-wet / Easy, Deciduous

A. FILIX-FEMINA cv. Cristatum.   Small-medium / Form 5 / Hardy / Low light / Garden soil or Potting mix / Moist-wet / Easy, Deciduous

A. FILIX-FEMINA cv. Frizelliae.   Small-medium / Form 5 / Hardy / Low light / Garden soil or Potting mix / Moist-wet / Easy, Deciduous

A. NIPONICUM cv. Pictum (*A. goeringianum* cv. Pictum). Japanese painted fern.   Medium / Form 3 / Hardy / High light / Garden soil or Potting mix / Moist-wet / Deciduous

A. JAPONICUM : see DIPLAZIUM

A. PROLIFERUM: see DIPLAZIUM

A. PYCNOCARPON. Glade fern.   Medium-large / Form 2 / Hardy / Medium light / Potting mix, Basic / Moist / Deciduous

A. THELYPTERIOIDES. Silver glade fern.   Medium-large / Form 2 / Hardy / Medium light / Garden soil or Potting mix / Moist / Deciduous

Azolla filiculoides
habit

AZOLLA.   Mosquito fern. A very small, mosslike fern of warm sluggish water. Grown as a novelty in aquariums or shallow ponds. Its rapid growth and ability to cover the surface of water discourages the reproduction of mosquitoes, hence the common name. Provide with adequate light, warm temperature, and still water with some organic matter.

A very small, floating, mosslike plant, the stem branching, bearing the fronds in two rows, the fronds lobed, the upper lobe fleshy, scalelike, the lower lobe inconspicuous, thin, colorless, submerged, the sori of two kinds, borne on the lower lobe, each enclosed by an indusium. Worldwide, 5 species.

A. CAROLINIANA   Small / Form 3 / Hardy / Low to high light / Aquatic

A. FILICULOIDES   Small / Form 3 / Hardy / Low to high light / Aquatic

Blechnum occidentale
habit

BLECHNUM.   Terrestrial, mostly medium-size coarse ferns. Erect ones with tree fern-like growth, useful as accents. Certain selections of *B. occidentale* useful as ground covers or in borders in mild climates, reddish brown when young. Deer fern (*B. spicant*) hardy and suitable for temperate climates, difficult in warm climates. For tree fern-like forms see Chapter 10, "Tree Ferns." See Joe 1960c for details on cultivated species.

Fronds usually pinnatifid to pinnate, the sorus long-oblong, dorsal, one on each side of the pinna midrib, the indusium shaped like the sorus, opening toward the midrib. Mostly southern hemisphere tropics, 220 species.

B. AURICULATUM   Medium / Form 4 / Semi-tender / Medium light / Potting mix / Moist

B. BRASILIENSE   Medium-large / Form 4-7 / Tender / Medium light / Potting mix / Moist

B. BRASILIENSE cv. Crispum.   Medium-large / Form 4-7 / Tender / Medium light / Potting mix / Moist

B. DISCOLOR   Medium / Form 4 / Semi-hardy / Medium light / Potting mix / Moist

B. GIBBUM   Medium / Form 4-7 / Tender / Medium light / Potting mix / Moist

B. GIBBUM, a wide-pinnae variant (*B. moorei* of trade).   Medium / Form 4-7 / Semi-tender / Medium light / Potting mix / Moist

B. OCCIDENTALE. Hammock fern.   Small / Form 4-6 / Semi-tender / High light / Garden soil or Potting mix / Moist

B. PENNA-MARINA   Small / Form 2 / Hardy / Medium light / Garden soil or Potting mix / Moist

B. POLYPODIOIDES *(B. unilaterale)*.   Small / Form 4-6 / Tender / Medium light / Potting mix / Moist / Difficult

B. SERRULATUM. Saw fern, Swamp fern.   Large / Form 1-2 / Semi-tender / Medium light / Garden soil or Potting mix / Moist-wet

B. SPICANT *(Lomaria spicant)*. Deer fern.   Medium / Form 5 / Hardy / Low light / Potting mix / Moist

BLOTIELLA: see LONCHITIS

Blechnum occidentale
frond

sori and indusia

Bolbitis cladorrhizans
sterile frond, fertile frond

BOLBITIS.   Rarely cultivated medium-size fern of coarse appearance, often growing along tropical waterways on rocks, soil, or up trees.

Rhizome mostly creeping, the fronds simple to pinnate, the veins netted, the fertile frond long-stalked, contracted, the sporangia covering the underside, no indusium. Tropics, 85 species.

B. CLADORRHIZANS   Medium / Form 2 / Tender / Medium light / Garden soil or Potting mix / Moist-wet

B. HETEROCLITA   Medium / Form 2 / Tender / Medium light / Garden soil or Potting mix / Moist-wet

sporangia
on back of a fertile pinna

habit

Botrychium virginianum
frond

sporangia.

BOTRYCHIUM. Grape fern. Small to medium terrestrial ferns, the native species used mostly in natural plantings in northeastern United States. Take transplants with ample soil to protect the fleshy roots; difficult to establish in gardens.

Fertile part branchlike, arising from near the base of the blade and bearing large round sporangia, the sporangia opening by slits, not protected, no indusium. Worldwide, 40 species.

B. VIRGINIANUM. Rattlesnake fern. Small / Form 4 / Hardy /
  Medium light / Garden soil or Potting mix / Moist / Deciduous

Camptosorus rhizophyllus
habit

sori and indusia

CAMPTOSORUS.   Walking fern. Small terrestrial ferns of limestone rocks, the fronds long tapered, forming new plants at their tip. Used in rock gardens or terrariums.

Frond simple, elongate, the tip long-tapered, bearing a bud, the base heart-shaped, the sori oblong, dorsal, scattered, the indusium the same shape as the sorus. North America and northeast Asia, 2 species.

C. RHIZOPYLLUS. Walking fern.   Small / Form 4-6 / Hardy / Medium light / Potting mix, Basic / Moist / Evergreen

C. SIBERICUS   Small / Form 4-6 / Hardy / Medium light / Potting mix, Basic / Moist / Evergreen

CAMPYLONEURUM: see POLYPODIUM

CERATOPTERIS.   Water fern. Subaquatic or floating annual fern often used in aquariums, a weed in some areas but the foliage edible.

Aquatic ferns, the frond mostly triangular, pinnately divided, broad, the fertile frond larger and more finely divided, the sporangia large, marginal, along the veins, protected by a continuous reflexed leaf margin indusium. Tropics and subtropics, 4 species.

C. PTERIDOIDES. American water fern.   Small / Form 4-6 / Tender /
    Medium light / Garden soil / Wet, Aquatic

C. THALICTROIDES. Oriental water fern.   Small / Form 4-6 / Tender /
    Medium light / Garden soil / Wet, Aquatic

CEROPTERIS: see PITYROGRAMMA

Ceratopteris pteridoides
fertile frond

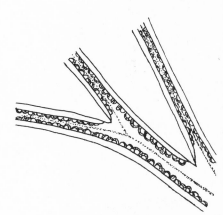

sori and indusia

habit of young plant

CETERACH.   Rusty back. Small terrestrial ferns with many scales on the underside, used in rock gardens. See Chapter 10, "Xerophytic Ferns."

Rhizome erect, the blade lanceolate, pinnatifid, or pinnate, thick, the many scales beneath broad, latticed, the veins forking, then netted near the margin, the sori dorsal, elongate along the veins, the indusium inconspicuous. Old World, 3 species. Recent authors unite this genus under *Asplenium.*

C. AUREUM   Small / Form 4 / Hardy / Medium light / Potting mix / Moist

C. OFFICINARUM   Small / Form 4 / Hardy / Medium light / Potting mix, Basic / Moist

Ceterach officinarum
habit

sori

Cheilanthes gracillima
habit

Cheilanthes gracillima
frond

CHEILANTHES.   Lip fern. Small evergreen rock-loving ferns often woolly or scaly beneath, preferring dry situations. Avoid water on the foliage. A number of United States natives in scattered cultivation and not all listed below. See Chapter 10, "Xerophytic Ferns," for more details on culture.

Small erect ferns, usually much divided and with woolly or scaly surfaces, the sori at the tips of the veins nears the margin of the segment, the indusium a reflexed leaf margin. Temperate areas and tropics, 180 species.

C. CALIFORNICA *(Aspidotis californica)*. California lace fern.   Small / Form 3 / Semi-hardy / High light / Garden soil / Dry / Difficult, Evergreen

C. FEEI. Slender lip fern.   Small / Form 3 / Hardy / High light / Drained garden soil or Drained potting mix, Basic / Moist-dry / Evergreen

C. FENDLERI (circulating in the trade as *C. lanosa* or *C. tomentosa*). Fendler's lip fern.   Small / Form 3 / Hardy / High light / Drained garden soil or Drained potting mix / Moist-dry / Evergreen

C. GRACILLIMA. Lace fern.   Small / Form 3 / Hardy / High light / Drained garden soil or Drained potting mix / Moist-dry / Evergreen

C. LANOSA (some of the trade material is *C. fendleri*). Hairy lip fern. Small / Form 2-3 / Hardy / Low light / Potting mix, Acidic / Moist

C. MYRIOPHYLLA   Small / Form 3 / Semi-tender / High light / Drained garden soil or Drained potting mix / Moist-dry

C. NEWBERRYI. Cotton fern.   Small / Form 3 / Semi-hardy / High light / Drained garden soil or Drained potting mix / Moist-dry

C. SILIQUOSA *(C. densa, Cryptogramma densa, Onychium densum, Pellaea densa, Aspidotis densa)*. Indian's dream, Cliff brake.   Small / Form 3 / Hardy / Medium light / Drained garden soil or Drained potting mix / Moist-dry / Evergreen

C. TOMENTOSA : see C. FENDLERI

Cheilanthes lanosa
sori, indusia pushed back

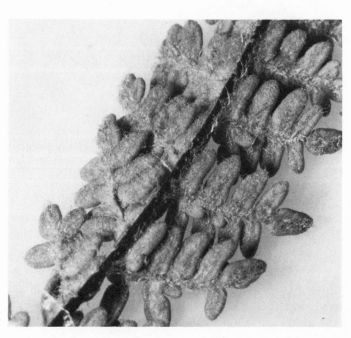

Cheilanthes gracillima
fertile leaflets with indusia

Cibotium glaucum
habit

stipes and trunk
with hairs

CIBOTIUM.   Tree ferns. Large to huge tree ferns, the Hawaiian species with well-defined trunks, the Mexican tree fern branching at the base to form clumps, sold as a potted plant when young, gracefully arching, light green. See Chapter 10, "Tree Ferns"; also Joe 1964d.

Stems densely covered with limp hairs, though mixed with stiffer ones in *C. menziesii*, the fronds broad triangular, the sori oblong, marginal, enclosed by a clamlike indusium of 2 parts. Asia, Hawaii, and Central America, 10 species.

C. BAROMETZ (most trade material by this name *Thelypteris torresiana*). Scythian lamb.   Large / Form 7 / Tender / Medium light / Potting mix / Moist

C. CHAMISSOI (*C. menziessi* of trade). Man fern.   Large / Form 7 / Semi-tender / High light / Potting mix / Moist

C. GLAUCUM (*C. chamissoi* of trade). Hapu, Hawaiian tree fern. Large / Form 7 / Semi-tender / High light / Garden soil or Potting mix / Moist

C. REGALE. Royal cibotium.   Large / Form 7 / Tender / Medium light / Potting mix / Moist

C. SCHIEDEI. Mexican tree fern.   Large / Form 7 / Semi-tender / Medium light / Potting mix / Moist

sori and indusia

Coniogramme japonica
habit

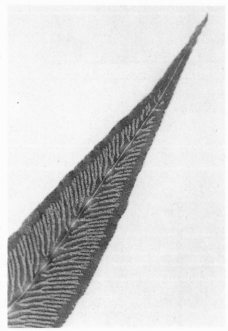

sporangia
along the veins

CONIOGRAMME.   Medium-large, creeping terrestrial ferns with strap-shaped leaflets. *C. japonica* like a large *Pteris cretica* in appearance, hardy, protect against snails and slugs.

Rhizome short to moderate creeping, the frond 1–3 pinnate, the leaflets few, large, the sori running along the veins except near the margin, no indusium. Old World tropics, Hawaii, Mexico, 20 species.

C. FRAXINEA   Medium-large / Form 2 / Hardy / Low light / Potting mix / Moist

C. JAPONICA. Bamboo fern.   Medium-large / Form 2 / Hardy / Low light / Potting mix / Moist

CRYPTOGRAMMA. Rock brake, Parsley fern. Small ferns used in rock gardens in cold temperate climates. Coarse parsleylike foliage.

Fronds 2–3 pinnate, the fertile fronds with podlike segments, the sori marginal, oblong, the margins of the fertile segments rolled over to form a reflexed leaf margin indusium. Rocky alpine and boreal areas of Europe, Asia, America, 4 species.

C. CRISPA *(C. acrostichoides).* Rock brake, Parsley fern. Small / Form 3 / Hardy / Medium light / Drained potting mix / Moist / Deciduous

C. DENSA : see CHEILANTHES SILIQUOSA

C. STELLERI. Slender rock brake. Small / Form 3 / Hardy / Medium light / Potting mix, Basic / Moist

Cryptogramma crispa
fertile pinnules

(left) sterile frond
(right) fertile frond

Ctenitis sloanei
habit

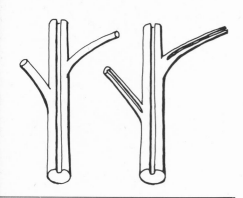

groove of rachis
not opening into costae,
(left) costae not grooved,
(right) costae grooved

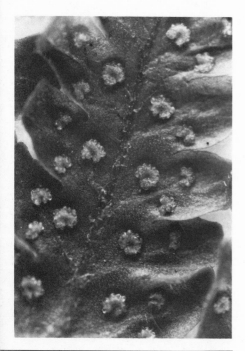

sori and indusia, *C. sloanei*

CTENITIS.   Medium to large ferns, terrestrial, the frond to several times divided. American tree fern of Florida forming a small trunk to 1½ feet high.

Rhizome creeping or erect, the leaf margin extending down the rachis as a wing, not as a ridge, the main rachis grooved, the grooves if present on the secondary rachis (costa) not opening into the groove of the main rachis, jointed reddish hairs present in the grooves, often minute and inconspicuous, the sori round, dorsal, the indusium kidney-shaped, attached by an infold. Pantropics, 150 species.

C. DECOMPOSITA: see LASTREOPSIS

C. PENTANGULARIS: see LASTREOPSIS

C. SLOANEI *(C. ampla, Dryopteris ampla).* American tree fern, Florida tree
    fern.   Large / Form 4-7 / Tender / High-medium light /
    Potting mix, Basic / Moist

CURRANIA: see GYMNOCARPIUM

CYATHEA.   Tree fern. Large tree ferns, *C. arborea* occasionally grown in south Florida. *C. costaricensis*, a rapid grower. See Chapter 10, "Tree Ferns"; also Tryon and Tryon 1959, Tryon 1970.

Stems covered with scales, the fronds large, wide-ovate or triangular, the sori round, dorsal, the indusium scalelike to globose. As now defined consisting only of species with the stipe scales having the marginal cells different from the central area cells in color, shape, orientation, and lacking a stiff hair at the tip. American tropics, 110 species.

C. ARBOREA. West Indian tree fern.   Large / Form 7 / Tender / Medium light / Potting mix / Moist

C. COLENSOI: see ALSOPHILA

C. COSTARICENSIS *(Hemitelia costaricensis).*   Large / Form 7 / Tender / High light / Garden soil / Moist

C. CUNNINGHAMII: see ALSOPHILA

C. DEALBATA: see ALSOPHILA

C. MEDULLARIS: see SPHAEROPTERIS

C. SMITHII: see ALSOPHILA

CYCLOPHORUS: see PYRROSIA

CYCLOSORUS: see THELYPTERIS

Cyathea costaricensis frond

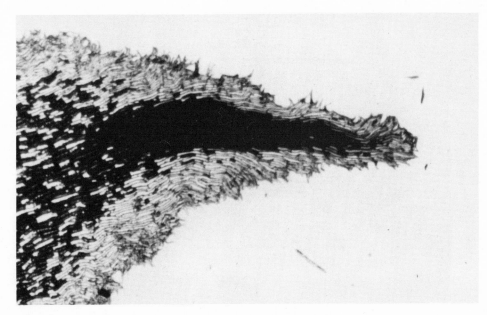

stipe scale
with rounded tip and
the marginal cells
different from the central cells

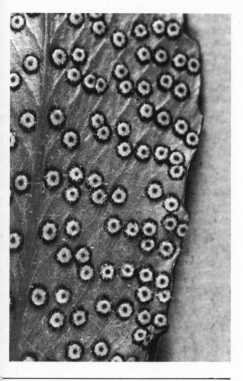

Cyrtomium falcatum
sori and indusia

CYRTOMIUM *(Phanerophlebia)*.   Medium-size coarse ferns with leathery durable foliage. The house holly fern much used as an indoor pot plant; its cultivar the Rochford fern, with its deeply incised-serrate margins, commonly grown. See Joe 1959b for details on cultivated species.

Rhizome nearly erect, the fronds pinnate, the pinnae broad at their base, tapered at the tip, the veins obscure but netted, the sori round, dorsal, scattered, the indusium peltate. Tropics and subtropics, 20 species.

C. CARYOTIDEUM   Medium / Form 4 / Semi-hardy / Medium light / Potting mix, Basic / Moist-dry

C. FALCATUM. House holly fern.   Medium / Form 4 / Hardy to Semi-hardy / High-medium light / Garden soil or Potting mix / Moist-dry / Easy, Evergreen

C. FALCATUM cv. Butterfieldii. Butterfield fern.   Medium / Form 4 / Hardy to Semi-hardy / Medium light / Garden soil or Potting mix / Moist-dry / Evergreen

C. FALCATUM cv. Mayi. May fern.   Medium / Form 4 / Hardy to Semi-hardy / Medium light / Garden soil or Potting mix / Moist-dry / Evergreen

C. FALCATUM cv. Rochfordianum. Rochford fern.   Medium / Form 4 / Hardy to Semi-hardy / Medium light / Garden soil or Potting mix / Moist-dry / Evergreen

C. FORTUNEI   Medium / Form 4 / Hardy to Semi-hardy / Medium light / Potting mix / Moist-dry

habit

Cystopteris fragilis
habit

CYSTOPTERIS.   Bladder fern. Mostly small ferns with delicate foliage used in shaded rock gardens and damp banks, deciduous in cold areas.

Fronds small, 2–4 pinnate, the sori dorsal, the indusium hood-shaped, fragile, fragmenting early. Subtropics, but mostly north temperate areas. 18 species.

C. BULBIFERA. Berry bladder fern, Bulblet bladder fern.   Medium / Form 3-6 / Hardy / Low light / Garden soil or Potting mix, Basic / Moist-wet / Deciduous

C. FRAGILIS. Brittle bladder fern, Fragile bladder fern.   Small / Form 3 / Hardy / Low light / Garden soil or Potting mix, Basic / Moist-wet / Deciduous

frond

sori and indusia

Davallia trichomanoides
habit

DAVALLIA.   Small to medium epiphytes with long, creeping, scaly rhizomes, the fronds coarse to finely divided, triangular. Planted in baskets or over rocks. *D. trichomanoides* also used as a ground cover in southern California. See Chapter 10, "Davallia and Relatives"; also Morton 1957 for key to cultivated species.

Long, creeping rhizomes covered with peltately stalked scales, the fronds falling from the rhizome when old, the grooves in the main rachis continuous with those of the secondary rachis, the sori submarginal, the indusium tubular, at the margin or nearly so. Mostly Old World tropics, 36 species.

D. CANARIENSIS (*D. portugal* of trade). Canary davallia.   Small-medium / Form 1-2 / Semi-tender / Low to high light / Drained potting mix / Moist-dry

D. DENTICULATA. Toothed davallia.   Medium / Form 1-2 / Tender / Low to high light / Drained potting mix / Moist-dry

D. DIVARICATA   Medium / Form 1-2 / Tender / Low to high light / Drained potting mix / Moist-dry

D. EMBOLSTEGIA (*D. japonica* of trade).   Medium / Form 1-2 / Semi-hardy / Low to high light / Drained potting mix / Moist-dry

D. FEJEENSIS. Fiji davallia.   Small-medium / Form 1-2 / Tender / Low to high light / Drained potting mix / Moist-dry

D. FEJEENSIS cv. Major.   Medium / Form 1-2 / Tender / Low to high light / Drained potting mix / Moist-dry

D. FEJEENSIS cv. Plumosa. Plume davallia.   Small-medium / Form 1-2 / Tender / Low to high light / Drained potting mix / Moist-dry

D. MARIESII *(D. bullata)*.   Small / Form 1-2 / Hardy / Low to high light / Drained potting mix / Moist-dry

D. PENTAPHYLLA : see **SCYPHULARIA**

D. PYXIDATA. Australian davallia.   Small / Form 1-2 / Semi-tender / Low to high light / Drained potting mix / Moist-dry

D. SOLIDA. Polynesian davallia.   Small-medium / Form 1-2 / Tender / Low to high light / Drained potting mix / Moist-dry

D. SOLIDA var. *lindleyi*.   Medium / Form 1-2 / Tender / Low to high light / Drained potting mix / Moist-dry

D. TRICHOMANOIDES. Squirrel's-foot fern.   Small / Form 1-2 / Semi-hardy to Semi-tender / Low to high light / Drained potting mix / Moist-dry / Easy

D. TRICHOMANOIDES, a larger, finer-cut variant.   Small-medium / Form 1-2 / Semi-hardy to Semi-tender / Low to high light / Drained potting mix / Moist-dry / Easy

Davallia trichomanoides
frond

sori and indusia

Dennstaedtia davallioides
habit

Dennstaedtia davallioides
leaflets bearing sori

Dennstaedtia bipinnata
sori and indusia

DENNSTAEDTIA.   Cup ferns. Medium to large terrestrial ferns with wide creeping rhizomes, used in foundation plantings or as bedding ferns, the hay-scented fern considered a weed in some temperate areas. See Joe 1965 for details on cultivated species.

Rhizome creeping, hairy, the stipe in cross section with a single fluted vascular bundle, the fronds medium to huge, many times pinnate, broad at the base, the sori marginal, the indusium cup-shaped, or nearly so, one side being formed from the leaf margin. Tropics, subtropics, 1 species in North America, 40 species.

D. BIPINNATA. Couplet fern.   Medium / Form 2 / Tender / Medium light / Potting mix / Moist

D. CICUTARIA *(D. rubiginosa)*.   Medium / Form 1 / Semi-tender / Medium light / Garden soil or Potting mix / Moist

D. DAVALLIOIDES. Lacy ground fern.   Medium / Form 1 / Semi-hardy / Medium light / Garden soil or Potting mix / Moist

D. PUNCTILOBULA. Hay-scented fern.   Medium / Form 1 / Hardy / Low to high light / Garden soil or Potting mix / Moist / Deciduous

DICKSONIA.   Tree fern. Large tree ferns with the fronds narrow and thin-leathery in texture, some species outdoors in mild, cool, wet climates. The Tasmanian dicksonia widely grown and cultivated outdoors in coastal California as far north as San Francisco. See Chapter 10, "Tree Ferns," also Tryon and Tryon 1959 for details on identifying cultivated species.

Stems clothed with bristlelike hairs, the fronds oblong or lanceolate, harsh, thin-leathery, the sori oblong, marginal, enclosed by a clam-shaped structure composed of a minute greenish reflexed leaf lobe and an indusium. Tropics and subtropics, 30 species.

D. ANTARCTICA. Tasmanian dicksonia.   Large / Form 7 / High-medium light / Garden soil or Potting mix / Moist

D. FIBROSA. Woolly tree fern, Fibrous dicksonia.   Large / Form 7 / High-medium light / Garden soil or Potting mix / Moist

D. SQUARROSA. Slender tree fern, Rough tree fern, New Zealand dicksonia. Large / Form 5-7 / High-medium light / Garden soil or Potting mix / Moist / Difficult

Dicksonia antarctica
sori and indusia

habit

DIDYMOCHLAENA.   Rarely cultivated medium-large terrestrial fern.
Frond subleathery, ovate, 2-pinnate, the segments rectangular, the sori elongate, dorsal, the indusium oblong-heart-shaped. Tropics, 1 species.

D. TRUNCATULA   Medium / Form 4 / Tender / Medium light / Potting mix / Moist

Didymochlaena truncatula
frond

sori and indusia

Diplazium lanceum
habit

Diplazium lanceum
indusia

DIPLAZIUM *(Athyrium).* Small to large ferns much like *Athyrium.* Prefer moist and humid areas.

Like *Athyrium* and often combined with it. Differing in having at least a few sori in pairs. The paired sori back to back, each sorus covered with an indusium, the indusia of a pair on the same vein, back to back. *Athyrium* having the sori and indusia single, or curved, not in pairs. Tropics and north temperate areas, 400 species.

D. ESCULENTUM *(Athyrium esculentum).* Vegetable fern. Medium / Form 4-6-7 / Semi-tender / High-medium light / Garden soil or Potting mix / Moist-wet

D. JAPONICUM *(Athyrium japonicum).* Medium / Form 3 / Hardy / Medium light / Potting mix / Moist-wet / Deciduous

D. LANCEUM var. CRENATUM *(D. subsinuatum* var. *crenatum, D. tomataroanum, Athyrium dubium* var. *crenatum).* Small / Form 2 / Semi-hardy / Medium light / Potting mix / Moist-wet

D. PROLIFERUM *(Athyrium proliferum).* Large / Form 5-6 / Tender / Medium light / Potting mix / Moist-wet

Diplazium sp.
frond

Doodia media
habit

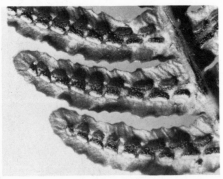

sori and indusia

DOODIA.   Hacksaw fern. Small to medium terrestrial ferns, the fronds erect, stiff, narrow, with many close-set leaflets. Slow-growing *D. media* used in terrariums, prefers slightly drier soil and humidity than most other ferns, the young fronds reddish, semitender. See Joe 1959a for details on cultivated species.

Fronds narrow, with many close-set pinnae, the margins sharply toothed, the sori oblong, dorsal, in one or more rows on each side of the pinnae midrib and parallel to it, the indusium shaped like the sorus. Polynesia to Ceylon, 11 species.

D. MEDIA (*D. aspera* of trade). Hacksaw fern.   Small-medium / Form 4 / Semi-tender / High light / Garden soil or Potting mix / Moist-dry

DORYOPTERIS.   Small to medium ferns usually grown in pots, interesting for their broad, often maple-leaf-like foliage borne on black polished stalks. *D. pedata* var. *palmata* easily grown from leaf buds.

Fronds simple, palmately lobed or entire, the stipes black and polished, the sori linear, marginal, the linear indusium a reflexed leaf margin. Tropical America, 35 species.

D. CONCOLOR   Small / Form 4 / Tender / Medium light / Potting mix / Moist

D. NOBILIS   Small-medium / Form 4 / Tender / Medium light / Potting mix / Moist

D. PEDATA var. PALMATA.   Small / Form 4-6 / Tender / Medium light / Potting mix / Moist

D. PEDATA var. TYPICA. Spear-leaved fern.   Small / Form 4 / Tender / Medium light / Potting mix / Moist

D. SAGITTIFOLIA   Small / Form 4 / Tender / Medium light / Potting mix / Moist

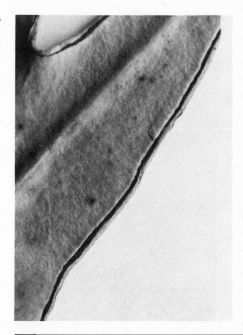

Doryopteris pedata
sori and indusia

Doryopteris concolor
basal part of frond

Doryopteris pedata
habit

Drynaria sparsisora
habit

Drynaria rigidula
habit

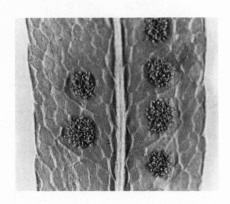

Drynaria rigidula
sori

DRYNARIA.   Oak leaf fern. Medium to very large epiphytic ferns with 2 kinds of leaves, humus-collecting leaves oak-leaf-like, foliage leaves long and divided. Humus-collecting leaves poorly developed in *D. rigidula* if kept too moist. See Chapter 10, "Polypodium and Relatives."

Distinct by the 2 kinds of leaves, the humus-collecting leaves short-broad, browning early, the foliage leaves long, pinnatifid or pinnate, the sori round, dorsal, the indusium absent. Old World tropics, 20 species.

D. QUERCIFOLIA *(Polypodium quercifolium).*   Oak leaf fern.   Large / Form 3 / Tender / High light / Drained potting mix / Moist-dry

D. RIGIDULA *(Polypodium rigidulum).*   Large / Form 3 / Tender / High light / Drained potting mix / Moist-dry

D. RIGIDULA cv. Whitei.   Large / Form 3 / Tender / High light / Drained potting mix / Moist-dry

D. SPARSISORA   Large / Form 3 / Tender / High light / Drained potting mix / Moist-dry

DRYOPTERIS.   Shield fern, Buckler fern. Mostly medium-sized ferns with thick rhizomes, the fronds in a crown, mostly thin-leathery, evergreen to deciduous. Hardy to tender species. Keep well drained. Many North American species used in temperate gardens. See Gleason 1952 for some natives, Joe 1963b for other species. Male fern and its many cultivars popular in temperate gardens; see Kaye 1968 for details. Many species transferred to *Thelypteris*, which see.

Rhizome thick, erect or ascending, the stipe with 3–7 vascular bundles, the fronds generally in a crown, 1 to 3 times pinnate, needlelike hairs absent on the frond, the upper side of the frond midrib grooved. The sori round, dorsal, the indusium kidney-shaped, attached by an infold. Worldwide, 150 species.

D. AMPLA: see CTENITIS

D. ARGUTA. Coastal woodfern, California shield fern.   Medium / Form 3 / Hardy to Semi-hardy / Low-medium light / Garden soil or Drained potting mix / Dry

D. ATRATA (*D. hirtipes* and *Nephrodium hirtipes* of trade). Shaggy shield fern.   Medium / Form 4 / Hardy to Semi-hardy / Medium light / Garden soil or Potting mix / Moist-dry

D. AUSTRIACA: see D. DILATATA

D. CRISTATA. Crested shield fern.   Medium / Form 4 / Hardy / Medium light / Garden soil or Potting mix / Wet to Moist-wet / Evergreen

D. DECOMPOSITA: see LASTREOPSIS

D. DILATATA (*D. austriaca, D. spinulosa* var. *dilatata*). Broad shield fern. Medium / Form 4 / Hardy / Low light / Garden soil or Potting mix / Moist / Evergreen

D. DILATATA cv. Grandiceps.   Medium / Form 4 / Hardy / Low light / Garden soil or Potting mix / Moist / Evergreen

D. ERYTHROSORA. Autumn fern.   Medium / Form 4 / Hardy / Low light / Garden soil or Potting mix / Moist

D. ERYTHROSORA cv. Prolifica.   Medium / Form 4-6 / Hardy / Low light / Garden soil or Potting mix / Moist

D. FILIX-MAS. Male fern.   Medium / Form 5 / Hardy / Low light / Garden soil or Potting mix / Moist / Deciduous

D. FILIX-MAS cv. Cristata. Crested male fern.   Medium / Form 5 / Hardy / Low light / Garden soil or Potting mix / Moist / Deciduous

Dryopteris erythrosora indusia

D. FILIX-MAS cv. Linearis.   Medium / Form 5 / Hardy / Low light / Garden soil or Potting mix / Moist / Deciduous

D. FILIX-MAS cv. Ramocristata.   Medium / Form 5 / Hardy / Low light / Garden soil or Potting mix / Moist / Deciduous

D. GOLDIANA. Goldie's fern.   Large / Form 4 / Hardy / High light / Garden soil or Potting mix / Moist / Deciduous

D. INTERMEDIA. Evergreen shield fern, Intermediate shield fern. Medium / Form 4 / Hardy / Medium light / Garden soil or Potting mix / Moist / Evergreen

D. LINNAEANA : see GYMNOCARPIUM

D. MARGINALIS. Marginal shield fern.   Medium / Form 4 / Hardy / Low light / Garden soil or Potting mix / Moist / Evergreen

D. NOVEBORACENSIS   Medium / Form 3 / Hardy / High light / Garden soil / Moist

D. PARALLELOGRAMMA   Medium / Form 4 / Semi-tender to Tender / Medium light / Garden soil or Potting mix / Moist

D. PSEUDOMAS cv. Crispa *(Lastrea pseudomas crispa)*. Hard male fern. Medium / Form 5 / Hardy / Low light / Garden soil or Potting mix / Moist / Evergreen

D. SPINULOSA. Spinulose shield fern.   Medium / Form 4 / Hardy / Low light / Garden soil or Potting mix / Moist

Dryopteris filix-mas cv. Cristata habit

Elaphoglossum crinitum
habit

ELAPHOGLOSSUM.   Seldom-cultivated ferns, small to medium, terrestrial or epiphytic, the fronds simple and entire.

Stipe jointed to the rhizome, the blade simple, entire, firm to hard, leathery, the veins immersed, mostly forked, then straight and parallel, the fertile fronds smaller, narrower, and often longer-stalked than the sterile, the sporangia on the whole undersurface unprotected. Tropics and subtropics, mostly American, 600 species. Several unidentified species in cultivation.

E. CRINITUM *(Hymenodium crinitum)*. Elephant-ear fern.   Small /
     Form 4 / Tender / Low light / Drained potting mix / Moist-wet

Elaphoglossum sp.
sporangial area

Equisetum hyemale
habit

"cones" bearing sporangia

EQUISETUM.   Horsetail, Scouring rush. A reedlike fern ally of wet places. See Chapter 10, "Fern Allies."

Stems finely grooved, jointed, the leaves papery scales around the joint, the spores in conelike structures produced at the tip of the stem. Worldwide, 23 species.

E. HYEMALE *(E. hiemale)*. Scouring rush.   Medium / Form 1 / Hardy / High light / Garden soil / Moist-wet / Evergreen

E. SCIRPOIDES. Dwarf scouring rush.   Small / Form 3 / Hardy / High light / Garden soil / Moist-wet / Evergreen

E. TELMATEIA. Giant horsetail.   Large / Form 1 / Hardy / High light / Garden soil / Moist-wet / Deciduous

GONIOPHLEBIUM: see POLYPODIUM

GONIOPTERIS: see THELYPTERIS

Gymnocarpium dryopteris
habit

sori

GYMNOCARPIUM.   Oak fern. Small to medium ferns with long creeping rhizomes and fronds spaced apart. The common oak fern used as a ground cover in eastern United States gardens.

Rhizomes slender, long-creeping, the stipes often minutely glandular with 2 vascular bundles, the blade triangular, pinnatifid to 3 pinnate-pinnatifid, without hairs, the pinnae jointed to the rachis, the sori submarginal, round, or oblong, not protected. Temperate areas, 5 species.

G. DRYOPTERIS *(Polypodium dryopteris, Phegopteris dryopteris, Dryopteris linnaeana)*. Common oak fern.   Small / Form 1 / Hardy / Low light / Potting mix / Moist / Deciduous

G. OYAMENSE *(Currania oyamensis)*.   Small / Form 1 / Hardy / Medium light / Potting mix / Moist

GYMNOGRAMMA: see **PITYROGRAMMA**

Hemionitis palmata
habit

sori

HEMIONITIS.   Small terrestrial ferns with broad leaves used in terrariums or in pots. *H. palmata* easily propagated from its buds.

Fronds simple, herbaceous, the veins netted, the sporangia borne along the veins, the indusium absent. India to the Philippines, but mostly American tropics, 5 species.

H. ARIFOLIA   Small / Form 4-6 / Tender / Medium light / Potting mix / Moist

H. PALMATA. Strawberry fern.   Small / Form 4-6 / Tender / Medium light / Potting mix / Moist

HEMITELIA: see ALSOPHILA and CYATHEA

HISTIOPTERIS.   Rarely cultivated, terrestrial, large ferns of rampant growth.

Rhizome wide-creeping, the fronds continually growing at the tip, the pinnae opposite, typically sessile, basal pinnules of each pinna often reduced, the sori and indusium like *Pteris*. Tropics, 7 species.

H. INCISA   Large / Form 1 / Semi-tender to Tender / Medium light / Potting mix / Moist

Histiopteris incisa
frond

pinna base,
sori, and indusia on pinnules

Humata tyermannii
habit

frond

indusia

HUMATA.   Small to medium epiphytic ferns like *Davallia*. Bear's-foot fern *(H. tyermannii)* a slow grower, a handsome basket fern with whitish rhizome scales, semihardy. See Chapter 10, "Davallia and Relatives."

Rhizome scaly, long-creeping, the fronds entire to several times pinnate, usually triangular, thin-leathery, the indusium roundish to kidney-shaped, attached only at the base or lowermost part of the sides, free elsewhere. Polynesia, Japan, Himalayas, Malaysia, Madagascar, 50 species.

H. GRIFFITHIANA   Small / Form 1 / Semi-tender / High-medium light / Potting mix / Moist-dry

H. TYERMANNII. Bear's-foot fern.   Small / Form 1 / Semi-tender / High-medium light / Potting mix / Moist-dry

HYMENODIUM: see ELAPHOGLOSSUM

HYMENOPHYLLUM: see MECODIUM

HYPOLEPIS.   Wide-creeping medium to large ferns with triangular finely divided fronds. Used as a ground cover or in foundation plantings in warmer climates. See Joe 1959c for details on some cultivated species.

Rhizome wide-creeping, hairy, the fronds triangular, thin, mostly finely divided, the sori marginal, roundish, usually protected by a tooth or reflexed leaf margin indusium. Tropics and subtropics, 45 species.

H. PUNCTATA   Medium-large / Form 1 / Semi-tender / Medium light / Garden soil or Potting mix / Moist / Easy

H. REPENS. Bramble fern.   Medium-large / Form 1 / Semi-tender / Medium light / Garden soil or Potting mix / Moist / Easy

H. TENUIFOLIA   Large / Form 1 / Semi-hardy / Medium light / Garden soil or Potting mix / Moist / Easy

Hypolepis tenuifolia habit

sori and indusia

LASTREA: see THELYPTERIS

Lastreopsis microsora
frond

groove of rachis
opening into grooves of costae,
the ridges an extension of
the leaf margin

sori and indusia

LASTREOPSIS.   Mostly medium-sized terrestrial ferns with broad, divided fronds. Used as pot or bedding plants in warm climates. See Tindale 1965 for taxonomic details.

Recently separated from *Ctenitis* by the leaf margin extending down the rachis as a ridge, the grooves of the secondary rachises (costae) opening into the grooves of the main rachis, otherwise like *Ctenitis*. Tropics, 25 species.

L. DECOMPOSITA *(Ctenitis decomposita, Dryopteris decomposita)*.   Small-medium / Form 2 / Semi-tender / High-medium light / Garden soil or Potting mix / Moist

L. MICROSORA ssp. PENTANGULARIS *(Ctenitis pentangularis, Dryopteris decomposita* of trade)*.   Small / Form 2 / Semi-tender / High-medium light / Garden soil or Potting mix / Moist / Easy

habit

Lemmaphyllum microphyllum
habit

LEMMAPHYLLUM.   Small creeping epiphytes with thick oval succulent leaves, used in terrariums, pots, or as novelties. Slow-growing.

Rhizome slender, creeping, the stipe jointed to the rhizome, the blade simple, ovate-lanceolate, entire, succulent, the veins netted, obscure, the fertile fronds narrower, the sori separate or running together and forming a row on each side of the midrib, protected by umbrella-shaped hairs when young, the indusium absent. East Asia, 5 species.

L. MICROPHYLLUM   Small / Form 2 / Semi-tender / Medium light / Drained potting mix / Moist

sori on fertile fronds

LITOBROCHIA: see **PTERIS**

Llavea cordifolia
habit

fertile pinnules

LLAVEA.   Rarely cultivated medium-size terrestrial fern, light green with canary-yellow scales on the stalk. See Joe 1959a for more details.

Rhizome and base of stipe conspicuously covered with pale-yellow scales, the fronds to 3 pinnate, the leaflets ovate, the fertile leaflets at the tip of the frond, contracted, linear, covered beneath with sporangia, partly protected by a reflexed leaf margin. American tropics, 1 species.

L. CORDIFOLIA   Medium / Form 4 / Tender / Medium light / Potting mix / Moist

LOMARIA: see **BLECHNUM**

LONCHITIS *(Anisosorus).* Rarely cultivated terrestrial fern of rather coarse appearance, the foliage likened to that of a young tomato plant. Separated from *Pteris* by the hairs rather than scales on the rhizome.

Rhizome creeping, thick and fleshy, bearing large flattened hairs, the stipe base with 2 vascular bundles, each bundle bent twice or nearly so, the veins free, the sorus marginal, borne between the sinus and the tip of a segment, the indusium marginal, linear. Tropical America and Africa, 2 species. Often confused with *Blotiella (B. lindeniana)*, which is not known in cultivation and has a hard erect rhizome and veins netted.

L. HIRSUTA *(Anisosorus hirsutus).* Medium-large / Form 3 / Tender / Medium light / Potting mix / Moist

Lonchitis hirsuta habit

pinnae

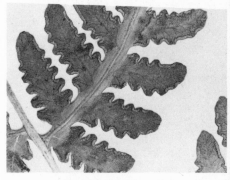

sori and indusia

Lorinseria areolata
(left) sterile frond
(right) fertile frond

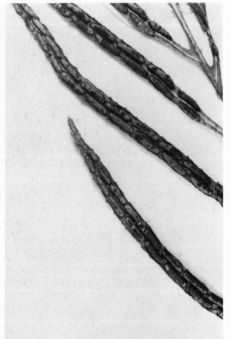

fertile pinnae

LORINSERIA.   Swamp fern. Coarse fern used in wet areas, of medium size, hardy. See Gleason 1952 for more details.

Like *Woodwardia* except the rhizome moderately creeping, the fertile frond much contracted. Eastern United States, 1 species.

L. AREOLATA (*Woodwardia areolata, W. angustifolia*). Narrow-leaved chain fern, Net-veined chain fern.   Medium / Form 1 / Hardy / Low-medium light / Garden soil or Potting mix, Acidic / Wet / Deciduous

LYCOPODIUM.   Clubmoss, Ground pine. One of the fern allies. Small to medium terrestrial or epiphytic plants with scalelike leaves and stems trailing, erect, or drooping, the foliage used in Christmas decorations. The tropical species in cultivation long, drooping, several times evenly forked. See Chapter 10, "Fern Allies."

Stems bearing small scalelike leaves, the sporangia large, of one kind, borne at the base of the leaves, the fertile leaves sometimes short or in conelike clusters borne at the tip of a stalk. Worldwide, 450 species.

L. CARINATUM   Medium / Form 3 / Tender / Medium light / Drained potting mix / Moist / Difficult, Evergreen

L. CLAVATUM. Running pine.   Medium / Form 1 / Hardy / Medium light / Drained potting mix / Moist / Difficult, Evergreen

L. COMPLANATUM. Ground cedar.   Medium / Form 1 / Hardy / Medium light / Drained potting mix / Moist / Difficult, Evergreen

L. LUCIDULUM. Shining clubmoss.   Small / Form 3 / Hardy / Medium light / Drained potting mix / Moist / Difficult

L. OBSCURUM. Ground pine.   Small / Form 1 / Hardy / Medium light / Drained potting mix / Moist / Difficult, Evergreen

L. PHLEGMARIA   Medium / Form 3 / Tender / Medium light / Drained potting mix / Moist / Difficult

L. SELAGO. Fir clubmoss.   Small / Form 3 / Hardy / Medium light / Drained potting mix / Moist / Difficult, Evergreen

L. SQUARROSUM   Medium / Form 3 / Tender / Medium light / Drained potting mix / Moist / Difficult, Evergreen

Lycopodium phlegmaria
habit

Lycopodium sp.
fertile leaves

Lygodium japonicum
habit

indusia

LYGODIUM.   Climbing fern. Tightly twining vine grown in pots or in the ground. Provide several strings or wires for the growth if foliage is to be shown off to the best advantage. The Japanese climbing fern (*L. japonicum*), the most commonly grown, produces new leaflets from dormant buds on old leaflets; eventually the old foliage dies to the base. See Joe 1960a for more details on this species.

Rhizome hairy, the fronds vinelike, the midrib twining, stemlike, the pinnae pinnate or palmate, the fertile lobes narrower, the individual sporangia near the margin, in 2 rows, covered by scalelike indusia. Tropics and subtropics except for 1 temperate species; 45 species.

L. FLEXUOSUM   Large / Form 3 / Tender / Medium light / Potting mix / Moist

L. JAPONICUM (*L. scandens* of trade). Japanese climbing fern. Large / Form 3 / Semi-hardy to Semi-tender / High-medium light / Garden soil or Potting mix / Moist

L. MICROPHYLLUM (*L. scandens*).   Large / Form 3 / Tender / Medium light / Garden soil or Potting mix / Moist

L. PALMATUM. Hartford fern.   Large / Form 3 / Hardy / Low light / Potting mix, Acidic / Moist / Difficult

(left) fertile pinna
(right) sterile pinna

Marattia sp.
habit

MARATTIA.   Rarely cultivated medium to large ferns.

Like *Angiopteris* except the fronds to 3 pinnate, the sporangia sub-marginal, fused into an oblong paired structure. Tropics, 60 species.

M. FRAXINEA   Large / Form 4 / Tender / Medium light / Potting
mix / Moist

Marattia fraxinea
fused sporangia

Marattia fraxinea
pinna

MARSILEA.   Water clover fern, Pepperwort. Leaves like a clover, used in aquariums or as a novelty plant. May be planted in pots; keep soil moist.
    Subaquatic ferns growing in mud, fronds sometimes floating, the blade of 4 leaflets, cloverlike. Worldwide, 60 species.

M. MINUTA   Small / Form 2 / Tender / High light / Garden soil or Potting mix / Moist-wet, Aquatic

M. QUADRIFOLIA   Small / Form 2 / Hardy / High light / Garden soil or Potting mix / Moist-wet, Wet, Aquatic

Marsilea minuta
habit

Matteuccia struthiopteris
habit

fertile pinnae

MATTEUCCIA *(Pteretis, Struthiopteris)*.   Ostrich fern. Medium-size ferns forming a vase-shaped cluster of fronds. See Gleason 1952, Lloyd 1971, for more details.

Sterile frond tapered at both ends, pinnate, the veins free, the fertile frond contracted, the sori in rows protected by a leathery leaf margin, the indusium inconspicuous. North temperate areas, 3 species.

M. STRUTHIOPTERIS *(M. struthiopteris* var. *pensylvanica, M. pensylvanica, Pteretis nodulosa, Onoclea struthiopteris)*. Ostrich fern.   Large / Form 4-6 / Hardy / Medium light / Garden soil or Potting mix / Moist-wet / Easy, Deciduous

Mecodium demissum
(left) habit
(right) frond

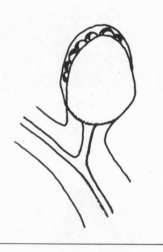

sorus and indusium

MECODIUM (*Hymenophyllum* in part).   Filmy fern. Rarely cultivated, used in terrariums. See Chapter 10, "Filmy Ferns."

Mostly small creeping epiphytic ferns of very humid places, the fronds only 1 cell layer thick in places, the sori roundish, marginal, surrounded by an urn-shaped or 2-valved indusium. Tropics and south temperate areas, 100 species.

M. DEMISSUM (*Hymenophyllum demissum*).   Small / Form 1-2 / Tender / Low light / Drained potting mix / Moist-wet

MENISCIUM: see THELYPTERIS

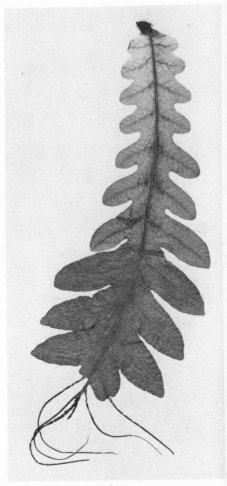

Merinthosorus drynarioides
habit

MERINTHOSORUS.   Large coarse epiphyte like *Aglaomorpha* but very rarely cultivated. See Holttum 1968 for more details.

Rhizome scales light red-brown, the frond like *Aglaomorpha* but the fertile lobes very narrow, restricted to the tip of the frond, entirely covered beneath with sporangia, the indusium absent. Malaysia to Solomon Islands, 1 species.

M. DRYNARIOIDES   Large / Form 2 / Tender / High light / Drained potting mix / Moist-dry

fertile frond.

MICROGRAMMA: see POLYPODIUM

Microlepia platyphylla
sori and indusia

Microlepia strigosa
habit

Microlepia firma
pinna

MICROLEPIA.   Medium to large terrestrial ferns planted in pots or in the ground. Useful in beds or foundation plantings. *M. strigosa* widely planted in southern California, a vigorous grower requiring periodic divisions of the clumps and removal of dead fronds. *M. platyphylla* coarser, larger, bluish green. See Joe 1962, Morton 1970, for more details.

Rhizome hairy, forming clumps, the fronds pinnately divided, usually hairy, the sori submarginal, covered with a shallow hood-shaped indusium, attached at base and sides. Tropics and subtropics, 45 species.

M. FIRMA   Medium / Form 2 / Semi-hardy to Semi-tender / Medium light / Potting mix / Moist

M. PLATYPHYLLA   Large / Form 3 / Semi-hardy to Semi-tender / Medium light / Garden soil or Potting mix / Moist-dry / Easy

M. SPELUNCAE cv. Corymbifera (*M. pyrimidata* of the trade). Medium / Form 3 / Tender / Medium light / Potting mix / Moist

M. STRIGOSA   Medium / Form 3 / Semi-hardy to Semi-tender / High light / Garden soil or Potting mix / Moist-dry / Easy

M. STRIGOSA f. MACFADDENIAE.   Small / Form 3 / Semi-hardy to Semi-tender / Medium light / Potting mix / Moist

MICROSORIUM: see POLYPODIUM

NEPHRODIUM: see DRYOPTERIS, THELYPTERIS

NEPHROLEPIS.   Sword fern. Widely cultivated epiphytic ferns normally with long narrow fronds. Best known for the Boston fern (*N. exaltata* cv. Bostoniensis) and the many cultivars derived from it. Used as a house plant or under glass in temperate areas. The tuber sword fern (*N. cordifolia)* commonly used in the ground and in pots in southern California and Florida. Plants reproducing by runners or stolons. The many cultivars of the Boston fern much confused as to names. See Morton 1958 for key to some species, also Chapter 10, "Boston Ferns and Relatives."

Fronds normally linear, narrow, pinnate, the pinnae many, jointed at the rachis and easily falling from it when dry or old, the sori round, submarginal, the indusium round or kidney-shaped, attached by its base. Tropics, 30 species.

N. BISERRATA *(N. ensifolium)*. Broad sword fern.   Large / Form 4-6 / Tender / Low to high light / Potting mix / Moist-dry

N. BISERRATA cv. Furcans. Fishtail sword fern.   Medium-large / Form 4-6 / Tender / Low to high light / Potting mix / Moist-dry

N. CORDIFOLIA. Tuber sword fern, Erect sword fern.   Medium / Form 4-6 / Semi-hardy to Semi-tender / Low to high light / Garden soil or Potting mix / Dry / Easy

N. CORDIFOLIA cv. Duffii. Duff's sword fern.   Small / Form 4-6 / Tender / Low to high light / Potting mix / Moist-dry

Nephrolepis cordifolia
habit

(left) *Nephrolepis exaltata*
(right) *N. cordifolia*
fronds

Nephrolepis cordifolia
sori and indusia

N. CORDIFOLIA cv. Tesellata (*N. cordifolia* cv. Plumosa). Tesellate sword fern.   Medium / Form 4-6 / Semi-tender / Low to high light / Potting mix / Moist-dry

N. EXALTATA. Common sword fern. Besides the cultivars listed below, others in recent trade include: cv. Elegantissima, cv. Piersonii, cv. Roosevelti, cv. Smithii, cv. Teddy Jr., cv. Tevillian, cv. Verona, cv. Whitmanii, and others. Generally the finer and more compact the form, the slower the growth.   Medium / Form 4-6 / Tender / Low to high light / Potting mix / Moist-dry

N. EXALTATA cv. Bostoniensis. Boston fern.   Large / Form 4-6 / Tender / Low to high light / Potting mix / Moist-dry / Easy

N. EXALTATA cv. Dwarf Boston. Dwarf Boston fern.   Small / Form 4-6 / Tender / Low to high light / Potting mix / Moist-dry / Easy

N. EXALTATA cv. Fluffy Ruffles. Fluffy ruffles.   Small-medium / Form 4-6 / Tender / Low to high light / Potting mix / Moist-dry

N. EXALTATA cv. Gracillima. Irish lace.   Small / Form 4-6 / Tender / Low to high light / Potting mix / Moist-dry

N. EXALTATA cv. Gretnae. Gretna sword fern.   Medium-large / Form 4-6 / Tender / Low to high light / Potting mix / Moist-dry

N. EXALTATA cv. Norwoodii. Norwood sword fern.   Medium / Form 4-6 / Tender / Low to high light / Potting mix / Moist-dry

N. EXALTATA cv. Piersonii. Pierson sword fern.   Large / Form 4-6 / Tender / Low to high light / Potting mix / Moist-dry

N. EXALTATA cv. Wagneri (*N. Wanamaker* of trade). Wagner sword fern.   Small / Form 4-6 / Tender / Low to high light / Potting mix / Moist-dry

N. EXALTATA cv. Wanamaker Boston. Wanamaker sword fern.   Large / Form 4-6 / Tender / Low to high light / Potting mix / Moist-dry

N. HIRSUTULA. Rough sword fern, Scurfy sword fern.   Medium-large / Form 4-6 / Tender / Low to high light / Potting mix / Moist-dry / Easy

N. PENDULA   Large / Form 4-6 / Tender / Low to high light / Potting mix / Moist-dry

NIPHIDIUM: see POLYPODIUM

NIPHOBOLUS: see PYRROSIA

NOTHOLAENA.   Cloak fern. Rarely cultivated small terrestrial xerophytic ferns used in rock gardens or as novelties. See Chapter 10, "Xerophytic Ferns."

Like *Cheilanthes* except the margins hardly reflexed, usually flat and not formed into a false indusium, the undersurface of the frond waxy in some species, though hairs or scales may be present. Worldwide, 60 species. Sometimes united with *Cheilanthes*.

N. AUREA. Slender cloak fern.   Small / Form 3 / Hardy to Semi-hardy / High light / Garden soil / Dry

N. HIRSUTA   Small / Form 3 / Semi-tender / High light / Garden soil / Moist-dry

Notholaena aurea
fertile pinnae

habit

Onoclea sensibilis
habit

fertile pinnae

ONOCLEA.   Sensitive fern. Medium-size, coarse-cut terrestrial fern spreading by running rhizomes, the fertile frond like a cluster of beads. Prefers moist situations. A temperate fern that grows well in southern California. See Gleason 1952 for details.

Sterile fronds triangular, the pinnae with wavy margins, the veins netted, the fertile frond contracted into roundish lobes enclosing the sori, the indusium inconspicuous. North America and Asia, 1 species.

O. SENSIBILIS. Sensitive fern, Bead fern.   Medium / Form 4-6 / Hardy / High light / Garden soil / Moist-wet / Easy, Deciduous

O. STRUTHIOPTERIS: see MATTEUCCIA

ONYCHIUM.   Claw fern. Small to medium terrestrial ferns forming clumps, the fronds finely divided. Grown in pots or in the ground. See Joe 1959b for more details.

Narrow fertile segments bearing linear sori on each side, the indusium a reflexed leaf margin, the indusium on one side of the segment meeting the indusium of the opposite side. Tropics and subtropics, 6 species.

O. DENSUM: see CHEILANTHES SILIQUOSA

O. JAPONICUM. Japanese claw fern, Carrot fern.   Small-medium / Form 3 / Semi-hardy / High light / Garden soil or Potting mix / Moist

O. STRICTUM   Medium / Form 3 / Tender / Low light / Potting mix, Basic / Moist

Onychium japonicum
habit

indusia

Ophioglossum petiolatum
habit

spike bearing 2 rows
of sporangia

OPHIOGLOSSUM. Adder's-tongue fern. Small ferns grown in natural gardens, in pots, or as novelties, reproducing vegetatively from buds on the thick roots. Various native species occasionally brought into gardens.

Sterile part entire, the fertile part springing from the base of the sterile blade and stalklike. Worldwide. 50 species.

O. PETIOLATUM   Small / Form 4-6 / Semi-hardy / High light / Garden soil / Moist

O. VULGATUM   Small / Form 4-6 / Hardy / High light / Garden soil / Moist

OSMUNDA. Medium-sized terrestrial ferns forming crowns of foliage, growing in moist soil. Some southern forms of the royal fern do well in southern California. See Gleason 1952 for details.

All or parts of the frond fertile, the fertile part contracted, without leaf blade tissue, the sporangia large, not in sori, not protected. Worldwide, 10 species.

O. CINNAMOMEA. Cinnamon fern.   Large / Form 5 / Hardy / Low light / Garden soil, Acidic / Moist-wet / Deciduous

O. CLAYTONIANA. Interrupted fern.   Large / Form 5 / Hardy / Low light / Garden soil, Acidic / Moist-wet / Deciduous

O. REGALIS. Royal fern.   Small-medium / Form 5 / Hardy / Low light / Garden soil, Acidic / Moist-wet / Deciduous

O. REGALIS cv. Cristata. Crested royal fern.   Small-medium / Form 5 / Hardy / Low light / Garden soil, Acidic / Moist-wet / Deciduous

Osmunda regalis
fertile pinnae

habit

Pellaea falcata
habit

PELLAEA. Cliff brake. Mostly small to medium rock-loving ferns of dry places, the broad leaflets often borne on hard, dark, polished stalks. Planted in rock gardens, pots, indoors or out in warmer climates. Plant in well-drained soils. See Chapter 10, "Xerophytic Ferns."

Stipes and rachises hard, normally polished, the frond pinnately divided, the leaflets and/or segments broad, mostly stalked or sessile, the sori marginal, oblong or joining linearly, the indusium a reflexed leaf margin, linear. Mostly America and South Africa, tropics and subtropics, 80 species.

P. ANDROMEDIFOLIA. Coffee fern.   Small / Form 3 / Hardy to Semi-hardy / High light / Drained garden soil or Drained potting mix / Moist-dry

P. ATROPURPUREA. Purple cliff brake.   Small / Form 4 / Hardy / Medium light / Drained potting mix, Basic / Moist-dry

P. BRACHYPTERA. Sierra cliff brake.   Small / Form 3 / Hardy / Medium light / Drained garden soil or Drained potting mix / Moist-dry

P. BRIDGESII   Small / Form 3 / Hardy / Medium light / Drained garden soil or Drained potting mix / Moist-dry

P. CORDATA: see P. SAGITTATA

P. DENSA: see CHEILANTHES SILIQUOSA

P. FALCATA. Australian cliff brake.   Small-medium / Form 2-3 / Semi-hardy to Semi-tender / High light / Drained garden soil or Drained potting mix / Moist-dry

P. MUCRONATA. Bird's-foot fern.   Small / Form 3 / Hardy to Semi-hardy / High light / Drained garden soil or Drained potting mix / Moist-dry

P. OVATA   Medium / Form 3 / Semi-hardy / High light / Drained garden soil or Drained potting mix / Moist-dry

P. ROTUNDIFOLIA. New Zealand cliff brake, Button fern.   Small / Form 3 / Semi-hardy / High light / Drained garden soil or Drained potting mix / Moist-dry

P. SAGITTATA var. CORDATA.   Small-medium / Form 3 / Semi-tender / High light / Drained garden soil or Drained potting mix / Moist-dry

P. VIRIDIS var. MACROPHYLLA (P. adiantoides).   Medium / Form 3 / Semi-tender / High light / Drained garden soil or Drained potting mix / Moist-dry

P. VIRIDIS var. VIRIDIS (P. hastata). Green cliff brake.   Medium / Form 3 / Semi-tender / High light / Drained garden soil or Drained potting mix / Moist-dry

Pellaea viridis var. viridis
fertile pinnules

Peltapteris peltata
(left) sterile frond
(right) fertile frond

PELTAPTERIS *(Rhipidopteris).*   Rarely cultivated small creeping epiphyte of humid areas.
Sterile frond palmately forked into narrow segments, the fertile frond roundish, two-lobed, covered beneath with sporangia, the indusium absent. Tropical America, 4 species.

P. PELTATA   Small / Form 2 / Tender / Low light / Drained potting mix / Moist-wet

PESSOPTERIS: see POLYPODIUM

PHANEROPHLEBIA: see CYRTOMIUM

PHEGOPTERIS: see GYMNOCARPIUM and THELYPTERIS

PHLEBODIUM: see POLYPODIUM

PHYLLITIS *(Scolopendrium)*.   Hart's-tongue fern. Small terrestrial, evergreen fern with tongue-shaped fronds. Susceptible to root rot, avoid overwatering, provide good drainage. Many garden forms, variable from spores or sterile, possible to propagate from basal pieces of the stipe. See Druery 1912, Kaye 1968, for details on the cultivars.

Frond simple, entire, strap-shaped, the base heart-shaped, the texture leathery, the veins 1 to 2 times forked, the sori linear, borne in pairs, one sorus on an upper and one on the lower branch of a vein, the indusium shaped like the sorus, opening toward its partner. North temperate areas, 8 species. Recent authors unite this genus under *Asplenium*, due to frequent hybrids with species of that genus.

P. SCOLOPENDRIUM *(Scolopendrium vulgare, Asplenium scolopendrium)*.   Hart's-tongue fern. Many cultivars in the trade including cv. Crispum, cv. Cristatum, cv. Fimbriata, cv. Marginatum, cv. Muricatum, cv. Ramo-cristatum, cv. Undulatum, cv. Variegatum, etc.   Small-medium / Form 4 / Hardy / Low light / Potting mix, Basic / Moist / Evergreen

P. SCOLOPENDRIUM var. AMERICANA.   Small-medium / Form 4 / Hardy / Low light / Potting mix, Basic / Moist / Difficult, Evergreen

Phyllitis scolopendrium
fronds

sori and indusia

PHYMATODES: see POLYPODIUM

habit

Pityrogramma argentea
frond

sporangia along veins

habit

PITYROGRAMMA *(Ceropteris, Gymnogramma)*.   Goldback fern, Silver-back fern. Small to medium terrestrial ferns, the stalks usually dark and polished, the fronds yellowish or whitish beneath. Prefer slightly drier conditions than most ferns, the plants short-lived, easy to grow from spores, hybridize freely in cultivation and in wilds. See Chapter 10, "Xerophytic Ferns," also Joe 1958b for details on some cultivated species.

Stipes stiff, dark, and polished, the blade with yellow or white powder beneath, the sporangia along the veins, the indusium absent. Africa, American tropics, 40 species.

P. ARGENTEA. Goldback fern.   Medium / Form 4 / Tender / High light / Garden soil or Potting mix / Moist-dry

P. CALOMELANOS. Silver fern.   Medium / Form 4 / Tender / High light / Garden soil or Potting mix / Moist-dry

P. CHRYSOPHYLLA. Gold fern.   Medium / Form 4 / Tender / High light / Garden soil or Potting mix / Moist-dry

P. HYBRIDA *(P. calomelanos* x *chrysophylla)*. Goldback fern.   Medium / Form 4 / Semi-tender / High light / Garden soil or Potting mix / Moist-dry

P. TARTAREA   Medium / Form 4 / Tender / High light / Garden soil or Potting mix / Moist-dry

P. TRIANGULARIS. California goldback fern.   Small / Form 3 / Hardy / High light / Garden soil or Potting mix / Dry

Platycerium willinckii
habit

PLATYCERIUM *(Alcicornium)*.   Staghorn fern, Elkhorn fern. Medium to large bizarre epiphytic ferns grown on walls or in baskets, rarely in pots. All degrees of intergradation exist among *P. bifurcatum, P. hillii, P. veitchii,* and *P. willinckii,* these species also with many cultivars, only a few listed here. The other species have fewer cultivars probably because they are less frequently cultivated. See Chapter 10, "Staghorn Ferns," also Joe 1964c, Franks 1969, Hoshizaki 1972, for more details.

Some fronds modified to form a base to support the plant and provide medium for the roots, the foliage fronds entire to many times forked, the sporangia in large patches, without definite sori, covered with minute star-shaped hairs, no indusium. Tropics, 18 species.

P. ALICICORNE: see P. VASSEI

P. ANDINUM   Large / Form 4-6 / Tender / High light / Drained potting mix / Moist-dry

P. ANGOLENSE. Angola staghorn fern.   Medium-large / Form 4-6 / Tender / High light / Drained potting mix / Moist-dry

P. BIFURCATUM. Common staghorn fern.   Medium / Form 4-6 / Semi-hardy to Semi-tender / High light / Drained potting mix / Moist-dry

P. BIFURCATUM cv. La Reunion.   Medium / Form 4-6 / Semi-tender / High light / Drained potting mix / Moist-dry

P. BIFURCATUM cv. Majus.   Medium / Form 4-6 / Semi-tender / High light / Drained potting mix / Moist-wet

P. BIFURCATUM cv. Netherland.   Medium / Form 4-6 / Semi-tender / High light / Drained potting mix / Moist-dry

P. BIFURCATUM cv. Roberts.   Medium / Form 4-6 / Semi-tender / High light / Drained potting mix / Moist-dry

P. BIFURCATUM cv. San Diego (*P. bloomei* and *P. Gresham's X*).   Medium / Form 4-6 / Semi-tender / High light / Drained potting mix / Moist-dry

P. BIFURCATUM cv. Ziesenhenne.   Medium / Form 4-6 / Semi-tender / High light / Drained potting mix / Moist-dry

P. CORONARIUM (*P. biforme*).   Large / Form 4-6 / Tender / High light / Drained potting mix / Moist-dry

P. COCONARIUM, a short form.   Medium / Form 4-6 / Tender / High light / Drained potting mix / Moist-dry

P. ELLISII   Medium / Form 4-6 / Tender / High light / Drained potting mix / Moist-dry

P. GRANDE. A 2-sporangial-patch species from the Philippines. For plants formerly by this name see *P. superbum* of Australia.   Large / Form 4 / Tender / High light / Drained potting mix / Moist-dry

P. HILLII   Medium / Form 4-6 / Semi-tender / High light / Drained potting mix / Moist-dry

P. HILLII cv. Bloom. (*P. bloomei*, not of *P. bifurcatum*).   Medium / Form 4-6 / Semi-tender / High light / Drained potting mix / Moist-dry

P. HILLII cv. Drummond (*P. diversifolium* of trade, not of botanical literature).   Medium / Form 4-6 / Semi-tender / High light / Drained potting mix / Moist-dry

P. HILLII cv. Pumile (*P. pumilum*).   Medium / Form 4-6 / Semi-tender / High light / Drained potting mix / Moist-dry

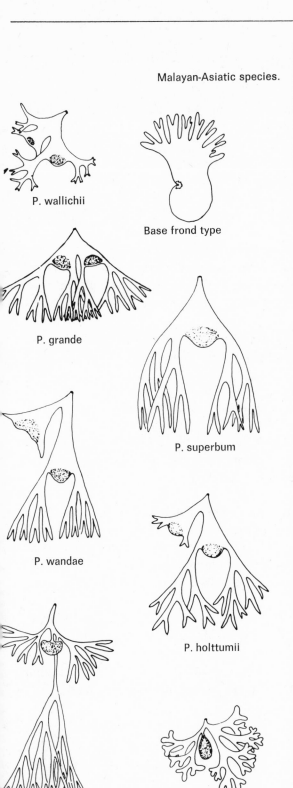

Malayan-Asiatic species.

P. wallichii

Base frond type

P. grande

P. superbum

P. wandae

P. holttumii

P. coronarium

P. ridleyi

Stipe cross-section

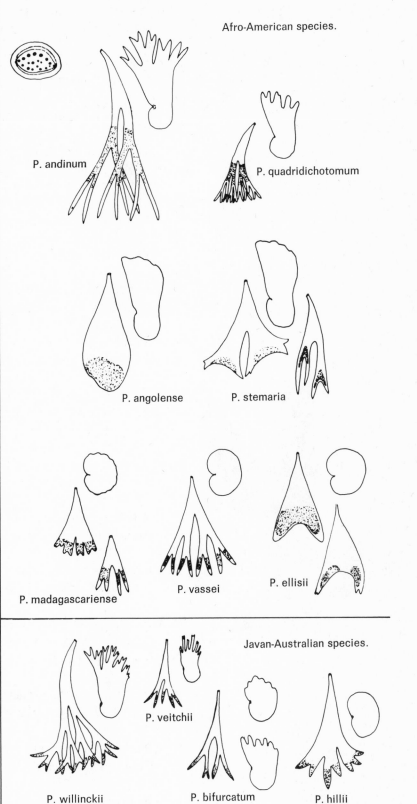

Afro-American species.

P. andinum

P. quadridichotomum

P. angolense

P. stemaria

P. madagascariense

P. vassei

P. ellisii

Javan-Australian species.

P. willinckii

P. veitchii

P. bifurcatum

P. hillii

species of *Platycerium*
after B. J. Hoshizaki,
Biotropica, 4(2), 93–117 (1972)

P. HOLTTUMII.   Large / Form 4 / Tender / High light / Drained potting mix / Moist-dry

P. MADAGASCARIENSE   Medium / Form 4-6 / Tender / High light / Drained potting mix / Moist-dry /Difficult

P. QUADRIDICHOTOMUM   Medium / Form 4-6 / Tender / High light / Drained potting mix / Moist-dry /Difficult

P. RIDLEYI   Medium / Form 4 / Tender / High light / Drained potting mix / Moist-dry

P. STEMARIA (P. aethiopicum). Triangular staghorn fern.   Medium-large / Form 4-6 / Tender / High light / Drained potting mix / Moist-dry

P. SUPERBUM (formerly P. grande).   Large / Form 4 / Semi-tender / High light / Drained potting mix / Moist-dry

P. SUPERBUM cv. Weitz Grande (P. weitz-grande).   Large / Form 4 / Semi-tender / High light / Drained potting mix / Moist-dry

P. VASSEI (P. alcicorne). The P. alcicorne of trade a dark green form of this species.   Medium / Form 4-6 / Tender / High light / Drained potting mix / Moist-dry / Easy

P. VEITCHII   Medium / Form 4-6 / Semi-tender / High light / Drained potting mix / Moist-dry

P. WALLICHII. Indian staghorn fern.   Medium / Form 4 / Tender / High light / Drained potting mix / Moist-dry / Difficult

P. WANDAE (P. wilhelminae-reginae).   Large / Form 4 / Tender / High light / Drained potting mix / Moist-dry

P. WILLINCKII (P. sumbawense of botanical literature). Java staghorn fern.   Large / Form 4-6 / Semi-tender to Tender / High light / Drained potting mix / Moist-dry

P. WILLINCKII cv. Lemoinei.   Large / Form 4-6 / Tender / High light / Drained potting mix / Moist-dry

P. WILLINCKII cv. Longwood Garden.   Large / Form 4-6 / Tender / High light / Drained potting mix / Moist-dry

P. WILLINCKII cv. Payton (P. sumbawense of trade).   Large / Form 4-6 / Semi-tender / High light / Drained potting mix / Moist-dry

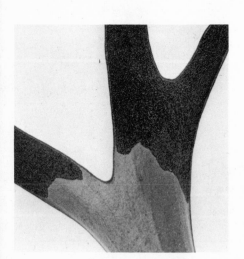

Platycerium willinckii
sporangial area

P. WILLINCKII cv. Pygmaeum.   Small / Form 4-6 / Tender / High
   light / Drained potting mix / Moist-dry

P. WILLINCKII cv. Scofield.   Large / Form 4-6 / Semi-tender / High
   light / Drained potting mix / Moist-dry

P. WILLINCKII cv. Walrus (*P. walrusii* of trade).   Medium / Form
   4-6 / Semi-tender / High light / Drained potting mix / Moist-dry

PLEOPELTIS: see POLYPODIUM

POLYPODIUM.   Polypody. A large group of diverse ferns, small to large, mostly epiphytes, the rhizome short or long creeping, branched, the fronds simple to once divided. Used in pots, baskets, or beds. The commonest species include the rabbit's-foot fern *(P. aureum)*, which is grown as a house plant or outdoors in warm climates, and members of the common polypody group *(P. vulgare* and relatives). The common fern growing from western U.S. shipments of green moss is the licorice fern *(P. glycyrrhiza)*. See Chapter 10, "Polypodium and Relatives," for details on the *P. vulgare* complex. Also see Lloyd and Lang 1964 and Shivas 1961.

Stipe jointed to the rhizome, the blade simple or pinnate, rarely more divided, the sori dorsal, round or dotlike, infrequently oval, the indusium absent. Worldwide, 75 species. By some authors separated into 20 different genera, and if so recognized, the commonly cultivated species would be distributed as follows:

CAMPYLONEURUM (tropical America, 25 species) to include:

P. ANGUSTIFOLIUM. Narrow-leaved strap fern.   Medium / Form 3 / Semi-hardy to Semi-tender / Medium light / Drained potting mix / Moist

P. COSTATUM. Strap fern.   Medium / Form 3 / Tender / Medium light / Drained potting mix / Moist

P. PHYLLITIDIS. Strap fern.   Medium / Form 3 / Semi-tender / Medium light / Drained potting mix / Moist

MICROGRAMMA (tropical America and Africa, 20 species) to include:

P. CILIATUM   Small / Form 2 / Tender / Medium light / Drained potting mix / Moist

P. HETEROPHYLLUM. Vine fern.   Small / Form 2 / Tender / Medium light / Drained potting mix / Moist

P. LYCOPODIOIDES   Small / Form 2 / Tender / Medium light / Drained potting mix / Moist

P. PALMERI   Small / Form 2 / Tender / Medium light / Drained potting mix / Moist

P. SQUAMULOSUM   Small / Form 2 / Tender / Medium light / Drained potting mix / Moist

P. VACCINIIFOLIUM   Small / Form 2 / Tender / Medium light / Drained potting mix / Moist

MICROSORIUM (Old World, 60 species, the large-sori species sometimes segregated into *Phymatodes*) to include:

P. ALTERNIFOLIUM   Medium / Form 1-2 / Tender / Medium light / Drained potting mix / Moist

P. DIVERSIFOLIUM   Medium / Form 1-2 / Semi-hardy / Medium light / Drained potting mix / Moist

P. MUSIFOLIUM   Large / Form 2 / Tender / Medium light / Drained potting mix / Moist

P. NIGRESCENS   Large / form 1-2 / Tender / Medium light / Drained potting mix / Moist

P. NORMALE   Medium / Form 1-2 / Semi-hardy / Medium light / Drained garden soil or Drained potting mix / Moist

P. POLYCARPON *(P. integrifolium, P. irioides, Microsorium punctatum)*. Medium / Form 2-3 / Tender / Medium light / Drained potting mix / Moist

P. POLYCARPON cv. Cristatum.   Medium / Form 2-3 / Tender / Medium light / Drained potting mix / Moist

P. POLYCARPON cv. Grandiceps. Climbing bird's-nest fern.   Medium / Form 2-3 / Tender / Medium light / Drained potting mix / Moist

P. SCANDENS *(P. pustulatum)*. Fragrant fern.   Small-medium / Form 1-2 / Semi-tender / Medium light / Drained potting mix / Moist

P. SCOLOPENDRIA *(P. phymatodes)*. East Indian polypody.   Medium / Form 1-2 / Semi-tender / High light / Drained garden soil or Drained potting mix / Moist

P. VIELLARDII   Medium / Form 1-2 / Tender / Medium light / Drained potting mix / Moist

NIPHIDIUM (tropical America, 10 species, formerly *Pessopteris*) to include:

P. CRASSIFOLIUM *(Pessopteris crassifolium)*. Medium-large / Form 3 / Tender / Medium light / Drained potting mix / Moist

P. CRASSIFOLIUM, crested form.   Medium-large / Form 3 / Tender / Medium light / Drained potting mix / Moist

PHLEBODIUM (tropical America, 2 species) to include:

P. AUREUM. Rabbit's-foot fern, Hare's-foot, Serpent fern, Golden polypody. Large / Form 2-3 / Semi-tender to Tender / High light / Drained garden soil or Drained potting mix / Moist

P. AUREUM var. ARANEOSUM.   Small-medium / Form 2-3 / Semi-tender / Medium light / Drained potting mix / Moist

P. AUREUM var. AREOLATUM.   Large / Form 2-3 / Semi-tender / High light / Drained garden soil or Drained potting mix / Moist-dry

P. AUREUM cv. Cristatum *(P. cristatum)*.   Large / Form 2-3 / Tender / Medium light / Drained potting mix / Moist

P. AUREUM cv. Glaucum *(P. glaucum)*.   Large / Form 2-3 / Semi-tender / Medium light / Drained garden soil or Drained potting mix / Moist-dry

P. AUREUM cv. Mandianum *(P. mandianum, P. manda)*.   Large / Form 2-3 / Tender / Medium light / Drained potting mix / Moist

P. AUREUM cv. Mexican Tasseled.   Large / Form 2-3 / Tender / Medium light / Drained potting mix / Moist

P. AUREUM cv. Undulatum *(P. mayii)*.   Large / Form 2-3 / Tender / Medium light / Drained potting mix / Moist

P. AUREUM cv. Variegatum.   Large / Form 2-3 / Tender / Medium light / Drained potting mix / Moist

P. DECUMANUM *(P. leucatamos)* and unnamed variant.   Large / Form 2-3 / Tender / Medium light / Drained potting mix / Moist

PLEOPELTIS (pantropical, 40 species) to include:

P. PERCUSSUM   Small / Form 1-2 / Tender / Medium light / Drained potting mix / Moist

POLYPODIUM (including *Goniophlebium*) species retained in POLYPODIUM:

P. AUSTRALE *(P. vulgare* in part). Several cultivars; some in the trade are: cv. Cambricum, cv. Pulcherrimum.   Small / Form 2-3 / Hardy / Medium light / Drained potting mix / Moist

P. BRASILIENSE *(P. triseriale* of some authors).   Large / Form 2-3 / Tender / Medium light / Drained potting mix / Moist

Polypodium interjectum
sori

P. CAMBRIOIDES (probably a sterile fancy-foliage form of *P. brasiliense*).   Medium / Form 2-3 / Tender / Medium light / Drained potting mix / Moist

P. FORMOSANUM   Small-medium / Form 2-3 / Hardy / Medium light / Drained potting mix / Moist

P. GLYCYRRHIZA (*P. vulgare* var. *occidentale*). Licorice fern. Cv. Malaha-
tense probably belongs here.   Small / Form 2-3 / Hardy /
Medium light / Drained potting mix / Moist

P. HESPERIUM. Western polypody.   Small / Form 2-3 / Hardy /
Medium light / Drained potting mix / Moist

P. INTERJECTUM (*P. vulgare* in part).   Small / Form 2-3 / Hardy /
Medium light / Drained potting mix / Moist

Polypodium interjectum
habit

P. KUHNII   Medium / Form 2-3 / Tender / Medium light / Drained potting mix / Moist

P. LEPIDOTRICHUM   Small / Form 2-3 / Semi-tender / Medium light / Drained potting mix / Moist

P. LORICEUM   Small-medium / Form 2 / Tender / Medium light / Drained potting mix / Moist

P. MARITINUM   Small-medium / Form 2 / Tender / Medium light / Drained potting mix / Moist

P. MENISCIIFOLIUM (*P. fraxinifolium* of trade).   Medium / Form 1-2 / Semi-tender / Medium light / Drained potting mix / Moist

P. MOSENII (*P. latipes* of trade).   Medium / Form 2-3 / Tender / Medium light / Drained potting mix / Moist

P. PECTINATUM. Comb polypody.   Medium / Form 3 / Tender / Medium light / Drained potting mix / Moist

P. PLEBEJUM   Small / Form 2-3 / Semi-hardy / Medium light / Potting mix / Moist

P. POLYPODIOIDES. Resurrection fern.   Small / Form 2-3 / Semi-hardy / Medium light / Drained potting mix, Acidic / Moist / Evergreen

P. PTILORHIZON   Small / Form 2 / Tender / Medium light / Drained potting mix / Moist

P. RHODOPLEURON   Small / Form 2 / Semi-hardy / Medium light / Drained potting mix / Moist / Difficult

P. SCOULERI. Leathery polypody.   Small / Form 2-3 / Hardy to Semi-hardy / Medium light / Potting mix / Moist

P. SQUAMULOSUM   Small / Form 2-3 / Tender / Medium light / Drained potting mix / Moist

P. SUBAURICULATUM. Jointed polypody.   Large / Form 2-3 / Tender / Medium light / Drained potting mix / Moist

P. SUBAURICULATUM cv. Knightiae. Knight's polypody.   Large / Form 2-3 / Semi-tender / High-medium light / Drained potting mix / Moist / Deciduous

P. THYSSANOLEPIS. Scaly polypody.   Small / Form 2-3 / Semi-hardy / Medium light / Drained garden soil or Drained potting mix / Moist

P. TRISERIALE   Medium / Form 2-3 / Tender / Medium light / Drained potting mix / Moist

P. VIRGINIANUM (*P. sempervivioides* of trade). American wall fern. Small / Form 2-3 / Hardy / Medium light / Drained potting mix / Moist / Evergreen

P. VULGARE. Common polypody. Also see P. AUSTRALE, P. GLYCYRRHIZA, P. INTERJECTUM, and P. VIRGINIANUM. Cv. Longicaudatum and cv. Ramosum Hillman (*P. bifido* of trade) may belong here.   Small / Form 2-3 / Hardy / Medium light / Drained potting mix / Moist

Species transferred to other genera:

P. CORONANS: see AGLAOMORPHA

P. DRYOPTERIS: see GYMNOCARPIUM

P. HERACLEUM: see AGLAOMORPHA

P. MEYENIANUM: see AGLAOMORPHA

P. QUERCIFOLIUM: see DRYNARIA

P. RIGIDULUM: see DRYNARIA

P. TENELLUM: see ARTHROPTERIS

Polystichum polyblepharum
habit

POLYSTICHUM. Shield fern. Small to medium terrestrial ferns forming a crown or cluster of foliage, the fronds narrow or oblong, the hardy species grown in borders or pots, some species evergreen and grown for their cut foliage. Propagated by buds in species bearing them, otherwise by spores or divisions in those species that clump. Also see *Rumohra* and *Arachniodes*. The hard and soft shield ferns form many variants; see Dyce 1963, Kaye 1968 for details.

Rhizome erect or ascending, the stipe with several vascular bundles, the frond 1 to several times pinnate, elongate, seldom wider at the base, the segments with spiny margins, the venation anadromic, the sori round, dorsal, the indusium peltate. Worldwide, 135 species.

P. ACROSTICHOIDES. Christmas fern.   Medium / Form 4 / Hardy / Low light / Garden soil or Potting mix / Moist / Evergreen

P. ACULEATUM. Hard shield fern.   Medium / Form 4 / Hardy / Medium light / Potting mix / Moist

P. ADIANTIFORMIS: see RUMOHRA

P. ANDERSONII. Anderson's holly fern.   Medium / Form 4-6 / Hardy / Medium light / Potting mix / Moist

P. ARISTATUM: see **ARACHNIODES**

P. BRAUNII. Braun's holly fern.   Medium / Form 4 / Hardy / Medium light / Potting mix / Moist / Evergreen

P. CAPENSE: see **RUMOHRA**

P. CORIACEUM: see **RUMOHRA**

P. DUDLEYI. Woodrustic fern.   Medium / Form 4-6 / Hardy / Medium light / Drained potting mix /Moist

P. LEMMONI.   Medium / Form 3 / Hardy / Medium light / Potting mix / Moist / Evergreen

P. LONCHITIS. Holly fern.   Medium / Form 3 / Hardy / Medium light / Potting mix / Moist / Evergreen

P. MUNITUM. Western sword fern.   Medium-large / Form 3 / Hardy / Low light / Potting mix / Moist

P. MUNITUM ssp. CURTUM.   Small-medium / Form 3 / Hardy / Low light / Potting mix / Moist

P. MUNITUM var. IMBRICANS.   Medium / Form 3 / Hardy / Low light / Potting mix / Moist

P. POLYBLEPHARUM (*P. setosum* of trade).   Medium / Form 4 / Semi-hardy / High-medium light / Garden soil or Potting mix / Moist-dry

P. PROLIFERUM   Medium / Form 4-6 / Hardy / Medium light / Garden soil or Potting mix / Moist / Easy

P. SETIFERUM *(P. angulare)*. Soft shield fern. Many cultivars in the trade including: cv. Angustatum, cv. Congestum, cv. Cristatum, cv. Cristatum-proliferum, cv. Cristato-gracile, cv. Plumosum, cv. Plumoso-divisilobum, cv. Proliferum, cv. Rotundilobum, etc.   Medium / Form 4 / Hardy / Medium light / Drained potting mix / Moist-dry

P. SETOSUM: see P. POLYBLEPHARUM

P. STANDISHII: see **ARACHNIODES**

P. TRIPTERON   Medium / Form 4 / Hardy / Medium light / Potting mix / Moist

P. TSUS-SIMENSE. Tsusima holly fern.   Small / Form 3 / Hardy / Medium light / Drained potting mix / Moist-dry

Polystichum pinnae (left to right) *P. proliferum, P. munitum, P. polyblepharum*

Polystichum proliferum sori and indusia

PSILOTUM.   Whisk fern. A medium-small plant, consisting of clusters of branched stems bearing inconspicuous leaves. See Chapter 10, "Fern Allies."

Green stems several times evenly forked, the leaves small and scale-like, few and far apart on the stem, the upper part of the stem bearing large 3-lobed sporangia. Subtropics and tropics, 3 species. Sometimes considered a fern rather than fern ally.

P. COMPLANATUM   Small-medium / Form 3 / Tender / High light / Drained potting mix / Moist

P. NUDUM   Small-medium / Form 3 / Semi-tender / High light / Drained potting mix / Moist

PTERETIS: see MATTEUCCIA

Psilotum nudum
sporangia

habit

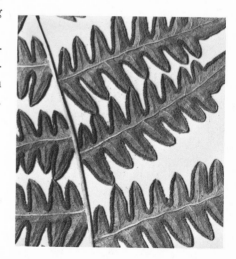

Pteridium aquilinum var. *pubescens* habit

frond

PTERIDIUM.   Bracken. Medium to large terrestrial ferns spreading from a slender, wide-creeping underground rhizome, the fronds spaced far apart, triangular, several times divided. A well-known native fern of open fields and slopes, rarely used as an ornamental because of its wide-spreading nature.

Rhizome slender, underground, hairy, the fronds 3–4 pinnate, triangular, the sori marginal, linear, protected by a reflexed leaf margin indusium and an inconspicuous linear indusium, the reflexed leaf margin continuous around the tips and bases of the lobe and smaller leaflets. Worldwide, 1 variable species.

P. AQUILINUM var. CAUDATUM.   Large / Form 1 / Semi-hardy / High light / Garden soil / Moist-dry / Deciduous

P. AQUILINUM var. LATIUSCULUM. Eastern bracken.   Large / Form 1 / Hardy / High light / Garden soil / Moist-dry / Deciduous

P. AQUILINUM var. PUBESCENS. Western bracken.   Large / Form 1 / Hardy / High light / Garden soil / Moist-dry / Deciduous

P. AQUILINUM var. PSEUDOCAUDATUM.   Large / Form 1 / Hardy / High light / Garden soil / Moist-dry / Deciduous

sori

Pteris cretica
habit

PTERIS.   Brake ferns. Small to large terrestrial ferns, the fronds in clusters, variously divided but not finely so. Popular ferns used in terrariums, pots, and planter beds. The very commonly cultivated species adapted to a wide range of soils but do not like to be kept too moist. See Joe 1958a, Walker 1970, for details on cultivated species. Cretan and spider brake with numerous cultivars.

Rhizome forming clumps, the fronds pinnately divided, the segments narrow, often sessile or adnate, the sori linear, the indusium a reflexed leaf margin, linear. Tropics and subtropics, 250 species.

P. ALTISSIMA   Large / Form 4 / Tender / Medium light / Garden soil or Potting mix / Moist

P. ARGYRAEA *(P. quadriaurita* var. *argyraea)*. Silver brake, Striped brake. Medium / Form 4 / Semi-tender / Medium light / Garden soil or Potting mix / Moist

P. CRETICA. Cretan brake. Some of the many cultivars in the trade include: cv. Albo-lineata, cv. Childsii, cv. Distinction, cv. Ouvrardii, cv. Parkeri, cv. Rivertoniana, cv. Wilsonii, cv. Wimsettii.   Medium / Form 3 / Semi-hardy to Semi-tender / High medium light / Garden soil or Potting mix / Moist / Easy

P. DENTATA *(P. flabellata, P. flaccida).*   Medium-large / Form 3 / Semi-hardy to Semi-tender / Medium light / Garden soil or Potting mix / Moist

P. ENSIFORMIS cv. Evergemiensis.   Small / Form 3 / Semi-tender / Medium light / Garden soil or Potting mix / Moist

P. ENSIFORMIS var. VICTORIAE. Victorian brake.   Small / Form 3 / Semi-tender / Medium light / Garden soil or Potting mix / Moist

P. LONGIFOLIA. Ladder brake. Most of the trade material by this name is *P. vittata.*   Medium / Form 4 / Tender / Medium light / Garden soil or Potting mix / Moist

P. MULTIFIDA *(P. serrulata).* Spider brake. Some of the many cultivars in the trade include: cv. Cristata, cv. Cristata Compacta, cv. Cristata Variegata.   Small / Form 3 / Semi-tender / Medium light / Garden soil or Potting mix / Moist

Pteris cretica cultivars
fronds
(top left to right)
cv. Albo-lineata,
cv. Distinction,
cv. Ouvrardii
(lower left to right)
cv. Parkeri,
cv. Rivertoniana,
cv. Wilsonii

fronds of different species
(left to right) *P. semipinnata*,
P. tremula,
P. dentata

sorus and indusium
P. vittata

P. QUADRIAURITA   Medium / Form 4 / Tender / Medium light / Garden soil or Potting mix / Moist

P. QUADRIAURITA var. ARGYRAEA : see P. ARGYRAEA

P. SEMIPINNATA   Medium / Form 3 / Semi-tender / Medium light / Garden soil or Potting mix / Moist

P. SEMIPINNATA var. DISPAR *(P. dispar)*.   Small / Form 3 / Semi-tender / Medium light / Garden soil or Potting mix / Moist

P. TREMULA. Australian brake.   Large / Form 4 / Semi-hardy to Semi-tender / High-medium light / Garden soil or Potting mix / Moist / Easy

P. TRIPARTITA *(Litobrochia tripartita)*. Trisect brake.   Large / Form 3 / Tender / Medium light / Garden soil or Potting mix / Moist

P. VITTATA *(P. longifolia* of trade). Chinese brake, Rusty brake. Medium / Form 4 / Semi-hardy to Semi-tender / High-medium light / Garden soil or Potting mix / Moist / Easy

PYRROSIA *(Cyclophorus, Niphobolus).*   Felt fern. Small creeping epiphytes with the fronds mostly undivided or deeply lobed, thickly covered beneath with a layer of hairs. The Japanese felt fern often grown in pots, baskets, or infrequently as a ground cover in southern California.

Rhizome creeping, the fronds simple and entire or deeply palmately lobed, densely covered beneath with star-shaped hairs, the sori dorsal, round, often merging, the indusium absent. Old World tropics and temperate areas, 100 species.

P. HASTATA *(P. tricuspis).*   Small / Form 2 / Hardy / Medium light / Drained potting mix / Moist-dry

P. LINGUA. Japanese felt fern, Tongue fern.   Small / Form 1-2 / Semi-hardy to Semi-tender / Medium light / Drained potting mix / Moist-dry / Easy

P. POLYDACTYLON   Small / Form 2 / Semi-tender / Medium light / Drained potting mix / Moist-dry

Pyrrosia lingua fronds

habit

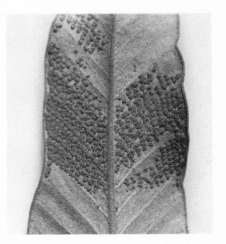

sori

Quercifilix zeilanica
habit of young plant

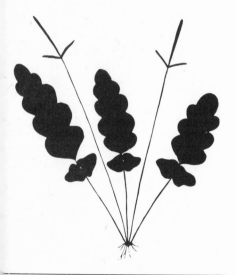

fronds,
the fertile tall and
contracted, the others sterile

QUERCIFILIX.   A small, little-known terrestrial fern. Rhizome creeping or ascending, the fronds of 2 kinds, the sterile lobed above, usually with a basal pair of pinnae below, the fertile long-stalked and contracted into a few linear segments, the sporangia along the veins and spreading to the blade surface, the indusium absent. Asiatic tropics, 1 species.

Q. ZEILANICA *(Q. zeylanicus)*.   Small / Form 4 / Tender / Medium light / Potting mix / Moist

RHIPIDOPTERIS: see PELTAPTERIS

RUMOHRA.   Leather fern. Medium-sized terrestrial or epiphytic ferns much used by florists for their durable cut-fronds, the broad fronds leathery, coarsely divided. Grown in beds, pots, or baskets, requiring only moderate watering and humidity.

Rhizome creeping, the fronds broad, smooth, triangular, 3 pinnate, the lower pinnae enlarged, the sori round, dorsal, the indusium peltate. Tropics of southern hemisphere, 1 species.

R. ADIANTIFORMIS *(Polystichum adiantiforme, P. coriaceum, P. capense, Aspidium capense)*. Leather fern.   Medium / Form 2-3 / Semi-hardy to Semi-tender / High-medium light / Garden soil or Potting mix / Moist-dry

R. ADIANTIFORMIS, unnamed variant (possibly *R. discolor*).   Medium / Form 2-3 / Semi-tender / High-medium light / Garden soil or Potting mix / Moist-dry

Rumohra adiantiformis
indusia

habit

SADLERIA.   Tree fern. Seldom-cultivated large tree fern, with oblong, leathery, little-divided fronds. Used outdoors in southern California as a tub or bed plant, more sensitive to root disturbance than other tree ferns. See Chapter 10, "Tree Ferns," also Joe 1960b.

Stem scaly, the fronds 2 pinnate or less, the veins netted along the midvein, elsewhere free, the sori dorsal, linear, and continuous on both sides of the midvein, the indusium shaped like the sorus. Pacific Islands, 6 species.

S. CYATHEOIDES   Large / Form 7 / Semi-tender / High light / Garden soil or Potting mix / Moist

Sadleria cyatheoides
sori and indusia

habit

Salvinia
habit

SALVINIA.   Very small floating plants used in aquariums. Same culture as for *Azolla*, which see.

Fronds roundish or elliptic, flat, half-inch or less long. Tropical and warm temperate areas of America and Africa, 10 species.

S. AURICULATA   Small / Form 2-3 / Hardy / Medium light / Aquatic

SCOLOPENDRIUM: see PHYLLITIS

Scyphularia pentaphylla
habit

sori and indusia

SCYPHULARIA.   Small davallialike ferns, epiphytic. See Chapter 10, "Davallia and Relatives."

Differing from davallia in the dark, nonciliate rhizome scales and the coarse-cut fronds. New Guinea to Malaysia, 8 species.

S. PENTAPHYLLA *(Davallia pentaphylla)*.   Small / Form 1-2 / Tender / High light / Drained potting mix / Moist-dry

SELAGINELLA.   Small to medium terrestrial or epiphytic fern allies. The foliage mossy or ferny, some metallic or iridescent yellow green, blue, or bronze. The stem creeping, trailing, erect, or drooping. Used as ground cover or potted plants. See Chapter 10, "Fern Allies."

Stem bearing small, scalelike leaves, the upper side of the leaf with a small inconspicuous flap of tissue near the base, the sporangia of two kinds, borne in terminal cones that are generally four-sided in cross section. Worldwide, 800 species.

S. EMMELIANA. Sweat plant.   Small / Erect and trailing / Tender / Low light / Garden soil or Potting mix / Moist-wet

S. EREMOPHILA. Desert spikemoss.   Small / Cushion-like / Hardy / High light / Garden soil or Potting mix / Moist-dry

S. INVOLVENS (S. caulescens). Many cultivars of Japanese origin. Small / Erect / Hardy / Medium light / Garden soil or Potting mix / Moist-wet

S. KRAUSSIANA (S. denticulata of trade). Spreading selaginella.   Small / Trailing / Semi-hardy to Semi-tender / Medium light / Garden soil or Potting mix / Moist-wet

Selaginella kraussiana
fertile leaves

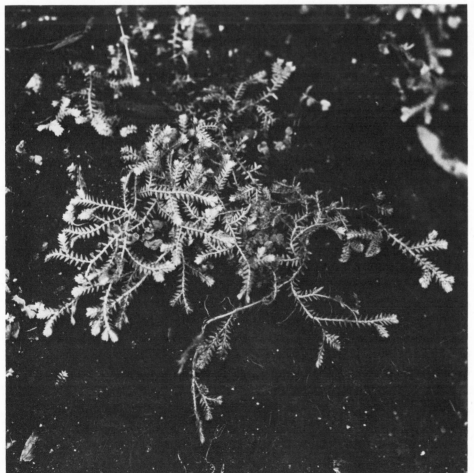

habit

Selaginella sp.
habit

Selaginella involvens
habit

S. KRAUSSIANA cv. Aurea.   Small / Trailing / Semi-tender / Medium light / Garden soil or Potting mix / Moist-wet

S. KRAUSSIANA cv. Brownii *(S. brownii).*   Small / Cushion-like / Semi-tender / Medium light / Garden soil or Potting mix / Moist-wet

S. LEPIDOPHYLLA. Resurrection plant.   Small / Rosette-like / Semi-hardy / Medium light / Garden soil or Potting mix / Moist-dry

S. MARTENSII   Small / Erect and trailing / Semi-tender / Medium light / Garden soil or Potting mix / Moist-wet

S. PALLESCENS   Small / Rosette-like / Semi-hardy / Low light / Garden soil or Potting mix / Moist-wet

S. PULCHERRIMA   Small / Trailing / Tender / Medium light / Garden soil or Potting mix / Moist-wet

S. UNCINATA. Rainbow moss, Peacock plant.   Small / Trailing / Semi-tender / Medium light / Garden soil or Potting mix / Moist-wet

S. WALLACEI   Small / Spreading cushion / Hardy / Medium light / Garden soil or Potting mix / Moist-dry

S. WILLDENOVII   Small / Erect and trailing / Tender / Medium light / Garden soil or Potting mix / Moist-dry

SPHAEROPTERIS.   Tree fern. Large tree ferns now including the much-planted Australian tree fern of trade. The Australian tree fern adaptable to a range of soil and coastal climates as far north as San Francisco. Takes some direct sun. The black tree fern needs more protection from sun and aridity. See Chapter 10, "Tree Ferns," also Tryon and Tryon 1959, Tryon 1970, for details on identification and classification.

Stem covered with scales, the fronds large, wide-ovate, or triangular, the sori round, dorsal, the indusium absent or present, if present cuplike, globose, or of scales. Includes some of the species formerly in *Alsophila*, *Hemitelia*, and *Cyathea* and now separated from them by the stipe scales having essentially similar cells throughout and not bristle-tipped. Tropics of India, Southeast Asia to New Zealand and South Pacific Islands, 120 species.

S. COOPERI (*Alsophila cooperi, A. australis* of trade). Australian tree fern, Cooper tree fern.   Large / Form 7 / Semi-hardy to Semi-tender / High light / Garden soil or Potting mix / Moist-dry

Sphaeropteris cooperi
sori

habit

Sphaeropteris cooperi
frond

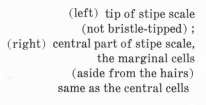

scales on stipes and trunk

S. COOPERI cv. Brentwood (*A.* 'Brentwood' of trade).   Large / Form 7 / Semi-tender / High light / Garden soil or Potting mix / Moist-dry

S. COOPERI cv. Robusta (*A.* 'Robusta' of trade).   Large / Form 7 / Semi-tender / High light / Garden soil or Potting mix / Moist-dry

S. MEDULLARIS (*Cyathea medullaris*). Black tree fern, Sago tree fern. Large / Form 7 / Semi-tender / High-medium light / Garden soil or Potting mix / Moist

(left) tip of stipe scale
(not bristle-tipped);
(right) central part of stipe scale,
the marginal cells
(aside from the hairs)
same as the central cells

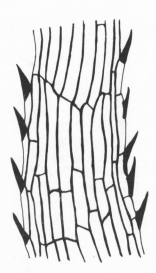

SPHENOMERIS.   Mostly delicate terrestrial plants of rocky areas, rarely grown.

Rhizome creeping, covered with narrow dark scales, the fronds close together, to 4 pinnate, the ultimate segments wedge-shaped, the sori marginal, the indusium fixed by the base and more or less by the sides. Tropics, 18 species.

S. CHINENSIS var. LITTORALE *(S. biflora).*   Medium / Form 3 / Tender / Medium light / Garden soil or Potting mix / Moist

S. CLAVATA   Small-medium / Form 3 / Tender / Medium light / Garden soil or Potting mix, Basic / Moist

Sphenomeris chinensis
segments and indusia

frond

Stenochlaena tenuifolia
habit

sterile frond

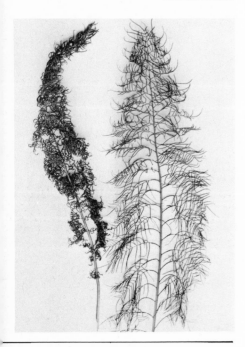

fertile fronds

STENOCHLAENA.   Scandent-climbing rhizome with the coarse fronds far apart. Used in baskets or permitted to climb trees and moss-covered poles, also used as a ground cover. See Joe 1959b for more details.

Rhizome long creeping, climbing, the sterile fronds pinnate, the fertile frond much contracted, covered with sporangia, the indusium absent. Mostly Malaysia and Africa, 40 species.

S. TENUIFOLIA (*S. palustris* of trade).   Medium / Form 1 / Semi-tender / High light / Garden soil or Potting mix / Moist

STRUTHIOPTERIS: see MATTEUCCIA

TECTARIA.   Medium to large terrestrial ferns with coarse fronds, used in pots or beds in warm climates. See Joe 1964b, Lellinger 1968, for more details.

Fronds widest at the base, 1–3 pinnate, coarsely divided, the leaflets broad, the veins irregularly netting, the sori round, dorsal, the indusium peltate or kidney-shaped and attached by its infold. Tropics, 212 species.

T. GEMMIFERA (*T. cicutaria* of trade). Button fern.   Medium / Form 4-6 / Semi-tender / Medium light / Garden soil or Potting mix / Moist

T. HERACLEIFOLIA. Halberd fern.   Medium-large / Form 4 / Tender / Medium light / Garden soil or Potting mix / Moist

T. INCISA   Medium / Form 4 / Tender / Medium light / Potting mix / Moist

T. MEXICANA   Medium / Form 4 / Tender / Medium light / Potting mix / Moist

Tectaria gemmifera.
frond

habit

venation, sori, the indusia shed

THELYPTERIS *(Lastrea).*   Wood fern, Hay fern. Mostly medium-sized terrestrial ferns with narrow fronds in clusters or distributed along a creeping rhizome. Used in borders or beds, infrequently as potted plants. The commoner tropical species (such as *T. dentata, T. normalis, T. torresiana*) often appearing as volunteers in spore cultures. The genus separated from *Dryopteris* and by some authors further divided into several smaller genera, such as *Cyclosorus, Goniopteris, Meniscium, Phegopteris,* etc. See Joe 1963a for details on some commonly cultivated species.

Rhizome various, the stipes with 1 or 2 vascular bundles, the blade mostly narrow pinnate-pinnatifid (broad 3 pinnate in *T. torresiana*), herbaceous, whitish needlelike hairs present, the midrib not grooved or if so, the groove not opening into the grooves of the pinnae, the sori dorsal, round, the indusium kidney-shaped, attached by its infold (absent in *T. angustifolia* and *T. torresiana*). Worldwide, 800 species.

T. ACUMINATA (*T.* 'K. O. Sessions' of trade).   Medium / Form 1 / Semi-tender / High light / Garden soil / Moist

T. ANGUSTIFOLIA *(Meniscium angustifolium).*   Medium / Form 4 / Tender / Medium light / Potting mix / Moist

T. AUGESCENS   Medium / Form 2 / Semi-tender / High light / Garden soil or Potting mix / Moist / Easy

T. DECURSIVE-PINNATA   Medium / Form 4 / Semi-hardy / Medium light / Garden soil or Potting mix / Moist-wet / Deciduous

T. DENTATA *(Nephrodium molle, Dryopteris dentata).* Downy woodfern. Medium / Form 5 / Semi-tender / Medium light / Garden soil or Potting mix / Moist / Easy

T. HEXAGONOPTERA *(Phegopteris hexagonoptera, Dryopteris hexagonoptera).* Southern beech fern, Broad beech fern.   Medium / Form 1 / Hardy / Medium light / Garden soil or Potting mix, Acidic / Moist / Deciduous

T. NEVADENSIS *(Dryopteris oregana, Lastrea oregana).* Sierra water fern. Medium / Form 3 / Hardy / Medium light / Garden soil or Potting mix / Moist-wet

T. NORMALIS   Medium / Form 2 / Semi-tender / Medium light / Garden soil or Potting mix / Moist / Easy

T. NOVEBORACENSIS. New York fern.   Medium / Form 1 / Hardy / High light / Garden soil or Potting mix / Moist / Deciduous

T. PARASITICA   Medium / Form 2 / Semi-tender / Medium light / Garden soil or Potting mix / Moist

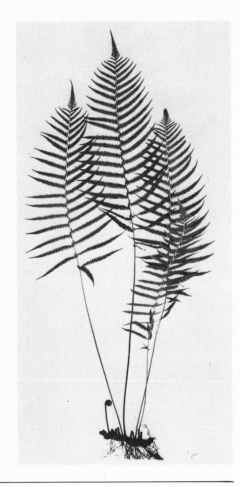

Thelypteris augescens
habit

T. PATENS   Medium / Form 4 / Tender / Medium light / Garden soil or Potting mix / Moist

T. PATENS cv. Lepida *(T. lepida, Dryopteris lepida).*   Medium / Form 4 / Tender / Medium light / Garden soil or Potting mix / Moist

T. PHEGOPTERIS *(Phegopteris connectilis).* Northern beech fern, Long beech fern.   Medium / Form 1 / Hardy / Low light / Garden soil or Potting mix, Acidic / Moist / Deciduous

T. PUBERULA var. *sonorensis.*   Medium / Form 2 / Semi-tender / Medium light / Garden soil or Potting mix / Moist

T. REPTANS. Creeping woodfern.   Small / Form 4-6 / Tender / Medium light / Garden soil or Potting mix, Basic / Moist

T. RESINIFERA. Glandular woodfern.   Medium / Form 2 / Tender / Medium light / Garden soil or Potting mix / Moist-wet

T. TETRAGONA   Medium / Form 5 / Tender / Medium light / Garden soil or Potting mix / Moist

T. THELYPTERIOIDES *(T. palustris).* Marsh fern.   Medium / Form 1 / Hardy / High-medium light / Garden soil or Potting mix / Moist-wet / Deciduous

T. TORRESIANA *(T. uliginosa, T. setigera* of trade).   Large / Form 5 / Semi-tender / Medium light / Garden soil or Potting mix / Moist

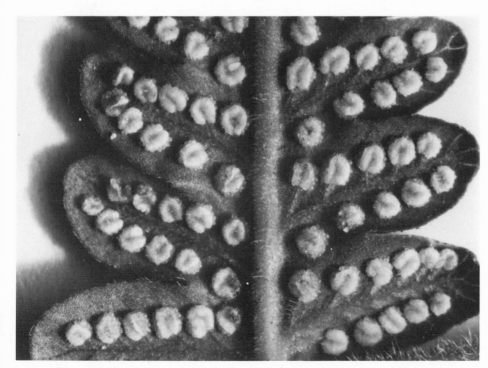

sori and indusia

Todea barbara
habit

pinnae and sporangia

TODEA.   Large terrestrial fern forming a crown of foliage, of moderate growth and size in southern California cultivation, handsome in pots.

Rhizome erect, clumping when old, the frond oblong, 2 pinnate, leathery, the fertile pinnae slightly contracted or not, the sporangia dorsal, scattered, large, no indusium. S. Africa, Australia, New Zealand, 1 species.

T. BARBARA   Medium / Form 5 / Semi-hardy to Semi-tender / High light / Garden soil or Potting mix / Moist

TRICHOMANES.   Filmy fern. Small terrestrial or epiphytic ferns with very thin fronds. Used in terrariums or conditions with high humidity. See Chapter 10, "Filmy Ferns."

Small fronds, membranous, bearing sori along the margin, the sori marginal, protected by a tubular or trumpet-shaped indusium. Mostly tropics and subtropics, 25 species.

T. RADICANS *(T. boschianum)*. Bristle fern.   Small / Form 2 / Semi-tender / Low light / Drained potting mix / Moist-wet

T. VENOSUM   Small / Form 2 / Semi-tender / Low light / Drained potting mix / Moist-wet

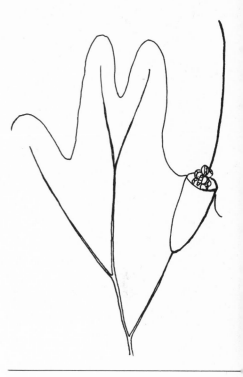

Trichomanes radicans
sorus and indusium

Trichomanes radicans
habit

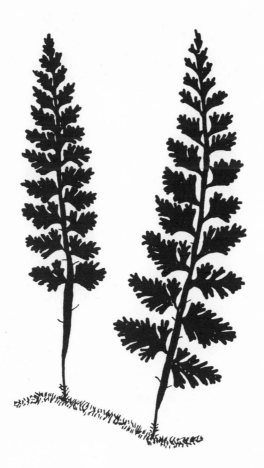

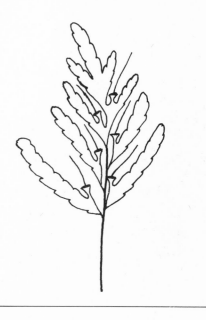

Trichomanes venosum
frond

Vittaria lineata
habit

sori

VITTARIA.   Shoestring ferns. Rarely cultivated epiphytes with long stringlike fronds. Grown in baskets or pots. Keep well drained; tender.

Fronds long, linear, firm, the sori submarginal, linear, parallel to the edge, immersed, the indusium absent. Tropics and subtropics, 50 species.

V. LINEATA   Medium / Form 3 / Tender / High light / Drained potting mix / Moist

WOODSIA.   Small terrestrial ferns with delicate foliage, used in damp rock gardens.

Fronds 1–2 pinnate, herbaceous, the sori dorsal, round, the indusium fragile filaments, scalelike or globose, surrounding the sorus at the base. Alpine, boreal, and temperate areas, 40 species.

W. ILVENSIS. Rusty woodsia.   Small / Form 3 / Hardy / Medium light / Garden soil or Potting mix, Acidic / Moist-wet / Deciduous

W. OBTUSA. Blunt-lobed woodsia, Obtuse woodsia.   Small / Form 3 / Hardy / Medium light / Garden soil or Potting mix, Basic / Moist-wet / Easy

W. OREGANA. Oregon woodsia.   Small / Form 3 / Hardy / Medium light / Garden soil or Drained potting mix / Moist-wet

W. SCOPULINA. Mountain woodsia.   Small / Form 3 / Hardy / Medium light / Garden soil or Drained potting mix / Moist-wet

Woodsia ilvensis
fertile pinnae

Woodsia scopulina
habit

sori with various indusia
(left to right)
W. obtusa, W. ilvensis, W. oregana

Woodwardia radicans
venation, sori, and indusia

Woodwardia orientalis
leaf buds

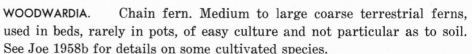

WOODWARDIA.   Chain fern. Medium to large coarse terrestrial ferns, used in beds, rarely in pots, of easy culture and not particular as to soil. See Joe 1958b for details on some cultivated species.

Fronds typically pinnate-pinnatifid, firm, the sori oblong, dorsal, in a row on each side of the midrib of the segment, the indusium shaped like the sorus. Europe, Asia, North America, 12 species.

W. ANGUSTIFOLIA: see **LORINSERIA**

W. AREOLATA: see **LORINSERIA**

W. FIMBRIATA *(W. chamissoi, W. radicans* var. *Americana)*. Giant chain fern.   Large / Form 5 / Hardy / High light / Garden soil / Moist / Easy

W. ORIENTALIS. Oriental chain fern.   Large / Form 4-6 / Hardy / High light / Garden soil / Moist / Easy

W. RADICANS. European chain fern.   Large / Form 4-6 / Hardy / High light / Garden soil / Moist / Easy

W. SPINULOSA. Mexican chain fern.   Large / Form 4 / Semi-tender / High light / Garden soil / Moist

W. VIRGINICA. Virginia chain fern.   Large / Form 1 / Hardy / High light / Garden soil, Acidic / Moist-wet / Deciduous

Woodwardia radicans
habit

GLOSSARY

ADNATE   grown to or united with another part.

ANADROMIC   when the basal branch or vein (as on a pinna) arises from the side toward the frond tip.

ANNULUS   a complete or partial ring or cluster of thick-walled cells on the spore case functioning to open the spore case.

ANTHERIDIUM   the male sex organ containing the sperm.

APOGAMY   production of sporophytes directly from the prothallium tissue rather than through fertilization of the egg and sperm.

APOSPORY   production of prothallia directly from young sporophyte tissue.

ARCHEGONIUM   the female sex organ containing the egg.

BINOMIAL   in reference to the species name which consists of two words, the genus name and species epithet.

BIPINNATE   twice pinnate, both primary and secondary divisions of the frond pinnate.

BIPINNATIFID   twice pinnatifid; the divisions of a pinnatifid frond again pinnatifid.

BLADE   the thin broad part of a leaf or frond.

BUD   on ferns the term usually applies to a proliferous bud or lump of tissue which grows into a new fern plant.

CATADROMIC   when the basal branch or vein (as on a pinna) arises from the side toward the frond base.

COMPOUND   a leaf of two or more leaflets.

COSTA   the main rib of a simple frond, or of the pinna (secondary rachis) or pinules of a compound frond.

CROZIER   the young uncoiling fern frond, the fiddlehead.

CULTIVAR   a plant variety originating in cultivation.

DECURRENT   when the base of a blade or division of a blade extends down the stipe, rachis, or costa as a winged expansion or ridge.

DORSAL   relating to the back or lower side of a leaf.

ENTIRE   with an even margin, not toothed or divided.

EPIPHYTE   a plant growing upon another plant yet not a parasite; the common polypody growing on a tree branch is an example.

FAMILY   a group of related genera.

FERN ALLIES   vascular plants reproducing by spores, like ferns, but having small leaves with simple unbranched veins; once thought to be closely related to ferns but now believed to be more distant relatives.

FLORA   a list of all the species growing in a region; also, a collective term for all the species growing in a region.

FOOT-CANDLE   a unit measuring light intensity; 1 foot-candle is equal to the amount of light cast by a standard candle 1 foot away from the flame.

FRIABLE   describing soil which is moist and loose.

FROND   the leaf of a fern, typically consisting of the stipe and blade.

GAMETOPHYTE   in ferns a small usually flat plant bearing the sex organs.

GENE   a unit on a chromosome determining the inheritance of a particular character.

GENUS   a group of related species.

HARDENED PLANTS   plants which have adjusted to more climatic exposure.

HYBRID   the offspring of parents differing in many characteristics.

IMMERSED   being sunken into the surrounding tissue.

INDUSIUM   the membrane surrounding or covering the sorus; a false indusium or a reflexed leaf margin indusium derived from the margin of the leaf rolling over and protecting the sorus.

JOINTED   separating naturally at a certain point and leaving a scar.

LANCEOLATE   lance-shaped.

LEAFLET   one of the divisions of a compound leaf.

LINEAR   long and narrow, the sides parallel or nearly so.

MARGINAL   relating to the margin or edge of a leaf.

MUTATION   a sudden heritable change appearing in animals or plants due to changes in the genes or chromosomes.

OVATE   with an outline like that of a hen's egg.

PALMATE   when the main veins, segments, or lobes radiate from a common point.

PEDATE   palmate with the side lobes cleft into two or more segments.

PELTATE   having a stalk attached at the center as the handle on an umbrella.

PINNA   the primary division of a pinnately divided frond.

PINNATE   having the arrangement of a feather with a single midvein from which leaflets arise.

PINNATIFID   having the frond pinnately cleft.

PINNULE   a secondary pinna.

PROTHALLIUM   the gametophyte, a small usually flat plant in the life cycle of the fern.

PUPS   a colloquial term referring to the young plants arising from older platycerium plants.

RACHIS   the midrib of a compound frond.

REFLEXED   abruptly bent downwards or backwards.

RHIZOME   a stem growing horizontally and anchored to the soil by roots on its underside.

ROOTSTOCK   that part of a short erect stem with roots attached.

SCALE   any small, flat, usually dry structure, such as those found on many fern rhizomes.

SEGMENT   as used in this work to mean the ultimate division into which a blade is divided.

SESSILE   not stalked.

SIMPLE   unbranched; the blade composed of one piece.

SINUS   a space or recess between two lobes of a frond or other expanded structure.

SORUS   a cluster of spore cases having a defined shape.

SPECIES   a category of individuals usually interbreeding freely and having many characteristics in common.

SPORANGIUM   the case enclosing the spores.

SPORE   a reproductive cell that may develop into a new plant.

SPORELINGS   young fern plants (sporophytes) arising from prothallia.

SPOROPHYTE   in ferns the familiar foliaceous plant bearing spores as opposed to the gametophyte or prothallium.

STIPE   the leaf stalk or petiole.

STIPULE   a basal appendage of a stipe or petiole, usually 2.

STOLON   a very long slender stem capable of producing a new plant at its tip or along its length.

SYNONYM   an alternate scientific name but not the legitimate name.

TERRESTRIAL   referring to plants growing on the surface of the ground in soil.

VASCULAR   pertaining to tissue specialized to conduct food and water in plants; VASCULAR BUNDLE   a bundle or strand of vascular tissue.

VEINS   the strands of vascular tissue in a leaf; FREE VEINS   veins having their ends free of other veins; NETTED VEINS   veins having their ends connected to other veins.

WING   a thin expansion or flat extension of an organ or structure.

XEROPHYTE   a plant very resistant to dry conditions, such as desert ferns.

APPENDIX I: MEASURING THE LIGHT

Special light meters may be purchased to measure foot-candles, but photographic light meters may also be used, according to the Agricultural Research Service of the U.S. Department of Agriculture. The following formula will convert photographic light meter readings to foot-candle readings:

$$\text{Foot-candles} = \frac{20\ (f)^2}{T\ S}$$

where f = the aperture in f stop, T = the shutter speed in seconds and S = the film speed in ASA units.

Place a large sheet of white paper on the surface to be measured for foot-candles. Set an appropriate ASA film speed on the meter and read the shutter speed required for proper exposure at a given f stop. Read the meter at about 12 inches from the paper under most conditions. For example, if the ASA film speed setting is set at 100 and the proper exposure is ½ second at an f stop of 16, the foot-candle value is 102:

$$102 \text{ foot-candles} = \frac{20\,(16 \times 16)}{\tfrac{1}{2} \times 100}$$

The formula provides a workable approximation. Results will vary according to the accuracy of the light meter and the cone of light accepted by the meter.

APPENDIX II: LIST OF SOURCES

FERN SOCIETIES

The American Fern Society
Dr. Terry R. Webster
Biological Sciences Group
University of Connecticut
Storrs, Connecticut 06268

The British Pteridological Society
Mr. J. W. Dyce
46 Sedly Rise
Loughton, Essex, England

The Los Angeles International Fern Society
Mr. Wilbur Olson
2423 Burritt Avenue
Redondo Beach, California 90278

Japanese Pteridological Society
Dr. K. Iwatsuki
Department of Botany
Kyoto University
Kyoto, Japan

Nelson, New Zealand, Fern Society
Mr. E. Ensor
562a Main Road
Stoke, Nelson, New Zealand

The Nippon Fernist Club
Prof. Satoru Kurata
Department of Forest Botany
Faculty of Agriculture
Tokyo University, Hongo
Bunkyo-Ku, Tokyo, Japan 113

South Florida Fern Society
P.O. Box 55-7275
Ludlam Branch
Miami, Florida 33155

FERN NURSERIES

Fern Sources in the United States—1972
By Donald G. Huttleston, printed in the
American Fern Journal 62(1):9–15

Sources of Ferns
By the LAIFS
Write to the
Los Angeles International Fern Society,
2423 Burritt Ave.,
Redondo Beach, California 90278

PLANT IMPORT INFORMATION

Plant Import Permit Station
United States Department of Agriculture
209 River Street
Hoboken, New Jersey 07030

PREPARED PLANTING MIXES

Horti-Pearl
Redco Incorporated
11831 Vose St.
North Hollywood, California 91605

Ron McLellan's Mix
1450 El Camino Real
San Francisco, California 94080

Mica-peat
Langley Peat Ltd.
496 West 40 Avenue
Vancouver 15, Canada

Pro-Mix B
Premier Peat Moss Corporation
25 West 45th St.
New York, New York 10036

pH PAPER

pHydrion Papers (Dual range Jumbo 1-11)
Micro Essential Laboratories
Brooklyn, New York 11210

(Or see Scientific Supply Companies,
listed below.)

TRACE ELEMENT MIX

(Also see Akira Chemical Service under
Scientific Supply Companies, below.)

Peter's Soluble Trace Element Mix
Robert B. Peters Company
2833 Pennsylvania Street
Allentown, Pennsylvania 18104

SCIENTIFIC SUPPLY COMPANIES

Akira Chemical Service
2542 W. 7th St.
Los Angeles, California 90057
(Chemicals only)

Carolina Biological Supply Co.
Burlington, North Carolina 27515

Carolina Biological Supply Co.
Powell Laboratories Division
Gladstone, Oregon 97027

Turtox
General Biological Supply House
8200 South Hoyne Avenue
Chicago, Illinois 60620

Van Waters and Rogers (VWR)
1363 S. Bonnie Beach Place
Los Angeles, California 90023

Wards Natural Science Establishment, Inc.
P.O. Box 1712
Rochester, New York 14603

Wards Natural Science Establishment
P.O. Box 1749
Monterey, California 93940

INTERNATIONAL CODES

*International Code of Nomenclature of
Cultivated Plants—1969*
(Cultivated Code)
Obtainable from:
The International Bureau for
Plant Taxonomy and Nomenclature
Tweede Transitorium
Uithof, Utrecht, Netherlands

The American Horticultural Society
Mount Vernon, Virginia 22121

Crop Science Society of America
Dr. Matthias Stelly
677 South Segoe Road
Madison, Wisconsin 53711

APPENDIX III: CLASSIFICATION OF FERNS AND FERN ALLIES

This classification arrangement is one of several proposals. No completely accepted arrangement is possible because botanists have not yet agreed upon the exact relationships (or "blood lines") of plants. Until all the needed data are gathered (and some, such as fossil data, may never be available) there will be differences of interpretation. Genera in italics rarely cultivated and not listed in text.

Kingdom Plantae (Plant Kingdom)
    Division Pterdophyta (Ferns and Fern Allies)
        Class Psilotinae
            Order Psilotales
                Family Psilotaceae (Whisk Fern Family)
                    Genus Psilotum

        Class Lycopodinae
            Order Lycopodiales
                Family Lycopodiaceae (Clubmoss Family)
                    Genus Lycopodium
            Order Selaginellales
                Family Selaginellaceae (Selaginella Family)
                    Genus Selaginella

        Class Equisetinae
            Order Equisetales
                Family Equistaceae (Horsetail Family)
                    Genus Equisetum

        Class Filicineae
            Order Ophioglossales
                Family Ophioglossaceae (Grapefern Family)
                    Genera Ophioglossum, Botrychium
            Order Marattiales
                Family Marattiaceae (Marattia Family)
                    Genera Angiopteris, Marattia

Order Filicales
    Family Osmundaceae (Osmunda Family)
        Genera Osmunda, Todea, *Leptopteris*
    Family Polypodiaceae (Polypody Family)
        Genera grouped according to their presumed relationships:
        Cupferns and Relatives—Dennstaedtia, Microlepia,
            Leptolepia, Hypolepis, Pteridium, *Paesia*, Lonchitis,
            Histiopteris, Sphenomeris, *Lindsaea*
        Davallias and Relatives—Davallia, Scyphularia, Humata,
            Leucostegia, Nephrolepis, Arthropteris
        Oleandras—*Oleandra*
        Maidenhair and Relatives—Onychium, Cryptogramma,
            Llavea, Ceratopteris, Coniogramme, Anogramma,
            Pityrogramma, *Bommeria*, Hemionitis, Adiantum,
            Cheilanthes, Notholaena, Pellaea, Doryopteris, Pteris,
            Actiniopteris, Acrostichum, Vittaria
        Blechnums and Relatives—Blechnum, Sadleria,
            Woodwardia, Lorinseria, Doodia, Stenochlaena
        Spleenworts and Relatives—Phyllitis, Camptosorus,
            Asplenium, Ceterach, Diplazium, Athyrium,
            Cystopteris, Woodsia
        Ostrich ferns and Relatives—Matteuccia, Onoclea
        Aspidiums—Dryopteris, Arachniodes, Rumohra,
            Polystichum, *Plecosorus*, *Cyclopeltis*, Cyrtomium,
            Didymochlaena, Lastreopsis, Ctenitis, *Polystichopsis*,
            Tectaria, Quercifilix, Thelypteris, Gymnocarpium,
            Bolbitis
        Polypodys and Relatives—*Drymoglossum*, Platycerium,
            Pyrrosia, Lemmaphyllum, Aglaomorpha, Drynaria,
            Merinthosorus, *Photinopteris*, Polypodium, *Grammitis*
        Elephant-ear fern and Relatives—Elaphoglossum,
            Peltapteris
    Family Schizaeaceae (Climbing Fern Family)
        Genera *Schizaea*, Lygodium, Anemia
    Family Gleicheniaceae (Gleichenia Family)
        Genera *Gleichenia, Dicranopteris*
    Family Hymenophyllaceae (Filmy Fern Family)
        Genera Trichomanes, Mecodium
    Family Cyatheaceae (Cyathea Family)
        Genera Sphaeropteris, Alsophila, Cyathea
    Family Dicksoniaceae (Dicksonia Family)
        Genera Dicksonia, Cibotium
Order Hydropteridales
    Family Marsileaceae (Water Clover Family)
        Genera *Regnellidium*, Marsilea, *Pilularia*
    Family Salviniaceae
        Genera Salvinia, Azolla

BIBLIOGRAPHY

ALDRICH, JR., DANIEL G., and W. R. SCHOONOVER, *Gypsum and Other Sulfur Materials*. California Agricultural Experiment Station, Circular 403, College of Agriculture, University of California, Berkeley, March 1951.

BOODLEY, JAMES W., "Soilless Mixes," *Horticulture, 50*, 38–39 (1972).

Brooklyn Botanic Garden, "Handbook on Ferns," *Plants and Gardens, 25 (1)*, 1–77 (1969).

DRUERY, C. T., *British Ferns and Their Varieties*. Routledge, London, 1912.

DYCE, J. W., "Variation in Polystichum in the British Isles," *The British Fern Gazette, 9 (4)*, 97–109 (1963).

FARRAR, DONALD R., "A Culture Chamber for Tropical Rain Forest Plants," *American Fern Journal, 58 (3)*, 97–102 (1968).

FOSTER, GORDON F., *The Gardener's Fern Book*, Van Nostrand Co., New York, 1964.

———, *Ferns to Know and Grow*, Hawthorn Books Inc., New York, 1971.

FRANKS, WENDY, *Platycerium-Fern Facts*, privately published, obtainable from The Los Angeles International Fern Society, Los Angeles, 1969.

GLATER, R. A. BOBRAV, "Smog Damage to Ferns in the Los Angeles Area," *Phytopathology, 46 (12)*, 696–698 (1956).

GLEASON, HENRY A., *The New Britton & Brown Illustrated Flora of the Northeastern United States and Adjacent Canada, 1*, 1–56, The New York Botanical Garden, 1952.

HARTMAN, HUDSON T., and DALE E. KESTER, *Plant Propagation Principles and Practices*, 3rd edition, 509–532, Prentice-Hall Inc., Englewood Cliffs, New Jersey, 1975.

HEVLY, R. H., "Adaptations of Cheilanthoid Ferns to Desert Environments," *Journal of Arizona Academy Science, 2 (4)*, 164–175 (1963).

HOAGLAND, D. R., and D. I. ARNON, *The Water-Culture Method for Growing Plants Without Soil*. California Agricultural Experiment Station, Circular 347, rev. January 1950, College of Agriculture, University of California, Berkeley, January 1950.

HODGE, W. H., "Fern Foods of Japan and the Problem of Toxicity," *American Fern Journal, 63 (3)*, 77–80 (1973).

HOLTTUM, R. E., *A Revised Flora of Malaya, 2*. "Ferns," 2d ed., Government Printing Office, Singapore, 1968.

253

————, "On the Significance of Some Name Changes in Ferns," *The British Fern Gazette, 10(2)*, 92–96 (1969).

HOSHIZAKI, B. J., "The Genus *Adiantum* in Cultivation (*Polypodiaceae*)," *Baileya, 17(3)*, 97–144 (1970).

————, "The Genus *Adiantum* in Cultivation (*Polypodiaceae*)," *Baileya, 17(4)*, 145–196 (1970).

————, "Morphology and Phylogeny of *Platycerium* Species," *Biotropica, 4(2)*, 93–117 (1972).

JOE, BARBARA, "Pteris Species Cultivated in California," *Lasca Leaves, 8(2)*, 26–29 (1958a).

————, "Ferns Cultivated in California: *Woodwardia, Aglaomorpha, Pityrogramma,*" *Lasca Leaves, 8(3)*, 60–65 (1958b).

————, "Ferns Cultivated in California: *Phyllitis, Doodia, Pyrrosia, Llavea,*" *Lasca Leaves, 9(1)*, 8–14 (1959a).

————, "Ferns Cultivated in California: *Cyrtomium, Onychium, Stenochlaena,*" *Lasca Leaves, 9(3)*, 61–67 (1959b).

————, "Ferns Cultivated in California: *Hypolepis,*" *Lasca Leaves, 9(4)*, 74–75 (1959c).

————, "Ferns Cultivated in California: *Lygodium,*" *Lasca Leaves, 10(4)*, 86 (1960a).

————, "Ferns Cultivated in California: *Sadleria,*" *American Fern Journal, 50(3)*, 232–236 (1960b).

————, "The Species of *Blechnum* in Cultivation," *Baileya, 8(3)*, 102–117 (1960c).

————, "Species of *Microlepia* Cultivated in California," *Lasca Leaves, 12(1)*, 8–12 (1962).

————, "Species of *Thelypteris* Cultivated in California," *Baileya, 11(3)*, 99–110 (1963a).

————, "Species of *Dryopteris* Cultivated in California," *Baileya, 11(4)*, 117–130 (1963b).

————, "Ferns Cultivated in California: *Asplenium,*" *Baileya, 12(1)*, 9–27 (1964a).

————, "Ferns Cultivated in California: *Tectaria,*" *Baileya, 12(2)*, 47–51 (1964b).

————, "A Review of the Species of *Platycerium* (*Polypodiaceae*)," *Baileya, 12(3)*, 69–126 (1964c).

————, "Cultivated Tree Ferns of the Genus *Cibotium* (*Dicksoniaceae*)," *Baileya, 12(4)*, 137–146 (1964d).

————, "Cup Ferns (*Dennstaedtia*) Cultivated in California," *American Fern Journal, 55(2)*, 58–62 (1965).

KAYE, REGINALD, "Variations in *Athyrium* in the British Isles," *The British Fern Gazette, 9(6)*, 177–204 (1965).

————, *Hardy Ferns*, Faber and Faber Ltd., London, 1968.

KLEINSCHMIDT, W. F., "A Method of Preparing Spores for Fern Culture," *American Fern Journal, 47(3)*, 95–97 (1957).

KNOBLOCK, IRVING W., "Gibberellic Acid and Ferns," *American Fern Journal, 47(4)*, 134–135 (1957).

LELLINGER, DAVID, "The Correct Name for the Button Fern (*T. gemmifera* not *T. cicutaria*)," *American Fern Journal, 58(4)*, 180 (1968).

LLOYD, ROBERT M., *Systematics of the Onocleoid Ferns*, University of California, Publications in Botany, *61*, 1–93 (1971).

LLOYD, ROBERT, and FRANK LANG, "The *Polypodium vulgare* Complex in North bility in Pterdophyta: Evolutionary Significance of Chlorophyllous Spores," *Biotropica, 2(2)*, 129–137 (1970).

LLOYD, ROBERT, and FRANK LANG, "The *Polypodium vulgare* Complex in North America," *British Fern Gazette, 9 (5)*, 168–177 (1964).

LOVIS, J. D., "Fern Hybridists and Fern Hybridising II, Fern Hybridising at the University of Leeds," *The British Fern Gazette, 10 (1)*, 13–20 (1968).

MAIRE, RICHARD G., and CLYDE L. ELMORE, "Liverwort Control on Liners," *Flower and Nursery Report*, Agricultural Extension, University of California, March 1973.

MATKIN, O. A., and PHILIP A. CHANDLER, "The U.C.-Type Soil Mixes," in Kenneth F. Baker, ed., *U.C. System for Producing Healthy Container-Grown Plants*, Extension Service Manual, *23*, 68–85, California Agricultural Experiment Station, September 1957.

MORTON, C. V., "Observations on Cultivated Ferns, IV, The Species of *Davallia*," *American Fern Journal, 47 (4)*, 143–148 (1957).

——, "Observations on Cultivated Ferns V, The Species and Forms of *Nephrolepis*," *American Fern Journal, 48 (1)*, 18–27 (1958).

——, "A New Form of *Microlepia speluncae*," *American Fern Journal, 60 (1)*, 28–29 (1970).

OHWI, JISABURO, *Flora of Japan*, Smithsonian Institution, Washington, D.C., 1965.

PATTERSON, PAUL M., and A. SEWELL FREEMAN, "The Effect of Photoperiodism on Certain Ferns," *American Fern Journal, 53 (3)*, 126–128 (1963).

SHIVAS, M. G., "Contributions to the Cytology and Taxonomy of Species of *Polypodium* in Europe & America, II Taxonomy," *Journal Linnean Society (Botany), 58 (370)*, 27–38 (1961).

STOKEY, ALMA G., "Duration of Viability of Spores of the *Osmundaceae*," *American Fern Journal, 41 (2)*, 111–115 (1951).

SUSSMAN, A. S., "Physiology of Dormancy and Germination in Propugles of Cryptogamic Plants," in W. Ruhland and A. Lang, eds., *Encyclopedia of Plant Physiology, 15 (2)*, 933–1025, Sprenger Verlag, Berlin, 1965.

SWINDELLS, PHILIP, *Ferns for Garden and Greenhouse*, J. M. Dent & Sons, Ltd., London, 1971.

THURSTON, SUSAN H., "Forcing a Collection of Native Ferns of New England and the Middle Atlantic States for Exhibition," *American Fern Journal, 29 (3)*, 85–94 (1939).

TINDALE, MARY D., "A Monograph of the Genus *Lastreopsis* Ching," Contributions from the *New South Wales National Herbarium, 3 (5)*, 249–339 (1965).

TRYON, ROLLA, "The Classification of the *Cyatheaceae*," Contributions from the *Gray Herbarium of Harvard University*, No. *200*, 1970.

TRYON, ROLLA, and ALICE TRYON, "Observations on Cultivated Tree Ferns: The Hardy Species of Tree Ferns (*Dicksonia* and *Cyatheaceae*)," *American Fern Journal, 49 (4)*, 129–142 (1959).

Turtox Service Dept., "Growing Plants in Nutrient Culture Media," *Turtox Service Leaflet*, No. *30*, General Biological Supply House, Chicago, 1957.

U.S. Department of Agriculture, *The Use of Sawdust for Mulches and Soil Improvement*, Circular No. 891, U.S. Government Printing Office, Washington, D.C., 1951.

U.S. Department of Agriculture, Agricultural Research Service, *Growing Plants Without Soil in Experimental Use*, Miscellaneous Publication 1251, U.S. Government Printing Office, Washington, D.C., 1972.

WALKER, T. G., "Species of *Pteris* Commonly in Cultivation," *The British Fern Gazette, 10 (3)*, 143–151 (1970).

WEIRBERG, ERIC, and BRUCE R. VOELLER, "External Factors Inducing Germination of Fern Spores," *American Fern Journal, 59 (4)*, 153–167 (1969).

WHERRY, EDGAR T., "The Soil Reaction of Certain Rock Ferns I," *American Fern Journal, 10 (1)*, 15–22 (1920).

————, "The Soil Reaction of Certain Rock Ferns II," *American Fern Journal*, *10(2)*, 45–52 (1920).

WHITTIER, D. P., "The Effect of Light and Other Factors on Spore Germination in *Botrychium dissectum*," *Canadian Journal of Botany, 51*, 1791–1794 (1973).

For a complete listing of ferns by genus and species, see pages 128–244. Page numbers in italics indicate illustrations.

i

PHOTOGRAPH CREDITS

Pages 150 (bottom right), 200 (left): G. Hampfler, Longwood Gardens; 157 (bottom right): F. Wertman; 168 (left): E. Bishop; 191 (top): R. Lloyd, Ohio University; 232: Barbara Joe Hoshizaki.

Color Section. 2 (bottom), 3 (top): John Wright; 6 (bottom): L. Alexander.

All other photographs are by Arthur Takayama.

ABOUT THE AUTHOR

Barbara Joe Hoshizaki is Professor of Botany at Los Angeles City College, Curator of Pteridophyta at the University of California at Los Angeles, and president of the Los Angeles International Fern Society, the country's largest organization of fern collectors and growers. She has done field work on ferns in the West Indies, Latin America, and various regions of the Pacific, and is the author of many scientific papers and articles. Mrs. Hoshizaki lives with her husband and two children in Los Angeles.

A NOTE ON THE TYPE

This book was set on the linotype in Century Expanded, designed in 1894 by Linn Boyd Benton (1844–1932). Benton cut Century Expanded in response to Theodore De Vinne's request for an attractive, easy-to-read typeface to fit the narrow columns of his *Century Magazine*. Early in the nineteen hundreds Morris Fuller Benton updated and improved Century in several versions for his father's American Type Founders Company. Century remains the only American typeface cut before 1910 still widely in use today.

Composed by Maryland Linotype Composition Co., Baltimore, Maryland.
Printed by Murray Printing Company, Forge Village, Massachusetts.
Bound by American Book–Stratford Press, Saddlebrook, New Jersey.
Color lithography by Universal Printing, St. Louis, Missouri.

Typography and binding design by The Etheredges.